The Holocaust and Memory in the Global Age

In the series

Politics, History, and Social Change

edited by John C. Torpey

Patricia Hill Collins, *From Black Power to Hip Hop: Racism, Nationalism, and Feminism*

Brian A. Weiner, *Sins of the Parents: The Politics of National Apologies in the United States*

Heribert Adam and Kogila Moodley, *Seeking Mandela: Peacemaking Between Israelis and Palestinians*

Marc Garcelon, *Revolutionary Passage: From Soviet to Post-Soviet Russia, 1985–2000*

Götz Aly and Karl Heinz Roth, translated by Assenka Oksiloff, *The Nazi Census: Identification and Control in the Third Reich*

Immanuel Wallerstein, *The Uncertainties of Knowledge*

Michael R. Marrus, *The Unwanted: European Refugees from the First World War Through the Cold War*

The Holocaust
and Memory
in the Global Age

Daniel Levy and
Natan Sznaider

Translated by Assenka Oksiloff

Temple University Press
Philadelphia

DANIEL LEVY is an Assistant Professor of Sociology at the
State University of New York, Stony Brook.

NATAN SZNAIDER is an Associate Professor of Sociology
at the Academic College of Tel-Aviv-Yaffo, Israel.

Temple University Press
1601 North Broad Street
Philadelphia PA 19122
www.temple.edu/tempress

Originally published as *Erinnerung im globalen Zeitalter: Der Holocaust*,
 © Suhrkamp Verlag Frankfurt am Main 2001, in a series
 edited by Ulrich Beck
Published 2006
Printed in the United States of America

♾ The paper used in this publication meets the requirements
of the American National Standard for Information Sciences—
Permanence of Paper for Printed Library Materials,
ANSI Z39.48-1992

Library of Congress Cataloging-in-Publication Data

Levy, Daniel.
    [Erinnerung im globalen Zeitalter. English]
    The Holocaust and memory in the global age / Daniel Levy
and Natan Sznaider; translated by Assenka Oksiloff.
        p. cm.— (Politics, history, and social change)
    Includes bibliographical references and index.
    ISBN 1-59213-275-8 (cloth : alk. paper)
    ISBN 1-59213-276-6 (pbk. : alk. paper)
        1. Holocaust, Jewish (1939–1945)—Influence.
    2. Holocaust, Jewish (1939–1945)—Personal narratives—History
and criticism.   I. Sznaider, Natan, 1954– .   II. Title. III. Series.
D804.3.L513 2005
940.53′18—dc22
                                            2005040045

2 4 6 8 9 7 5 3 1

Contents

1

Revised Introduction to the English Edition

THE MAIN REASON GLOBALIZATION causes so much anxiety is that it is steadily dissolving the coordinates we have been using to make sense of experience. This anxiety is by nature almost impossible to articulate and instead is expressed as a series of interrelated fears. People fear a worldwide homogenization of cultures, which will inexorably entail the loss of their own. They fear that without these cultural buffers, individuals will be set adrift, without any anchors, bonds, or values. In short, they fear that because all human attachments are particular, globalization will standardize and destroy everything in our collective life that is worth having. From this perspective, globalization presents itself as a huge trap. Collective memories persist as a bulwark against encroaching globalization. They serve as a foundation for stabilizing group and national memories that are linked to a particular place and time. After all, is the concept of collective memory not an integral component of the fixed national and ethnic sense of identity that people have of themselves?

From all this, it seems axiomatic that global collective memory and global society are impossible. But is this theoretically and empirically true? That is the subject of this book. Aside from the fact that this view of the global transformations of the past two decades is simplistic, it also tends to overlook the changing modes of temporality and memory associated with globalization. The study of collective memory usually regards these memory structures as being bound by tight social and political groups such as the "nation" or "ethnos" (Halbwachs 1980; Smith 1995). But what happens when an increasing number of people, primarily in consumer societies, no longer define themselves (exclusively) through the nation or their ethnic belonging? Can we imagine collective memories that transcend national and ethnic boundaries? If so, we must ask, how do these transnational memory forms come about, and of what do they consist?

This book examines the distinctive forms that collective memories take in the age of globalization. The conventional concept of "collective memory" is firmly embedded within what we call the "container of the nation-state." We argue that this container is in the process of slowly being cracked. It is commonly assumed that memories, community, and geographical proximity belong together. We direct our attention to global processes that are characterized by the de-territorialization of politics and culture. We observe a process in which issues of global concern are able to become part and parcel of everyday local experiences and moral life worlds. Does this open up new "memoryscapes"? Can solidarities and mutual responsibilities transcend territorial boundaries? Rather than restricting the conceptualization of collective memory to a national context, we argue, it is possible, and necessary, to uncover memoryscapes that correspond to emerging modes of identification in the global age.

We pursue these questions by studying the transition from national to cosmopolitan memory cultures. Cosmopolitanism refers to a process of "internal globalization" through which global concerns become part of local experiences of an increasing number of people (Beck 2004). To avoid later misunderstandings, we should emphasize that our conception of cosmopolitanization differs from the Kantian concept of cosmopolitanism and other philosophical variants that entail a universalistic notion and envision a polis extending around the globe. The Enlightenment understanding of cosmopolitanism was a universal project limited to elites and insufficiently responsive to the underlying power relations that have shaped the diversity, particularity, and history of humanity (Hollinger 2001). The Kantian outlook and the universalism that sustains it predicate equality on sameness.

Such normative concepts are of little use for sociologists looking for global social processes. "To be useful for our purposes," according to Ulrich Beck (2004: 183 ff), "the Enlightenment concept of cosmopolitanism has to be freed from its origins in imperial universalism, such as we find in Kant and many others. It has to be opened up to the recognition of multiplicity. . . . To do this, cosmopolitanism has to lose its fixation on the purely global and be redirected to the interconnection between the global and the local."

Cosmopolitanization relates to processes that take place within national societies. The internalization of globalization takes roots as global concerns provide a political and moral frame of reference for local experiences (Beck 2002: 17–19). In a global context, "cosmopolitanism means first of all rooted cosmopolitanism," Beck writes. "There are several things to be learned from this. One is that it presents the clearest historical example of what actually happens when universalistic philosophy and particularistic local cultures exist side by side: they mix and produce new forms of both. They produce new forms of rooted cosmopolitanism, and they produce new forms of localism that are open to the world. By rooted cosmopolitanism, we mean universal values that are emotionally engaging, that descend from the level of pure abstract philosophy and into the emotions of people's everyday lives. It is by becoming symbols of people's personal identities that cosmopolitan philosophy becomes a political force. Cosmopolitanism thus disregards the prevailing opposition between cosmopolitans and locals: Cosmopolitanism does not exist without local particularities" (Beck 2000: 98–99). Conceptually, the notion of cosmopolitanization thus provides an analytic prism that captures a key dynamic in the global age—namely, the relationship between the global and the local (or, for our purposes, the national). Accordingly, we suggest that national and ethnic memories are transformed in the age of globalization rather than erased. They continue to exist, of course, but globalization processes also imply that different national memories are subjected to a common patterning. They begin to develop in accord with common rhythms and periodizations. But in each case, the common elements combine with preexisting elements to form something new. In each case, the new global narrative has to be reconciled with the old national narratives, and the result is always distinctive.

This book traces the theoretical and empirical foundations for the emergence of "cosmopolitan memories" through an examination of how the Holocaust has been remembered in Germany, Israel, and the United States in the past fifty years. We suggest that shared memories of the Holocaust, the term used to describe the destruction of European Jewry by Nazi Germany and a formative event of the twentieth century, provide the foundations for a new cosmopolitan memory. It is a memory that harbors the possibility of transcending ethnic and national boundaries. Can an event defined by many people as a watershed in European history (Bartov 1996; Diner 1999) be remembered outside the ethnic and national boundaries of the Jewish victims and the German perpetrators? Can this event be memorialized by people who do not have a direct connection to it? At the beginning of the third millennium, memories of the Holocaust facilitate the formation of transnational memory cultures, which in turn have the potential to become the cultural foundation for global human-rights politics (Levy and Sznaider 2004). This nation-transcending dynamic stands at the center of our sociological analysis. We are studying not the historical event called the Holocaust but how changing representations of this event have become a central political and cultural symbol facilitating the emergence of cosmopolitan memories.

The choice of the Holocaust is not arbitrary. The Holocaust—or, rather, the representations that produce shared memories—is a paradigmatic case for the relationship of memory and modernity. Modernity, until recently one of the primary analytic and normative frameworks for intellectual self-understanding, is itself questioned through memories of the Holocaust. In this view, the mass murder of European Jews by the Nazis is regarded not as a German–Jewish tragedy but as a tragedy of reason or of modernity itself (Adorno and Horkheimer 1999 [1944]; Arendt 1992 [1963]; Bauman 1989). We go beyond the critique of modernity and argue that, in an age of ideological uncertainty, these memories have become a measure for humanist and universal identifications. Hence, it is precisely the abstract nature of "good and evil" that symbolizes the Holocaust, which contributes to the extraterritorial quality of cosmopolitan memory.

Initially, revulsion about the Holocaust was prominent in Europe, as shown by Europeans' continuously negative attitudes toward nationalism and their corresponding willingness to let a set of transnational ideas and institutions take over certain aspects that had been under the firm sovereignty of the nation-state. However, as our findings show, by the 1990s the Holocaust had been reconfigured as a decontextualized event oriented toward nation-transcending symbols and meaning systems such as the United Nations' Universal Declaration of Human Rights of 1948. Memories of the Holocaust helped shape the articulation of a new rights culture. Once that culture was in place, however, it no longer needed to rely on its original articulation to take on strong normative powers. Jeffrey Alexander (2002) has referred to the Holocaust as the dominant symbolic representation of evil in the late twentieth century and as a foundation for a supranational moral universalism. Holocaust memory and the new rights culture have been mutually constitutive. The Holocaust is now a concept that has been dislocated from space and time, resulting in its inscription into other acts of injustice and other traumatic national memories across the globe.

References to the Holocaust abound in debates about slavery and colonialism. Many African intellectuals borrow from a Holocaust vocabulary to advance their own claims about European guilt and reparations (Soyinka 2000). Black Americans' demands for reparations for slavery frequently invoke references to the way Jewish organizations negotiated reparations with Germany (Torpey 2001). In China, "study of the Holocaust is linked to memory of the Japanese invasion and the Nanking massacre, as well as to the emerging consciousness of human rights" (Miles 2001: 511). To name but a few other examples that show the Holocaust's global reach: the United Nations' war-crimes tribunal for Rwanda referred to the Holocaust explicitly in a media trial when it accused three men of inciting Hutus to murder Tutsis and moderate Hutus; debates about the "stolen generation" in Australia have repeatedly drawn on the comparison (Moses 2003); and the major document on human-rights abuses in Argentina is titled "Nunca Mas (Never Again)." It is the universal nature of evil associated with the Holocaust that fuels its metaphorical power and allows it to be appropriated in referring to human-rights abuses that bear little resemblance to the original event.

Representations of the Holocaust have thus become a major point of reference for debates about memory in the 1990s. Memories of the Holocaust have been invoked to justify military interventions, provided a model for various measures of restitution, and contributed significantly to the formation of an international human-rights regime (Levy and Sznaider 2004). In what follows, we study the circulation of Holocaust memories beyond the conventional references to particular groups (such as nations) in an attempt to theorize collective memory in relation to globalization processes. In doing so, we hope to contribute not only to the study of memory but also to a broader debate about the cultural effects of globalization in general.

THE SOCIOLOGICAL RELEVANCE of Holocaust remembrance lies, among other things, in the fact that it is situated at a crucial juncture in the transition from First Modernity to Second Modernity. This distinction provides a useful heuristic device to address the methodological and empirical implications of global processes. Following Beck, the difference between First and Second Modernity is that modernity has begun to modernize its own foundations—it has become reflexive, directed at itself. This causes huge new problems both in reality and in theory. First, modernity depended tacitly but crucially on many non-modern structures for its clarity and stability. When modernization begins to transform those structures and make them modern, they cease to be useable foundations. To be sure, this process should not be construed as an evolutionary periodization; nor do those epochal distinctions imply that they are mutually exclusive.

A spatially fixed understanding of culture so thoroughly pervades classic works in sociology that it is rarely remarked on (Tomlinson 1999). It is a conception that goes back to sociology's birth amid the nineteenth-century formation of nation-states. Ironically, the territorial conception of culture—the idea of culture as "rooted"—was itself a reaction to the enormous changes that were occurring as the nineteenth century turned into the twentieth. It was a conscious attempt to provide a solution to the "uprooting" of local cultures that the formation of nation-states necessarily involved. Sociology understood the new symbols and common values above all as means of integration into a new unity.

The triumph of this perspective can be seen in the way the nation-state has ceased to appear as a project and a construct and, instead, has become widely regarded as something natural, something that has always existed. The nation-state has been accepted as the normal (and normative) state of affairs, abstracted into a conceptual language that frequently obscures the historical malleability of sovereignty. According to this view, the nation-state reflects a "spatial understanding of the possibility of political community, an understanding that necessarily gives priority to the fixing of processes of historical change in space. Not only does the principle of state sovereignty reflect a historically specific resolution of questions about the universality and particularity of political community, but it also fixes that resolution within categories that have absorbed a metaphysical claim to timelessness. . . . Time and change are perceived as dangers to be contained" (Walker 1990: 172–73).

At the beginning of the twenty-first century, globalization is posing a challenge to the idea that binding history and borders tightly together is the only possible means of social and symbolic integration. This revised idea of space is part of a long-standing historical process. It is for this reason, says Charles Maier (2000: 87), that the twentieth century is characterized most accurately by the emergence, rise, and subsequent crisis of so-called territoriality. Accordingly, the cosmopolitanization of collective memories serves as an example of how the concepts of nationhood and statehood are uncoupled.

Memories of the Holocaust revolve around the dichotomy of "particularism" and "universalism." Was the Holocaust a Jewish catastrophe with German perpetrators, or was it a universal catastrophe, a breakdown of civilization in modernity? These two forms of interpretation and their respective cultures of remembrance grew out of two historical events in the aftermath of the Holocaust that, at first glance, have nothing in common: the founding of the State of Israel and the issuing of the Universal Declaration of Human Rights. Both occurred in 1948 and refer to the particular as well as the universal interpretations that until recently have determined the image of the Holocaust. Both interpretations "make sense." Although they are not mutually exclusive, one is usually emphasized at the expense of the other.

Within the context of global Second Modernity, the meanings of universalism and particularism are transformed, as is the relationship of the two terms to each other. When we talk about Holocaust memories becoming more cosmopolitan in this book, we are not suggesting that they are now "universal" in the sense that one unified interpretation exists. The Holocaust will certainly not become a "totalizing" referent that means the same thing to everyone. Just as globalization leads to regional transformations and cosmopolitanism cannot do without the local in second modernity, meanings of the Holocaust emerge through encounters between the global and the local. In the process, the nation-state no longer maintains its hegemony over the interpretation of memories. The Holocaust becomes everyone's common property and allows people from different places to deal with it in the most diverse ways. Globalization and cosmopolitanization refer to concrete social spaces that are determined by an increasing degree of reflexivity and the everyday intermingling of different cultures. Here, the particular and universal are not opposing forces. Instead, they act together to determine a horizon of experiences that is fraught with discontinuities and uncertainties.

We replace the either–or perspective that dominated in First Modernity with a view of the relationship between universalism and particularism as a series of "as well as" options that extend over the second half of the twentieth century. In contrast to the earlier, Enlightenment universalism, one can now justify cultural and religious distinctions through a universal insistence on difference. During first modernity, particularities were relegated to the private sphere, and members of society were expected to acknowledge a generally valid (national) universalism. A "contextual universalism" (Beck 1997) that increasingly accepts transnational connections (such as dual citizenship and bilingualism) prevails in Second Modernity.

Analyzing Holocaust remembrance in the age of globalization serves as a means for examining the relationship between the universal and the particular. A dynamic relationship between the local and the global increasingly has become determined by cosmopolitan memory. The majority of studies insist that Holocaust memories are shaped by national imperatives, a view expressed in the proliferation of works on national memorial sites (Young 1997). While this focus on national sites of commemoration is important, it remains confined to territorial conceptions of memory. It does not sufficiently take into account how global *topoi* are inscribed into local and national discourse. Many scholars who acknowledge the influence of international politics and other external factors interpret them in terms of an instrumentalization of the Holocaust. They criticize the effects of globalization by equating them with the Holocaust's Americanization. (For examples of this tendency, see Cole 1999; Junker 2000; Loshitzky 1997; Rosenfeld 1997; Shandler 1999.)

The characterization of global culture as ostensibly timeless and without memory is based on a limited understanding of globalization, in which culture falls prey to worldwide homogenization. Such unification exists, however, primarily in the minds of the critics, whose bogeyman is "McDonaldization," or the reign of the Big Mac as the symbol of cultural homogenization (Ritzer 1993). Real, existing global culture is anything but homogeneous. Empirical studies show that global culture does not replace the local but engages with it through a process of hybridization (Friedman 1990; Nederveen Pietersee 2003). The same symbols have different meanings in different countries. Even the Big Mac is often mixed into national culture and politics and is adapted to local tastes. Our goal, of course, is not to redefine the Big Mac as a symbol of national aspirations. Rather, we will demonstrate that even this symbol of standardization is not in reality standardized. If national and global cultures intermingle even in this case, the idea of one homogeneous, global culture is hardly tenable. A far more meaningful approach would involve acknowledging that we are dealing with hybrid formations composed of both global and national elements.

Thus, we analyze globalization as an endogenous factor in current political culture. We are displacing the concept of collective memory from its former, purely national context and linking it to the process of cosmopolitanization. As mentioned, cosmopolitanization is a process of "internalized globalization" (Beck and Willms 2004). This means that it is a nonlinear, dialectical process in which the global and local exist not as cultural opposites but, rather, as mutually binding and interdependent principles. The process not only entails connections that break down old boundaries but also extends to the quality of the social and the political within national communities (Beck and Willms 2004). The cosmopolitanization of collective memory influences the self-image of various groups, whose identity is no longer dominated solely by the nation-state. Globalization leads to the "intensification of the self-awareness of the world as a whole entity" (Robertson 1995). Drawing on the work of Roland Robertson, we call the dialectical relationship that forms the basis of cosmopolitan memory "glocalization." Glocalization creates new connections that situate our political, economic, and social experiences in a new type of supranational context. As we will show, however, this process through which the global becomes internalized does not lead to a convergence and homogenization of Holocaust memories.

A central feature of this process of cosmopolitanization relates to the rise of rapid, electronically based communication, which has led to an interlocked system without national borders. This brings events that are far away from us close to home, which substantially influences the way people perceive their locality. The immediate speed and imagery of the new global communications facilitate a shared consciousness and cosmopolitan memories that span territorial and linguistic borders. A moral proposal is made to the viewer—a proposal that can be accepted or rejected but can hardly be ignored. In global times the media also becomes a mediator of moral affairs. (For a discussion of the moral consequentiality of the media, see Tester 1999.)

Here the global becomes a cultural horizon by which we measure our (local) existence. As mentioned, this de-territorialization (and, hence, de-nationalization) of memory does not entail abandoning the national perspective. Instead, it points to a transformation of the national through a more complex relationship between the global and the local, a relationship in which different groups react to globalization in different ways. While "national memory" is determined by identity that is produced within clearly defined borders, "cosmopolitan memory" is characterized by shifting boundaries and a process of de-territorialization.

The United States, Germany, and Israel as Empirical Examples

Both the historiography and the commemoration of the Holocaust have exploded in the past two decades. At the same time, we must emphasize that the central meaning of the Holocaust has been different in every country. Even the term "Holocaust" is surrounded by different taboos in different countries. The fact that the word has become sacred in this way is a sign that it has a central place in each country's set of central beliefs. Yet it is no accident that the same word is used in all of them. These different national meanings evolved at the same time. With the growth of cosmopolitanism and the circulation of activists, scholars, and media images, cross-fertilization has been increasing.

We examine three countries in which the Holocaust has played a foundational role in their self-images: Germany, Israel, and the United States. We will show how collective memories in those countries have undergone significant changes that warrant an analysis that transcends the nation-state. In the political cultures of Germany, Israel, and the United States, memories of the Holocaust are a prominent theme (Novick 1999; Olick and Levy 1997; Segev 1993). They are expressed in a reciprocal relationship of particular and universal forms of memory (Levy 1999). As noted earlier, in the past memories of the Holocaust were organized around a dichotomy of universalism and particularism (Young 1993). Instead of reducing these terms to their ideological assumptions, we treat them as important objects in our investigation. We historicize ideas of particularism and universalism, thereby de-moralizing them while retaining them as valuable sociological tools. As noted earlier, our primary objective is to disentangle these terms from their conventional "either–or" perspective and understand them in terms of "as well as" options.

Consequently, speaking about the cosmopolitization of Holocaust memory does not imply progressive universalism that is subject to a unified interpretation. The Holocaust does not become one totalizing signifier containing the same meanings for everyone. Rather, its meanings evolve from the encounter of global interpretations and local sensibilities. The cosmopolitization of Holocaust memories thus involves the formation of nation-specific and nation-transcending commonalities. These cosmopolitanized memories refer to concrete social spaces that are characterized by a high degree of reflexivity and the ongoing encounter with different cultures. According to this view, it is no longer the dichotomy but the mutual constitution of particular and universal conceptions that determine the ways in which the Holocaust can be remembered. The cosmopolitization of memory does not mean the end of national perspectives so much as their transformation into more complex entities where different social groups have different relationships to globalization. The inscription of Holocaust memories into local contexts thus produces processes not only of de-territorialization but also of re-territorialization. Hence, one of the central questions relates to the "right" or "appropriate" way to commemorate the event. Who does the Holocaust "belong" to in the global age? Can it belong only to the Jewish victims of the German perpetrators? How, for example, do immigrants to Germany remember the Holocaust? Or does the Holocaust belong to all who want to define themselves as victims?

The very principles of the United States correspond to the time-honored universalization of Holocaust memories: America is a land of immigrants. In contrast to Israel, the United States is the very *embodiment of universalism* in the sense that (ideally) anyone who legally resides in the United States or is born there can become an American citizen. Of course, in reality there are many restrictions; nevertheless, in the American conception of "good" and "evil," as inscribed in U.S. law and self-perception, it is always considered "wrong" to discriminate against an individual on the basis of his or her origins. The specifically American treatment of the Holocaust as a great crime—as the most horrific of all crimes—against humanity that has had a worldwide impact has its foundations in this principle. It is here that the general as well as the universal meanings of the Holocaust intersect, constituting the roots both of universal human rights and of cosmopolitan memory. But there is more to it. To prevent another Holocaust, human rights can be invoked, thereby restricting the autonomy of individual states. Thus, the "Americanization" of the Holocaust, notwithstanding debates within the United States, is also its universalization. The way in which a state treats its citizens is now a matter of general public interest, and the conflict between international law, which guarantees the sovereignty of the state, and human rights, which can undermine this sovereignty, is reflected in the latest developments in world politics. To whom the Holocaust "belongs" is the key issue in this conflict over memory.

In contrast to the heterogeneous United States, Israel is a Jewish state. It is the *embodiment of particularism* in that ethnic heritage is the decisive factor in determining citizenship. For this reason, particularism is the dominant form of remembrance in Israel. Germany lies between these two extremes. Its laws on citizenship and ethnic-identity politics move between universalism and particularism. In all three countries, the interpretation of the Holocaust is part of the political culture. This becomes quite apparent when one takes a quick look at museums and memorials. In Israel's central memorial, Yad Washem, the particular meaning of the Holocaust dominates, and the only relevant victims who are remembered are the Jewish ones. In Germany, the so-called perpetrator nation—a country that is ambivalent about its own national identity—the meaning of the Holocaust is a point of contention in debates on national history that keep resurfacing. In both Israel and Germany, Jews remain Jews (victims) and Germans remain Germans (perpetrators). At the U.S. Holocaust Museum in Washington, D.C., the Holocaust experience of the Jewish victims serves as a symbol for victims in general.

In sum, the Holocaust has been confronted by various forces that have attempted to universalize it, to particularize it, and to nation-alize it. Recently this memory has persisted on a global level. Its strength as a global collective memory has been powered and main-tained precisely through the fiery interaction between the local and the global. We argue that this dual process of particularization and universalization has produced a transnational symbol that is based on a cosmopolitanized memory—one that does not replace national collective memories but exists as their horizon.

THIS BOOK SITUATES our theoretical project within a comparative his-torical context. Part I is a theoretical analysis of memory and the nation-state and the dissolution of the connection between the two. We propose a new conceptual vocabulary for studying collective memories in the global age. In chapter 2, we historicize existing theories of mnemonics and suggest a rethinking of collective memory outside its usual national parameters.

In the past few years, the term "globalization" has been hotly debated. It has been assumed that collective memory, community, and geographical proximity must go together. We direct our attention to global processes that are characterized by their increasing separation, by the de-territoralization of politics and culture. Globalization thus changes the structure of collective memory. And just as we have abandoned the older, anthropological understanding of culture as internally coherent and holistic, we will have to abandon the sociological confinement of collective memory to the memory of territorially bounded nations.

Critics of globalization argue that the global is too broad a category to produce real identifications. There is no doubt that collective memory has been studied exclusively as pertaining to a group or a nation. Indeed, one can interpret the preoccupation with collective memory in the past two decades as a national reaction to the discourse of globalization and as an attempt to replace the increasingly discredited concept of the nation with that of collective memory. Other nations confronting a similar disintegration of national sensibilities have also turned to this type of memory work, examining the relationship between history and memory within the ongoing tension of tradition and modernity (Schulze and François 2000; Schwartz 2000; Yerushalmi 1983; Zerubavel 1995). Pierre Nora's *Realms of Memory* (1996), a touchstone in the literature of collective memory, is an excellent example of this point of view. Nora distinguishes between the social environments, or milieux, of memory, and the sites that have been set up to preserve the memory of events. He sees the latter as a substitute for living traditions. According to Nora and others, globalization leads to the dissolution of collective memories—or, more precisely, to inauthentic, rootless, superficial substitutes for them. But our argument is that the status of collective memory is now changing precisely because the nation and its purposes are losing their hegemony over the interpretation of memory. The traces of memory now travel freely across borders. The discourse of human rights is the vehicle on which this memory travels.

A similar argument can be applied to the analysis of time. Global culture does not wipe out local memories; instead, it mixes with them. The claim that the nation-state is the only container for a true understanding of memory is based on an ahistorical point of view. In the past few decades, a consensus has emerged in the historiography that acknowledges the "invention" of tradition (Anderson 1991; Hobsbawm and Ranger 1983). Ironically, when national cultures were invented, they were open to the same criticisms as those directed at global culture today. They were dismissed as superficial and inauthentic substitutes for local cultures that were once rich in tradition, and they were criticized as being much too large and alienating. Surely, it was argued, nobody would ever identify with the impersonal image of the nation. As history has shown, this prediction was wrong. By tracing the historical transformations of national and cosmopolitanized memories, we propose a conceptual tool kit that provides a perspective for studying collective memory in a globalized context.

Chapter 3 is a brief historical detour that explores changing conceptions of cosmopolitanism through the example of Jewish diaspora life. Memories of the Holocaust are bound up with the fate and the paradigmatic role of a de-territorialized existence of Jews. Before World War II, Jews lived the tension between universalism and particularism. They were present without really belonging, the kind of strangers described by Georg Simmel (1999 [1908]). This "not belonging" enabled the Jews to become the cosmopolitans of Europe but also the defenseless victims of the Nazis. The fate of European Jews was closely tied to that of the European nation-state. The Jews of Europe called into question the three premises of homogeneity on which the nation-state was always determined and defined: "homogeneity of space and time; homogeneity of space and population; and the homogeneity of past and future" (Beck and Bonss 2001: 22).

A central manifestation of this cosmopolitanism is expressed in the idea of diaspora. It offers itself as an alternative to rootedness, fixedness, the essence of belonging. Diaspora rejects the necessity of geographically defined nations. Diaspora opens possibilities for memory that reach beyond national modes of identification. We observe an elective affinity between the contours of cosmopolitan memories and the properties of diaspora. The defining elements of

Jewish existence before the Holocaust and before the establishment of the State of Israel—a mixture of longing for territorial independence and longing for the universal message of diaspora—are seen no longer as specifically Jewish issues but as more general arenas in which nationality, civil society, and cultural identities move. "Diaspora," a term that originated in Jewish tradition, has become detached from its Jewish roots through contemporary social-science usage.

Because there is less pressure to assimilate, and because cultural identity is legitimized within a pluralistic framework, minority groups are no longer forced to define themselves in terms of their new homeland. At the beginning of the twenty-first century, with improved means of transportation and communication, the overarching idea of diaspora has become an identity-forming concept that appeals to a growing number of people who have experienced a form of displacement, voluntary or forced. While the original concept referred to a community sent into exile, today "diaspora" is a desiderata and metaphor for many minority situations. Connection to a group with roots outside the coordinates of the host country, whether ethnic, national or religious, is now often a matter of choice and even a source of pride.

In Part II, we present our historical analysis of the transformation that led up to the cosmopolitization of memories during the 1990s. This periodization takes into account specific developments in the individual countries. Various historical events led to substantial changes in the political and cultural spheres of these nations. While our historical analysis reflects the developments in the three countries under investigation, it also transcends national boundaries and recognizes epochal commonalities that allow people to identify with cultural representations that originate elsewhere.

Our analysis of this transformation identifies four crucial time periods during which representations of the Holocaust were recast. We begin with the decade immediately following the end of World War II. This period was marked by silence concerning the destruction of European Jewry, which at that time did not even have a name and was broadly subsumed under the atrocities of the war. To be sure, Auschwitz was addressed by intellectuals and others, but the Holocaust did not permeate public discourse, nor was its commemoration institutionalized. Germany, Israel, and the United States had different reasons to be silent about this past, but there were also nation-transcending commonalities that informed postwar references to the Holocaust.

The second period encompasses the 1960s and early '70s, when awareness of the Holocaust began to grow. During this period, the foundations of the iconographic status of the Holocaust were established. This period constitutes a turning point for the reception and institutionalization of Holocaust memory. Against the background of a series of important trials of former Nazis, such as the trial of Adolf Eichmann in Jerusalem in 1961 and the Auschwitz trial in Frankfurt in 1963–65, detailed accounts and widespread media representations of the Holocaust reached a broad audience.

In the third period, during the late 1970s and early '80s, we observe a flood of commemorative events. A major turning point in media representation and the "Americanization" of the Holocaust came with the broadcast of the television series *Holocaust* at the end of the 1970s. Characteristic of these changes was the temporal duality of memory. Memories of the Holocaust came to be regarded simultaneously as unique with reference to the past and universal with reference to the future. That is, the Holocaust of the past was something that happened predominantly to the Jews, whereas the Holocaust of the future might happen to anyone.

Following this comparative analytic path of the Israeli, German, and U.S. landscapes of remembrance, the last part of our study deals with the 1990s. This fourth period, which commands the center of our analysis, culminates in the cosmopolitanization of Holocaust memories in the late 1990s. The end of the Cold War was a decisive turning point for the normative formation and institutionalization of cosmopolitanized memories. When the uniting interests and values of anticommunism vanished, international cooperation had to be reorganized on a new basis. The attempt to articulate and organize around new values has been a conscious one over the past ten years, and it is no accident that the Holocaust has come to play a major role in that reorganization. It has emerged precisely because of its status as an unquestioned moral value on which all people supposedly can agree. With the fall of the Iron Curtain and the crisis in Yugoslavia at the beginning of the 1990s, the Holocaust has provided a political and cultural basis for establishing new sensibilities and solidarities. This tendency reached a high point during the Kosovo conflict in 1998, when "military humanism" (Beck 1998) was legitimized through the slogan, "Never again Auschwitz."

The need for a moral touchstone in an age of uncertainty and the absence of master ideological narratives have pushed the Holocaust to prominence in public thinking. The Holocaust has become a moral certainty that now stretches across national borders and unites Europe and other parts of the world. Here, we focus on the role of "distant suffering" and newly formed "victim cultures" in the emergence of cosmopolitan landscapes of memory. Our main focus is not so much on the Holocaust as such. What interests us is not only how Holocaust memories endure but also how, through awareness of particular historical realities, they are transformed into meaningful political and cultural symbols.

One important feature of this nonlinear development is that the past does not determine the future in the same way. Rather than homogenizing and reducing the number of views, globalization divides each national political culture into several competing worldviews, some of which are more globalized than others. The central characteristic of the social carriers of global memory is that their personal relationships are determined less by the nation-state than by the world of which it is a part, and this leads them to interpret the world in a different way. Not only critical historians but also people who work for international nongovernmental organizations (INGOs), such as Human Rights Watch, have to be put into this category. Their political priorities are no longer the internal affairs of their nations. On the contrary, they seem to be working collectively to abolish the very meaning of domestic affairs, to make all human-rights transgressions by definition the world's affair. The sovereignty of nation-states is increasingly being challenged when human rights are at stake. Thus, we believe that those who argue that there is now a surfeit of memory that blocks actual politics ignore that debates about human rights, restitution, and justice on the global level cannot function without it.

These new narrative frameworks, and their mediation through political and cultural institutions, reconfigured the Holocaust as a decontextualized event and contributed to its focal position for a cosmopolitanized European memoryscape that has extended its normative reach. The end of the bipolar word ushered in a new phase of human-rights advocacy. The formation of a human-rights regime and the concomitant cosmopolitanization of sovereignty have become features of the post–Cold War period with political and cultural consequences. Once in place, this human-rights regime greatly informs the ongoing juridification of international politics and the cosmopolitanization of nation-states' sovereignty (Levy and Sznaider 2004). In contrast to the nation-state–forming characteristics of the international period a century earlier, the cosmopolitanization of the past two decades indicates a recasting of states' sovereignty. While the "old internationalism" regulated the relations between nation-states and sanctified their sovereignty, the "new cosmopolitanism" challenges the primacy of the nation and emphasizes the underlying interdependencies in a global age.

THIS BOOK WAS CONCEIVED in 1999, long before the so-called midlife crisis of the human-rights regime (Ignatieff 1999) and before the first epochal event of the twenty-first century—namely, the terrorist attacks of September 11, 2001. The blurring of peace and war and of civilians and combatants in the aftermath of the September 2001 terrorist attacks have given a new urgency to discussions about the political status of human rights and sovereign prerogatives (Calhoun et al. 2002). Suffice it to say that September 11 has propelled debates about human rights to the forefront of international and domestic rhetoric. Antiterrorist measures frequently infringe on civic rights and have given rise to demands that sovereignty be less conditional (Ignatieff 2001). Conversely, these attempts have also created strong opposition from international NGOs and other non-state actors seeking to preserve the role of human rights as a measure of legitimacy in the international community.

The juridification of international politics is a corrective to the arbitrariness that inheres in the application of human rights. The widespread internalization of human-rights norms through the collaboration of states and non-state actors also implies that disregard or violation of human rights incurs political liabilities for states both domestically and in their international relations. This is not a normative point but a conceptual one—that is, nation-states' sovereignty is no longer the only, or possibly even the decisive, political and normative category that shapes loyalties and solidarities. This holds true even in the age of global terrorism.

This book, then, is about the historical link between memories of the Holocaust and the emergence of a moral consensus about human rights. Against those who will wave the twin flags of cynicism and Realpolitik, it should be emphasized that even in times of terror and the fight against it, human rights cannot be done away with. Even a superpower such as the United States must take aspects of "soft power" into consideration, and the struggle for international legitimacy remains a central element for political success (Kagan 2004). Cosmopolitan memories have left their cage and become unbound.

Part I

2

Cosmopolitan Memory

FUTURE-ORIENTED MEMORIES emerge very slowly and compete continuously with national and ethnic memories. In the process, debates arise about the "right" memories. Who were the perpetrators? Were Jews the only victims, or were other groups victims, as well? How guilty can and should a country such as Germany feel? How long can a sovereign state such as Israel define itself in terms of "victimhood"? Such ongoing debates about appropriate ways to remember the Holocaust contribute substantially to shaping a self-reflexive and ultimately cosmopolitan form of memory.

For some time now, Israeli, German, and American debates have not revolved exclusively around the origins and nature of the Holocaust. Instead, they have focused on how the Holocaust was remembered in the past, how it should have been remembered, and, consequently, how it can be remembered in the future. Such controversies are not merely academic. Films, documentation, speeches, museum exhibits, and other media highlight these issues. In fact, it is precisely those popular representations of the Holocaust that have made the political and malleable nature of memories apparent to the broad public.

Does this mean, then, that concepts such as "collective memory" are losing their significance? Is this yet another "zombie" category that simply refuses to vanish from the sociological vocabulary? Can one even still talk about one "collective" that remembers? Does not globalization imply that collectives have dissolved and that we have become homeless, ahistorical individuals who collect memories in an ad hoc fashion—from TV, history books, movies, and friends and acquaintances—as if we were browsing supermarket shelves? All this raises another question: Does "collective memory" refer only to "national memory"? Or does it refer to a new incarnation of memory that transcends national boundaries and internalizes the global, challenging the foundation of national consciousness and memory at its very core? Pervasive migration flows and transnational experiences, for example, offer alternative forms of memory that transcend the physical borders of states. The impact of electronic communication, with its endless string of new images, is even more decisive in accelerating this boundary-transcending process. The media constantly remind us that the stories we tell ourselves are not the only sources of identification. Even the viewer who resists identifying with "other" stories must in some ways come to terms with them.

In the specific case of the Holocaust, the images that are tied to national identities—Germany as perpetrator, Israel as victim, and the United States as liberator—are no longer the only relevant ones. The lines between victim and perpetrator have become blurred. For instance, immigrants who become German citizens cannot and will not accept the label "perpetrator." As these boundaries begin to dissolve, generational ties are also loosened. Grandchildren do not feel responsible for the crimes of their grandparents. Palestinians, both inside and outside Israel, are no longer willing to view themselves as perpetrators and Israelis as victims. On the contrary, they turn the Holocaust on its head, placing themselves in the role of the "Jewish" victims, with the Israelis as the "German" criminals. Even the glorious narrative about the pristine image of the United States as liberator is being scrutinized by internal and external forces. Minority groups in the United States remind the nation about the crimes it perpetrated against Native Americans and African Americans. These and similar issues are part of the process in which the Holocaust is continuously reformulated, reinterpreted, discussed, evoked, and even, at times, denied. Along the way, the Holocaust is reaffirmed as the touchstone for a disoriented, de-territorialized humanity searching for moral clarity amid constant uncertainty. So is *this* perhaps what is meant by "collective memory" today? Could it be that the zombie actually lives?

Rather than discarding the concept of collective memory, we are transposing it from the confines of its formerly national context to a broader global one. The emphasis on global forms of memory stresses the temporal (i.e., whose past plays a decisive role, and for whom?) as well as the spatial (i.e., which geographic and political "borders" determine the cultural lives of groups?) transition from First to Second Modernity. As parameters shift, the images change. National frameworks and recollections have changed and continue to change as certainties begin to crumble. This does not imply, however, that memories become meaningless. The concept of memory should not be dispensed with in favor of fragmentation and ahistorical representations, as is frequently the case among postmodernists and even their critics. Some celebrate the loss of binding signifiers while others mourn it. Beyond these two poles, however, a framework is emerging in which these images can be understood and interpreted. The storehouse of memories can be considered empty only if one ignores how collective memory functions in a global world. On the one hand, those who embrace the notion of collective memory tend to ignore the global element, since they are oriented toward a national context and lack the necessary vocabulary to situate the collective outside the parameters of nationhood. On the other hand, if one gives up the concept of collective memory altogether, one plays into the hands of those globalists who identify it with the outdated nation-state and regard memory as merely a barrier against a global consumer culture. But in our opinion, there is no need to throw out the baby with the bathwater. Instead of rejecting collective memory because of its alleged murkiness or questionable ideology, the challenge is to redefine its sociological conditions of possibility and specify its relevance to the question of memory in the global age.

Global Representations

Collective memory is based on representations that need to be understood in temporal and spatial terms. Space and time are the coordinates that people use to organize their experiences. Specifically, cultural representations enable social groups to develop historical self-awareness and thereby also determine their relationship to other groups. Representations of memory are particularly important in this context. Different eras develop distinctive mnemonic forms and content (Hutton 1993). While these representations were previously determined almost exclusively through the community of the nation-state, processes of globalization, in their concrete manifestations as well as in their ideological aspirations, have greatly contributed to the reconfiguration of memory cultures. The following questions are central to our inquiry: How does globalization influence the circumstances and conditions necessary for the production of meaningful images? How are these images related to the experience of space and time? What influence do these images have on collective identities, and how do the changes affect memories that were originally produced in a local context? Can global images emerge in new arenas that are challenging the nation-state from below and from above?

The De- and Re-territorialization of Memories

Globalization transforms culture and the vocabulary used to produce meaning. This transformation becomes most evident when the particularities that make up a culture are ripped from their original spatial (i.e., local and national) contexts. Culture can no longer be understood as a closed national space, because it now competes constantly with other spaces. Transnational media and mass culture such as film and music are loosening the national framework without eliminating it entirely. In the process, conceptions and ideas about the world come into conflict with conceptions and ideas about the nation. Even the television viewer who never leaves his or her hometown must integrate global value systems that are produced elsewhere into his or her national frame of reference.

Globalization sets a process in motion that dislodges the idea of "society," understood as a territorially bounded system, from its traditional spatial and temporal social contexts. In our global age, cultural memory cannot be reduced, conceptually or empirically, to a territorially fixed approach. Consequently, cosmopolitan memory also reflects the search for new certainties, replacing those provided by the state during First Modernity. As we will argue, the slogan "Never again Auschwitz" has become this kind of assurance, extending beyond the countries and groups that have a direct connection to the Holocaust.

Today's media highlight the increased mobility of our society and the influence of electronic media that defies borders. This has also become a focus for some sociologists, who regard networks as an important boundary-transcending property (Castells 1996). Nevertheless, most people's experiences continue to be bounded by local coordinates. These processes are not mutually exclusive. Empirical research has shown that global culture does not replace local culture (Friedman 1990; Nederveen Pieterse 2003). But to incorporate these results into our theory, we have to stop thinking about "global" and "local" as mutually exclusive categories. They are, instead, two aspects of a single dialectical process. For this reason, when we want to talk about the universalizing side of this process, we refer not to "global" but to "globalizing" culture—something that influences, transforms, and patterns local culture. When we want to grasp the particularizing side of this process, we need a word that emphasizes that local cultures, after they are globalized, maintain distinctive identities. As we noted in the introduction, we draw on the work of Roland Robertson in calling this side of the process "glocalization." The creation of multiple connections that place our political, economic, and social experience in a new, supranational context starts with improved transportation and communication. The resulting nearness of the faraway changes the level at which people experience their localities. Globalization results in an "intensification of the consciousness of the world as a whole" (Robertson 1992: 8). This does not mean that we all become cosmopolitans, and it does not mean that we all participate in a single, homogenous culture. Rather, the global exists as a cultural horizon within which we interpret our existence.

This implies that one forms numerous ties that lead to political, economic, and social experiences in new supra-, trans-, and postnational contexts. Faraway events influence our local experiences. In the process, we do not become "enlightened" cosmopolitans; nor are we confronted with an unstoppable or unified global, hegemonic culture. De-territorialization always goes hand in hand with re-territorialization, which is made possible partly by awareness of catastrophes that threaten all of humanity. New certainties also arise

in the wake of uncertainties that affect everyone and could turn anyone into a potential victim. These uncertainties could be environmental, nuclear, or disease-related crises, to name a few. This sense
of insecurity can feed off the past and anticipate the future: Danger
lurks around every corner.

There is one type of catastrophe, however—one that occurred on
European soil—that encapsulates the idea of catastrophe per se: the
Holocaust. The ongoing transformation of Holocaust memories is
a result of farther-reaching processes of change, dissolution, and re-
building of traditional realms of life experience. As we will argue in
our empirical analysis, the de-territorialization of Holocaust memories in no way implies the end of nationally based structures of
remembrance. Rather, it implies the transposition of memories onto
a complex cultural terrain, where different groups offer distinctive
interpretations of the global and the nation.

The Effect of Glocalization on the Historical Understanding of Time

Place is not the only thing that loses its meaning and specificity.
The temporality of the nation-state, of ethnic groups—indeed, of
memory per se—is accelerated through global processes. The connection of past, present, and future to a particular place is loosened.
The presence of transnational migrants, a viewership drawn together
by globally televised spectacles and shared consumption of mass culture, has become pervasive; "our" past suddenly is also "their" future.
What kind of memories do Turkish Germans, Palestinians in Israel,
or African Americans claim as their own? Geographic and temporal distances are fading as many events are transmitted globally and
almost instantly. Distant suffering suddenly becomes visible to all.

Of course, the global individual is not completely self-sacrificing,
concerned solely with the suffering of others. Nevertheless, global
media offer up a selection that can be accepted or rejected. The
individual can choose to feel others' suffering or remain detached,
but choosing to ignore events is also a form of participation. The
current suffering of others must be made comprehensible, however;
it must be integrated into a cognitive structure that is connected to the

"memory" of other people's suffering. In this way, earlier catastrophes become relevant in the present and can determine a future that is articulated outside the parameters of the nation-state.

As mentioned, the Holocaust, as the definitive catastrophe, is caught up in this non-synchronous time—a point that is frequently overlooked by those who talk about a "Holocaust industry" and see the proliferation of commemorative sites as a purely economic phenomenon (Finkelstein 2000). The privatization of media and the vast reach of the Internet have resulted in an unstoppable torrent of information into which Holocaust memories are also swept. A quick glance confirms that Holocaust experts, pseudo-experts, deniers, memorials, museums, and so on cohabit on the Internet in global harmony and discord. The consumer faces an overwhelming amount of information. Unlike in First Modernity, however, the information is no longer hierarchically structured, and the uninformed user frequently has no way to know its source—whether it comes from the U.S. Holocaust Memorial Museum, from a pocket of neo-Nazis, or from the website of a serious historian. The power of memory is no longer centrally driven and becomes fragmented.

In the age of globalization, social and cultural differences become more apparent and start to influence the way memories are formed. This in no way implies that the revival of ethnic identities is merely a knee-jerk reaction to the supposedly homogenizing efforts of globalization. On the contrary. What we are dealing with is a self-aware, reflexive outlook that recognizes the world as an arena of experiences and involves an awareness of the welfare of others and of global conditions rather than actual contact with others. In this case, the world encroaches on the local scene, be it through actions occurring at the other end of the world that influence our existence or through a vision of an interconnected world. These different approaches to globalization lead to a multiplicity of temporal models and, above all, to the breakdown of a time line determined by past, present, and future.

There are two camps: those who view the "acceleration of time" as a threat, and those who integrate it into their everyday experience. For those who take the latter, reflexive attitude, their choice of identities is no longer necessarily based on existing continuities. Instead, it is based on informed preferences. This outlook has nothing to do with

evolutionary theories of modernization maintaining that particularism is a holdover from a premodern past. Here, universalism and
particularism exist side by side.

This nexus of time changes and the need for representational
mechanisms is acknowledged in the work of the French sociologist
Maurice Halbwachs, a foundational figure in the field of collective-
memory studies. Halbwachs (1980) distinguishes between social
memory and historical memory. Social memory is the memory of
things that one has experienced personally and that the group of
which one is a part has experienced. It is history before it becomes
history, the present experienced through a group and then remembered. For example, the social memory of the Holocaust is limited
to the generation who lived through the war. Historical memory, by
contrast, is memory that has been mediated by films, books, schools,
and holidays. For most people in most countries, national experience
is overwhelmingly based on such represented memories. In the case
of the Holocaust, only a small minority of people who experienced
Nazism firsthand is alive. Most people's experience on a national
scale—in the sense of extraordinary, history-making events—is based
on representative memories. Thus, the Nazi era is not part of most
people's lived experience, and memories of the Holocaust are based
exclusively on representations.

But this is not the only reason representations have become central to the formation of collective memories. Representations are
also taking on an increasingly important role in view of the worldwide network of global media and a weakening of the nation-state
as the dominant ideological force of meaning production. For this
reason, representation, conceived as an intersubjective process of
understanding, is central to the de-territorialization of memory.

Collective Memory in the Age of Mechanical Representation

Literature inspired by the Frankfurt School tends to critique representations as superficial and lacking authenticity (Benjamin 1969). Accordingly, social memory is perceived as authentic, lived experience,
whereas historical memory, which is propped up by representations,

is merely a mnemonic substitute. Critics of globalization regard mediated representations as something that dissolves collective memory and sets up inauthentic and rootless substitutes in its stead. Anthony Smith puts it as follows: "A timeless global culture answers to no living needs and conjures no memories. If memory is central to identity, we can discern no global identity in the making" (Smith 1995: 24). Why can a "timeless global culture" conjure no memories? Because, Smith says, timelessness is of its essence: "This artificial and standardized universal culture has no historical background, no developmental rhythm, no sense of time and sequence. . . . alien to all ideas of 'roots,' the genuine global culture is fluid, ubiquitous, formless and historically shallow" (Smith 1995: 22). Smith's statement is emblematic of two recurring assertions. One restricts memory to the symbolic boundaries of the nation; the other situates it in a normative dichotomy of real lived experiences and inauthentic mediated representations.

To say that nations are the only possible containers of true history is a breathtakingly un-historical assertion. Religious traditions and institutions such as the Catholic church and Judaism are good examples. In addition, there is now a vast literature on national tradition, and it is clear that every single national tradition has gone through a moment of "invention" (Hobsbawm and Ranger 1983). What makes the irony especially rich is that, when national cultures were being invented, they were attacked using exactly the same arguments that are leveled at global culture today: that they were superficial and inauthentic substitutes for rich local culture, and that no one would ever identify with such large and impersonal representations. Notwithstanding the fact that this turned out to be spectacularly wrong, the perception that representations are substitutes for "authentic" experiences persists.

Pierre Nora is a prime exponent of this point of view. As noted earlier, he distinguishes between the social environments, or milieux, of memory and the sites that have been set up to preserve the memory of events. He sees the latter as a substitute for living traditions. "Memorial sites exist because the social environment of memory exists no longer, the surroundings in which memory is an essential component of everyday experience" (Nora 1996: 1). This distinction between authentic memories and their substitutes is a necessary pre-condition to a view such as Smith's that global culture is producing an "eternal present" (Smith 1995: 21). To be sure, face-to-face interaction is different from mediated interaction. The story of the Holocaust told by survivors to their children is different from what one learns from a movie or in school. But there is a fallacy in thinking that impersonal representations are somehow fake and not connected to our real emotions and real identities. Once again, the history of the nation-state is instructive. Nora's view essentially restates the late–nineteenth-century opposition of *Gesellschaft* and *Gemeinschaft*, which placed the new, nationwide political and economic structures in opposition to those of local communities. It claimed that larger structures were soulless. Part of this soullessness lay in their imper-sonal means of communications, such as the newspapers. But the argument turned out to be a romantic and nostalgic one. Mechani-cal representations did not stand in the way of strong identification. They fostered it.

Our critique of Nora is directed against his implicit norma-tive claim and the fixation on the nation-state as the sole possible (and imaginable) source for the articulation of collective memories. Hence, he laments, "The acceleration of history, then, confronts us with the brutal realization of the difference between real memory and history, which is how our hopelessly forgetful modern societies, propelled by change, organize the past" (Nora 1989: 8). He constructs an opposition that is reminiscent of the *"fin de siecle syndrom,"* based on the abstract assumption that modernity destroyed tradition, with its microsociological equivalent focusing on alienation and anomie among individuals without social bonds. The same objections that were raised against the modern nation-state at the end of the nine-teenth century now serve as the last resort in its defense. However, in both transitions—to the national and to the global—representations are playing a central role.

In *Imagined Communities* (1991), Benedict Anderson describes how all communities, and especially nations, are unities that are funda-mentally imagined. The very belief that there is something funda-mental at the bottom of them is the result of a conscious myth-building process. To come into existence, the nation-state depended at the turn of the twentieth century on a process by which existing societies used representations to turn themselves into new wholes that would act immediately on people's feelings and on which they could base their identities—in short, to make them into groups with which individuals could identify. The essential point of Anderson's thesis, which is often overlooked, is that a new system of values requiring self-sacrifice and willingness to live together is necessary in the transition to nationhood. In the premodern era, solidarity was based primarily on direct contact with the "Other" (ethical boundaries correlate to village boundaries); with the "nationalization of the masses," it became necessary to identify with many other people whom one could not possibly get to know personally via an "imagined community." We do not know each other, and yet we feel united as citizens of the same country.

This nation-building process parallels what is happening through globalization at the beginning of the twenty-first century. The nation *was* the global when compared with the local communities that preceded it. However, this did not render the nation inauthentic. The ability of representations to give a sense to life is not ontologically but sociologically determined. So if the nation is the basis for authentic feelings and collective memory—as the critics of global culture seem almost unanimous in maintaining—then it cannot hold that representations are a superficial substitute for authentic experience. The nation was literally inconceivable without an imagined community. So to the contrary, representations are the basis of that authenticity, and there is nothing theoretically or empirically inconceivable about their providing such a basis on a global level.

Hence, rather than privileging one form of memory over the other, it seems more fruitful to identify the different historical and sociological conditions of memory cultures. Jan Assmann's distinction between two memory types is instructive. He differentiates between communicative memory, which is based on group-specific carriers, and cultural memories that can exist independent of their carriers: "What is at stake is the transformation of communicative, i.e. lived and in witnesses' embodied memory, into cultural, i.e. institutionally shaped and sustained memory, that is, into 'cultural mnemotechnique'" (Assmann 1991: 343).

Far from leading to a form of collective amnesia, these transformative processes actually lead to the proliferation of memories. Aleida Assmann points out that

> the reason for this is that the eyewitnesses' memory of their experiences, if it is not to be lost to posterity, must be translated into the cultural memory of future generations. Living memory thus gives way to a media-oriented memory, which is supported by such material symbols as monuments, memorial sites, museums, and archives. While certain types of memories are waning, such as the memory based upon formal learning and cultural traditions, and, in connection with the Shoah, lived memories, others, such as those generated by media and politics, are clearly on the rise. (Assmann 1999: 15)

The transformation and proliferation of these cultural memories provide an interesting historical and analytic lens to compare both transitions—that is, the materialization of nationalism toward the end of the nineteenth century and the emergence of cosmopolitan orientations at the end of the twentieth century. Anderson identifies three cultural models that lost their significance before the nation could be imagined: the decline of the written word as a privileged carrier of ontological truth; the decline of cosmological time; and the decline of dynasties. All of these elements are reemerging today under a new guise. National newspapers now compete with ubiquitous global images. Books, magazines, and newspapers that had promoted and reflected national loyalty are up against global media that can reorient their readers toward an international perspective. On the one hand, time is more unified; on the other, we are witnessing the construction of a mélange of times (Nederveen Pietersee 2003). In other words, the dis-simultaneity of simultaneities has become perceptible. The time of the nation-state (history) is no longer identical with the time of the citizen of that state, which results in the breakup of the nation's linear chronology. People are increasingly constructing their biographies without regard to the prescribed rules of the state. This can appear in the form of family time or work time. More important for our argument is the fact that experiences, including local ones, are also oriented toward a global horizon. This, of course, is not a homogeneous time, since globalization is a process of internalization that revolves around the local appropriation of global values rather than a mere superimposition of the latter on the former, as some scholars of homogenization would have it. There are a number of ways to find a fitting system of reference. One can turn inward (to one's own ethnic or religious group) or look outward (to global value systems such as human rights). The time of the nation-state is thus undermined both from within and from outside.

The Pluralization of Memories: The Fragmentation of Memory and the Decline of the Nation-State

The real issue is the purported dearth not of representations but, rather, of their source. According to Nora, memories are becoming increasingly fragmented and are no longer solely a product of the nation-state. Along with this transformation, Nora recognizes that the transmission of memory has expanded to social forces outside the realm of the state. He writes: "The coupling of state and nation was gradually replaced by the coupling of state and society" (Nora 1989: 11). No longer is the nation-state the uncontested privileged site for the articulation of collective identity. Nora points to and deplores the erosion of the state's ability to impose a unitary and unifying framework of memory. Consequently, he laments the fact that our time is no longer spent celebrating the nation; it is spent studying the ways in which we celebrate it. Much of our present political and cultural discourse is devoted to debunking the myth of the nation. Nora observes: "While challenging a tradition may be a worthy enterprise, it also means that that tradition can no longer be handed down in an unaltered state" (Nora 1989: 10). This does not in any way suggest that the era of the nation-state is over. Rather, it suggests that the nation-state's hegemonic reign as the central producer of meaning has come to an end. National memories are now mixed with collective memories culled from other, collective expressions of solidarity such as ethnicity, gender, and religion.

One of the central characteristics of collective memory in Second Modernity is its reflexivity. This reflexive transformation is the product of a transition from social memories to historical recollection. In German debates, this is highlighted via the distinction between memory (*Erinnerung*) and recollection (*Gedächtnis*): "Through their specific identity, memory signifiers, signifiers of a culturally specific mnemotechnique, take on the character of a code. They are proof that one is a member of a specific group. In contrast, signifiers of recollection are not about short-term memories; they are about the processing of these memories" (Dabag and Platt 1995: 12).

What characterizes the transformation of collective recollection in second modernity is precisely this processing of memory. At its core lies the distinction between memory and history, a distinction that Nora does not recognize. He maintains that

> recollection is a phenomenon that is always in the moment.... [H]istory, in contrast, is a representation of the past. Since recollection is affective and magical, it is made up solely of details, which is what give it its force.... As an intellectual, secular enterprise, history demands analysis and critical debate. Recollection takes memory into the realm of the sacred, whereas history drives it out. History strives for demystification. (Nora 1998: 13)

The signs that lead Nora to conclude that there is a lack of authenticity in the present are, for us, the very wellspring of a self-reflexive culture of recollection. Recollection and memory blend together, a phenomenon that is particularly evident in the history and remembrance of the Holocaust. This is why the literature of remembrance, which is increasingly dissolving the old historical narratives, plays such a dominant role here.

Media Events and the Technological Conditions of Globalization

Media events on a global scale are possible only because of technological breakthroughs in electronic media. Patrick Hutton (1993) outlines how developments in the field of communications go hand in hand with new forms of memory. According to Hutton, oral cultures rely on memories of lived experiences. In cultures of literacy, however, we "read" to retrieve forgotten wisdom from the past. The invention of the printing press to produce books and newspapers was crucial in this process of reconstructing the past.

How do the new global media transform collective memory? The technological revolution that introduced the printing press textualized culture. The printed text led to an externalization of knowledge and laid the foundation for reference to shared knowledge. The global media have led to yet another revolution in the reception of knowledge, values, and memories: They have promoted a visual culture. We now remember things with the aid of images, which helps to explain why exhibitions, films, memorials, and other media are becoming so important. This development is highlighted by the increase in so-called media events. According to Daniel Dayan and Eliahu Katz (1992), these events can be understood as something like holidays that provide viewers with the opportunity to concentrate on shared principles and collective memory. They are characterized by the impression they give of being "live." Even when the focus is on conflicts, the media serve to shape a common understanding of the "event." Media events are often regarded as important dates that are meaningful to large groups of people.[1] Through these events, news from the entire world enters local life worlds. Not only is the local seen as part of a larger global context, but the world itself is presented as a meaning-creating political, cultural, and moral force. Given the intensity and extensiveness of such media events, Dayan and Katz suggest, the globalized media play a significant role in the formation of an imagined world community.

This resonates with Anderson's description of how the nation was made into a "horizontal society" and how various symbols through which this society was represented to itself played a key role. It was precisely the now lambasted media that produced the requisite solidarity through constant repetition of images and words. Technological changes in the means of communications are of central importance for the structuring of memory time and culture. In the era of the nation-state, the central institution was the press. In the era of globalization, the electronic media play an analogous role (Thompson 1995). A distinctive element of the new media is the rise of "media events," through which a live and concentrated local action can be shared by the world (Dayan and Katz 1992). This is how

---

1. This is outlined on an empirical and theoretical level in Gebhardt 2000.

the world is transported into the local. Distant others can be part of the strong feelings of everyday life. But we have to emphasize here the overriding importance of the local context. People do not simply identify with what they see on television. Strong identifications are produced only when distant events have local resonance. But paradoxically, this ethnocentric focus on events is precisely the process that causes a belief in, then a willingness to act on, universal values. The basis of a wider shared morality is identification with distant others. However, this is produced through a connection of the global with the local. The new identity is produced not instead of the old but by transforming it—just as in the building of nations.

3

Holocaust and Diaspora

The Holocaust: Product or Crisis of Modernity?

WHY HAS THE HOLOCAUST captured so much more attention than any other catastrophe in the past two decades? The enormity of the atrocity would seem reason enough, but there must be more to it than that. The proliferation of Holocaust discussions in the United States, Europe, and Israel at the end of the twentieth century coincided with an important phase in the transition from First to Second Modernity. Why has this catastrophe become a catalyst for cultivating a global consciousness? By global conscience we do not mean a unitary, universal, and homogeneous conscience but, rather, a mixture of patterns of Holocaust memory and various local manifestations of how the Holocaust is remembered, if at all.

Other catastrophes have not had the same impact. For example, Hiroshima as a symbol of nuclear disaster has not become a medium for cosmopolitan remembrance. There are a number of reasons for this. For one thing, cosmopolitanism was formerly limited to Europe and the United States, and the Holocaust is a European phenomenon. This seems counterintuitive at first. The Japanese seem not only to have developed victim consciousness long before anyone else did in the 1960s, but they actually called it by that name and supplied it with a very detailed metaphysics (Buruma 1994). Most important of all, Japanese remembrance had very different fundamental assumptions: It began with universalism. That is, it began with the idea that modern warfare made everyone victims, no matter who wins or loses the war. Therefore, war itself was the object to be wiped out.

The Japanese thought of themselves as the ultimate victims because they had experienced nuclear war, which in the aftermath of World War II was perceived as the most likely scenario for future warfare. That is what the lessons of Japanese victimhood were designed to prevent—another world war that would draw everyone into its orbit. By contrast, memories of Jewish victimhood were supposed to prevent another Holocaust. The big difference, of course, is that in the "nuclear Holocaust" scenario there ultimately is no difference between victors and vanquished. World War III will make victims of us all. In Holocaust-derived victim consciousness, by contrast, there is an essential divide between innocent victims and evil perpetrators.

This dichotomy is important in the new global politics of the late twentieth and early twenty-first century. It will supply the foundation for what is called "military humanitarianism." It might be more accurate to redefine the dichotomy as a parallel—and somewhat incompatible—conception of victimhood, one universal and one particular. The particular one highlights the crimes of the aggressor; the universal one downplays them through the very idea that we are all victims. Because of increasing globality—that is, the global flow of information and a growing sense of interconnectedness—the rate of cultural transfer and exposure has expanded far beyond the European and North American horizons. Nevertheless, European and U.S. experiences continue to play a central role. This is one of the reasons that the war in Bosnia and Kosovo caused such a stir, whereas the reaction to the genocide in Rwanda was relatively muted and slow in coming, as the ten-year commemorations of that genocide in April 2004 clearly demonstrated.

The main reason for the prominence of Holocaust remembrance is the transformation of existing national memories. A historical development has taken place in Israel, the United States, and Germany that did not occur in Japan. Of course, it was in the political interests of the United States to keep Hiroshima out of the international spotlight. It was the United States, together with other nations—a fact that is often overlooked—that defeated Nazi Germany. But it was also the Americans who dropped the atomic bomb on Hiroshima. In the case of other catastrophes, such as natural disasters and environmental issues of global scope, it usually is not possible to identify one responsible party. In the case of the Holocaust, in contrast, a number of elements converge. The issue of guilt is clear-cut. But guilt is not the only factor. On a much more fundamental level, civilization, modernity, the self-image of Europe and America, and, with it, the self-image of almost the entire world hang in the balance.

Social scientists and theorists turned their attention toward universal (and thus generalizable) features of Nazism. It was within the broader theme of modernity that social theorists started to pay attention to the Holocaust and its effects on the relationship between modernity and social theory. In looking at some of the principal social theorists who have tackled the phenomenon of the Holocaust, we can identify two ambivalent conceptualizations of modernity. One perceives modernity as the realization of progress and is firmly embedded in Enlightenment ideals; the other focuses on barbarism as the flip side of these processes. A central question that links the two is whether barbarism constitutes a separate breakdown of civilization or is part of modern rationalization and bureaucratization itself.

The founding fathers of sociological theory are firmly embedded in the first camp. For them, civilization is the guiding principle of modern society; barbarism is its counter-principle. Progress and civilization are not merely the outcome of modernity; they are its constitutive principles. Preindustrial societies are seen as lacking in reason, rationality, and progress, to mention a few of the core ideas of modernization theories that dominated the social sciences after World War II. To be sure, these founding fathers were aware of the costs that modernity could incur: Max Weber's "Iron Cage," Karl Marx's "alienation," and Emile Durkheim's "anomie," to name but a few, are evidence of the ambivalence with which modernity was perceived. But ultimately they all stressed the potential of modern society to become the bearer of Enlightenment ideals. Accordingly, most social scientists viewed the Holocaust as an aberration and a perversion of those ideals. In contradistinction, social theory since the Holocaust has been debating the relationship between barbarism and modernity. Rather than viewing the Holocaust as a deviation from the emancipatory path, some perceive barbarism and civilizational

breaks as qualities inherent in, and sometimes even as inevitable out-
comes of, modernity and the Enlightenment.

Hannah Arendt embodied both the Enlightenment and a strong
skepticism in her political and social theory. An article published
in 1950, "Social Science Techniques and the Study of Concentration Camps," provides first clues. In it, Arendt claims that the concentration camps are beyond understanding if one remains within
the conventional social-science assumptions of rationality. Why?
Because, she says, most of our actions are utilitarian in nature.
Totalitarianism—or in this case, the camps—do not fit this utilitarian-
ism. To Arendt, the Nazis seemed more concerned with running extermination factories than with winning the war. Her later works *The
Origins of Totalitarianism* (1958 [1951]) and *Eichmann in Jerusalem* (1992
[1963]) echo these initial thoughts on the Holocaust. The ambivalence
between these frames of civilization and barbarism remained the primary organizing principle for Arendt's thoughts on the Holocaust.
For Arendt, the Nazis, and Eichmann as Nazism's personification,
represented the breakdown of the Enlightenment and democracy, of
critical judgment, and of reason. Nazism was not particularly German
but, rather, a manifestation of totalitarianism.

Universalizing the phenomenon did not keep Arendt from rec-
ognizing its singular features. She perceived the uniqueness of the
Holocaust not only in the scope and systematic nature of the killings,
but also in the very attempt to deny humanity as such. Conventional
categories of crime become irrelevant, a view that was later incorporated into the legal canon via the concept "crimes against humanity."
Arendt's own ambivalence about whether the Holocaust was beyond
comprehension or required a new vocabulary is shown in her shifting
understanding of the nature of evil. In her work on totalitarianism she
called attention to the idea of "radical evil," but by the time she observed the Eichmann trial in 1961 she was emphasizing the "banality
of evil" and Eichmann as its personification.

However, Arendt was not willing to endorse wholeheartedly the
position taken by Theodor Adorno and Max Horkheimer in *Dialectic of the Enlightenment* (1999 [1944]). According to Adorno and
Horkheimer, barbarism is an immanent quality of modernity rather
than its corruption. According to their view, civilizational ruptures

inhere—at least, potentially—in the processes of rationalization and bureaucratization that characterize modernity. It is the breakdown of reflexivity within modernity that facilitates the destructive potential of modernity. This has little to do with German peculiarities, but it is related to the Western process of instrumental reasoning and Enlightenment.

Unlike Adorno and Horkheimer, Arendt did not regard the Holocaust as a culmination of modernity. She is often misread because of her thesis on the "banality of evil," which claims that it is not necessary to have monsters for the monstrous to become reality.[1] This approach allows one to remove the perpetrators of the Holocaust from their original cultural and national contexts and to focus instead on structures of modernity. This is one more step in decontextualizing the Holocaust. It is dislodged from its historical framework and thereby rendered more "accessible."

A comparable de-contextualization can also be observed with respect to the victims. Who were the victims? Or, more precisely, who are the victims, and who will they be in the future? By rethinking the Holocaust, the Jewish victims can come to represent victimhood in general. The Jew is the "Other," whereas the perpetrator is the "Non-Other," so to speak. In what way is the position of the stranger thereby altered?

Just as Arendt attempted to universalize the Nazi criminal, Zygmunt Bauman universalizes the victim. In *Holocaust and Modernity* (1989), Bauman suggests a radicalization of the modernity-equals-barbarization thesis. Here we have traveled from one extreme of the continuum (the assumption that barbarism is a counter-principle of modernity) to another extreme (Bauman's view that modernity equals barbarism). The Holocaust is no longer a perversion of the

---

1. Contrary to Arendt's own intentions, her thesis formed the ideological and theoretical basis of a historiographical approach that became known as "functionalism" (see Mason 1979). This should not be confused with the sociological method of the same name, even though the two have some things in common. Historiographical functionalism explains the Holocaust through impersonal bureaucratic forces and collective processes—or, in the words of its leading proponent, "cumulative radicalization" (Mommsen 1983) that was based on fragmented decision-making processes and competition within the Nazi regime. Anti-Semitism plays a secondary role in this analysis; the "Final Solution" is considered a result of bureaucratic processes.

principles of rationality. Rather, it is its direct outcome insofar as it provides the necessary logistics for its execution. Furthermore, Bauman suggests that the inability of the social sciences to grasp the essence of the Holocaust is also a function of its sociological approach to morality as such. He objects to a historical understanding of the moral foundations of modern society and argues that distance between people prevents all moral relations between them. Instead, he stipulates a presocial morality or an unsocialized self based on unconditional responsibility for the other. Consequently, he views modernity not as the foundation of morality but as a main source of its corruption. For Bauman, the lessons of the Holocaust have to lead to a postmodern ethics, making his arguments part of the postmodern turn. If Arendt focuses on the *human condition*, emphasizing the social and political environment by which morality is circumscribed, Bauman stresses *human nature*, conceived as an ahistorical and ultimately ontological category.

Both arguments undermine attempts to situate the Holocaust within one precise historical and cultural context. But these approaches ultimately remain dependent on the polarity of universalism and contextualization. We, by contrast, want to show how the Holocaust is contexualized and appropriated for particular readings while also giving it conceptual wings so it can break out of its historical context and be connected to a more universal appropriation. We are no longer dealing with the either–or between particularism and universalism but are taking an inclusive approach. Specifically, we are attempting to think Auschwitz within the framework of a contextualized universalism. It is not sufficient, in our opinion, merely to denounce modernity as the source of barbarism. Instead of dismissing out of hand the role of the Other in modernity, as Bauman does, we will demonstrate how the relationship to the "Jewish Other" in Second Modernity has, in light of specific forms of Holocaust remembrance, been transformed from a term loaded with negative connotations to a positive one, operating as a kind of moral imperative.

Bauman also "universalizes" the Jewish philosopher Emanuel Levinas by failing to see his connection to a specifically Jewish philosophy. Ethics, for Levinas, is first and foremost Jewish ethics. In contrast, Bauman regards a "moral universalism" with no specific social context as the only appropriate answer to the "immoral universalism" of modernity. Levinas recognized, however, that the Jewish state of uprootedness could give rise to very specific moral convictions: "The Jewish person discovers individuals before he discovers landscapes and cities. He is at home in a society before he is at home in his own house" (Levinas 1990: 23). Through Levinas we are introduced to a perspective that can be interpreted as thoroughly cosmopolitan. In our opinion, the Jewish diaspora can serve as a paradigm for de-territorialization as such. A particular awareness of place and the relationship to being Other are played out on an immediate experiential level here.

But how other is this Other the new hero of universal identity politics? The diaspora was never a closed-off sphere. Lived Jewish culture was not only mixed with other cultures; it was itself a mixture of cultures. In a certain sense, its cosmopolitanism lay in Judaizing the mixture of cultures it absorbed: It gave them a unifying cast without negating them. This is part of why Jewish culture is so well adapted to be the background model of second-wave modernity. The experience of diaspora, of life in exile, is the clearest example modernity offers of a sustained community life that did not need a territorial container to preserve its history. In Jewish experience, life outside the nation-state is nothing new. That is precisely why the Jewish genocide has become the central theme in the mnemonic structure of Second Modernity.

For Levinas, the social is an expansion of the interpersonal. Bauman misinterprets Levinas's ethics as something that exists outside society. Consequently, he understands "Being with Others" as a moral principle that acts independently from—or even *against*—socialization processes. Hence, the Holocaust should not be interpreted as a universal experience. It should be understood for what it was: an attempt to annihilate the European Jews. This does not undermine the globalization of memories. On the contrary. These memories are part of the globalization process and even surface in anti-globalist discourses. The parallels in the rhetoric of anti-Semitism and anti-globalism are striking. In the former case, the "Jew as Other" was often taken up as a symbol of rootless urban modernity. From this perspective, the Jewish experience forms the antithesis to the sentimentalized anti-modernity of Germans (and others). The work of the German sociologist Werner Sombart illustrates this position quite well. Sombart equates the city with the desert and places the Jews in both: "The big city is a direct extension of the desert—both are equally far removed from the steaming clump of native soil and both force its inhabitants to become nomads" (Sombart 1911: 423). The Jewish desert and the Jewish big city form a counterpoint to the German forest, where heroes dwell. Already during World War I, Sombart regarded the battle against the British as a struggle between heroes and merchants. For the heroes, society provides ethical boundaries, whereas for the merchants, the boundaries may stretch to infinity. From this perspective, the Jews were always without a home, without a fatherland, without honor. In the anti-Semitic fantasy, the Jews were also portrayed as feminized, commercialized, and, like money, abstract. These same *topoi* persist under the surface in right- and left-wing forms of anti-Americanism and anti-globalism—in their aversion to abstraction and, in particular, the abstract nature of money. If there are similarities between anti-Semitism and anti-globalism, then the "global" remembrance of the Holocaust is also a memory that connects back to the Jewish victims.

Cosmopolitanism and Jewish Victims: The De-territorialization of Memory

Cosmopolitanism and Holocaust Remembrance

Which group, then, could carry such cosmopolitan memories? Social scientists have concentrated primarily on two: the elite (e.g., intellectuals in the media and business leaders), and transnational migrant workers (Castells 1996). We will look at a third group, whose impact on the de-nationalization of memory is not necessarily a result of their physical presence so much as of their function as representatives of victimhood and the Other. Holocaust memories have taken on a cosmopolitan scope because they enable diverse oppressed groups to recognize themselves in the role of the Jewish victims. It is for this reason that the Holocaust—or, specifically, the equating of current victims with the Jewish victims—plays a major role in the cosmopolitanism of Second Modernity.

It is important to reiterate that cosmopolitanism is no longer merely a philosophical approach. Identifications are anchored in ritual and commemorative practices that appeal to people through visual and emotive channels. It is by embodying philosophy in rituals that cosmopolitan identities are created, reinforced, and integrated into communities. This is what happened in the transition from Greek philosophy to syncretistic religions. But this is not a purely historical point. It is something that still affects us. The most important syncretistic religion to grow out of the Hellenistic period was Christianity, a clear combination of universalistic, Hellenistic Greek philosophy (especially stoicism and neo-Platonism) and local religious beliefs (notably, Jewish Messianism). The combination changed the elite ethos of stoicism into the mass religion of Christianity. As we will argue later, much of what we now take for granted as cosmopolitan morality is a secularized form of Christianity. Of course, one could say the same about the Enlightenment—that it represented a secularization of Christian morality. The Enlightenment is conventionally regarded as quite the opposite: as the rise of a rationalism that was militantly antireligious. Now we know that this is an exaggeration. What the Enlightenment called deists and atheists we now call religious people.

The argument that the Enlightenment was in many ways a continuation of the Christian tradition should not in itself excite too much comment today. But what difference does it make to the spread of cosmopolitan ideas? Calling the Enlightenment a secularized religion rather than an abstracted philosophy emphasizes the centrality of emotional engagement and social integration. It also emphasizes that both are bound up with symbol and ritual, not just with spoken ideas. It is symbol and ritual that turn philosophy into personal and social identity.

In what follows, we will show how, in the context of globalization, the role of the Jews as the paradigmatic Other has contributed to a positive reorientation of the concept of cosmopolitanism. The identification of other victim groups with the Jewish victims of the Holocaust has altered the significance of contemporary cosmopolitanism. This has occurred at least partly because the Jewish experience was a paradigmatic example of cosmopolitanism during First

Modernity. The only difference was that during modernity's heyday, the de-territorialization of Jewish identity—evident in the primacy awarded religion and, later, Zionism—was interpreted by liberals and nationalists alike as a sign of the Jews' inability to assimilate within a national framework.

Therein lies the bitter irony of today's cosmopolitanized form of remembering the Holocaust: The Jews were persecuted and murdered precisely because of their cosmopolitanism. Prior to the Holocaust and to the founding of the State of Israel, the Jewish experience was determined by a mixture of yearning to be territorially independent and to be universal ambassadors of the diaspora. Nowadays, however, these can no longer be considered specifically Jewish concerns. Instead, they constitute the broader arena in which issues of citizenship, civil society, and cultural identity are played out. Particularly in Europe, Jews were simultaneously cosmopolitan and citizens of a particular country. The annihilation of European Jews was the fanatic attempt of ethnonationalist Germany to eliminate transnational Jewish cultures and societies from the heart of Europe. In the anti-Semitic consciousness of the first, nationally oriented modernity, European Jews represented everything that nationalism considered dangerous. They were viewed as representatives of the universal, the rootless, the international, and the abstract, in contrast to the local, the rooted, and the concrete. They were seen as representatives of bourgeois commerce, which thought and acted without consideration for the borders of the nation-state and was symbolized in the abstract power of money, a medium that dissolves the hierarchical "community of honor" and can create a functionally differentiated society of "equal" individuals.

Although the Jews were more aware of the need to straddle the poles of universalism and particularism, this state of tension has increasingly become the norm in today's world. Identification with the Jewish victims of the Holocaust allows cosmopolitanism to rise to a new level. As we indicated earlier, part of the reason is that Jewish experience was the original, paradigmatic case of cosmopolitanism during the first wave of modernity. Jewish existence before the Holocaust, and before the founding of the State of Israel, mixed longing for territorial independence with attraction to and enmeshment in other cultures. This condition of diaspora grew not out of Judaism per se but out of tensions among citizenship, civil society, and cultural identity. European Jews were both a nation and cosmopolitan. Jews therefore lived in a tension between universalism and particularism that is increasingly becoming the norm for all nations. Franz Rosenzweig once said that Jews lived in two dimensions: the Now and the Eternal. But this tension between territorial identity (the Now) and de-territorialized existence (the Eternal) is increasingly the destiny—or, in modern terms, the danger and opportunity—of all people (Hertzberg 1998).

"Cosmopolitanism" is often confused with "universal enlightenment," which undermines individual national culture. Formerly, the enlightened community of thinkers unflinchingly led the search for "truth." Today, the producers of mass culture strive for universal profit and entertainment markets. One need only think of Karl Popper's *The Open Society and Its Enemies*, a seminal Cold War text published in 1945 that defended the openly cosmopolitan imperialism of the West. As Malachi Hacohen's analysis of Popper shows (Hacohen 1999), anti-Semitism prevented this type of universalism from mediating between nationalism and cosmopolitanism.

If we accept that universalism and particularism mutually influence and define each other, then, according to Roland Robertson (1992), we can recognize two concurrent processes: a particularization of the universal and, conversely, a universalization of the particular. The result is cosmopolitanization, a product of various historical stages that often occurs against the very intentions of those who attempt to understand the Holocaust. In the course of history, the Holocaust has been universalized, particularized, and nationalized. Its power as cosmopolitan memory has grown and multiplied through the interaction of local (i.e., national) and global claims.

Diaspora as a Jewish Perspective

Diaspora Communities in Second Modernity

The experience of the diaspora is the counterpoint to living in a group defined by territory and nationality. It produces a sense of belonging and connectedness to groups and places that are outside the national borders of where one has settled. The de-territorialization of social identities poses a challenge to the nation-state, with its demand for absolute loyalty. Multiple identities and sometimes even multiple citizenships are becoming increasingly widespread in the context of globalization. In these cases, opponents of diaspora formations talk about conflicting loyalties; supporters regard these types of affiliations as prototypes for defining the global citizens of the future. Whichever way one looks at the issue, clearly defined diaspora communities strengthen the tendency by which identities are not necessarily formed through exclusive allegiance to a single political or geographic entity. Instead, there emerge multiple loyalties to various entities (e.g., other countries, religious communities, and so on). As James Clifford (1994) notes, within the framework of globalization diaspora communities sustain many more ties than merely those to a particular homeland. Lateral connections among diaspora members in different locations are typical in this type of network.

We will summarize only a few of the most important factors connected to this development. In addition to improved transportation and communication networks and the integrated global economy, the growth of "global cities" (Sassen 2001) and the de-territorialization of social identities (Clifford 1994) are catalysts for this movement. While these processes aid in the development of a new diaspora, they are also identified as factors leading to the decline of existing communities. Multiculturalism has relieved the pressure to assimilate, and the preservation of cultural identity has become more legitimate. Consequently, minority identity is no longer necessarily defined by one's connection to a homeland.

The Jewish Diaspora

The concept of the diaspora that has taken hold in the social sciences refers directly to the Jewish experience. In Jewish history, the idea of a life outside the nation-state is nothing new (Boyarin and Boyarin 1993). Prior to the Holocaust and to the founding of the State of Israel, there was a mixture of longing for territorial independence (Zionism) and fascination and direct contact with and in other cultures (assimilation, new religious trends). This state of affairs came about not only because of Judaism but also because of the tension among civil rights, citizenship, and cultural identities. From early on, European Jews saw themselves both as citizens of a country and as cosmopolites—they experienced directly the tension between universalism and particularism. This state of affairs was not common at the time, but, as we have noted, it has increasingly become the norm in Western democracies. The diaspora was never, nor is it now, a closed culture; hence, Jewish culture has always mixed with others. If one understands culture as something open to the outside (and not homogeneous), one can see how the newly emerging cosmopolitan culture is becoming "Jewish." This why remembering the Holocaust plays such a crucial role today. The Jew as "Other" could also result in an apparent dilemma—that is, an Otherness that is becoming cosmopolitan, that does not require a spatial (national) container to preserve its historical memory.

At the beginning of the twentieth century, the Jewish diaspora experience and its cosmopolitan exponents stood in crude opposition to the national–territorial forms of memory that constituted the European nations. By the end of the twentieth century, this relationship had changed significantly. We can talk about an elective affinity between Jewish memory and newly emerging forms (and practices) of memory in Second Modernity. The basic idea behind the diaspora concept increasingly revolves around providing a sense of identity for disfranchised peoples. Whereas the diaspora was initially associated with a community living in forced exile, in Second Modernity it has become a preferred metaphor for the situation in which many minorities find themselves. In the present day, identification with a group (be it ethnic, national, or religious) whose historical roots are outside the spatial and temporal coordinates of the adopted homeland is often a matter of preference and, frequently, of pride. In addition to its social impact, this stance has political repercussions. In the face of oppression or real disadvantage, maintaining a status that is not based on fixed geographical boundaries fuels political strivings and protests (Clifford 1994). At the very least, identification with national forms of memory is not automatic, and sometimes it is even rejected. Past experiences of oppression play a vital role in this process of identity formation.

Lifting the Taboo of the Holocaust

The emergence of new Holocaust memories and life in second modernity are closely intertwined. Memory is not something static; it is "fluid" and constantly in flux. National, historical, and other contexts have an impact on these changes. A key discursive mechanism in this process is the transformation of the Holocaust's "sacredness" and the taboos surrounding it. What do we mean by this? As we will elaborate in the historical chapters, the first response to the genocide in the immediate aftermath of World War II was very similar to our contemporary reaction to the massacre in Rwanda. But those reponses did not, in and of themselves, produce the Holocaust, because the framework within which the Holocaust could be understood as such first had to be constructed. The original images and facts affected the world almost exactly the way the recent images and facts about the Rwandan genocide have touched us. Everyone was horrified; then they moved on. The slaughter did not get a name of its own.

The clearest sign that the Holocaust is unique is that it has its own name. There is the Holocaust, then there are all the other massacres. People can argue all they want about how theoretically this is not true, but as long as they use the word—and as long as no other massacre gets its own word—they are designating the Holocaust as unique. The social structure that is language constrains them to do so. If they use another term, they will just have to explain that they are actually referring to the Holocaust. The clearest sign that "the Holocaust" is sacred is that using the term lightly can give offense. Although hyperbole is the name of the game, if one uses "the Holocaust" lightly, one feels it. That is what it means to be a sacred word: to be somehow cut off from profane speech, to be surrounded by a charged space.

In other words, the Holocaust is surrounded by taboos, and taboos provide insight into the dominant culture of a society. They determine the limits of what are considered legitimate forms of identification. In many respects, the transformation of memory is closely tied to the lifting of taboos imposed on certain public topics. The content of these anamnetic revisions is different from case to case. Nevertheless, the mechanism driving these transformations is similar, a phenomenon that we will discuss in more detail. First, however, we must stress that we are not reducing "taboo" to something individual and psychologically based. Instead, we will focus on the interplay between taboo and collective memory. The distinction between taboo and prohibition is instructive in this context, for it provides insight into the changes that have taken place in Holocaust remembrance:

> Taboos involve moral principles and definitional claims which are beyond debate, not because there are not alternatives, but because these issues are not decided by rational argument. Taboos are usually obdurate: they may change gradually, or may be transformed dramatically, but they make their claims as absolutes; one does not debate with a taboo, one either obeys or transgresses its proscriptions. Prohibitions, in contrast, operate through appeals to calculative rationality and exogenously constituted interests. (Olick and Levy 1997: 924)

In what follows, we will show how these taboos have been erected and subsequently dismantled precisely in those countries where the Holocaust historically has played a pivotal role. The history of Holocaust remembrance in Germany, Israel, and the United States is a history of how a quasi-mythological perception of the Holocaust has lost its status as taboo and been transformed into a prohibition. This metamorphosis corresponds to a shift from the Holocaust as sacred to a profane field of signifiers. For some, this signals a trivialization of the Holocaust; for others, it opens the possibility of using its moral force to contend with contemporary political crises.

Germany, Israel, and the United States are societies that have different types of taboos based on their particular histories and politics. Nevertheless, the Holocaust is a hotly debated topic in all three countries. This is a fairly recent phenomenon. Immediately after World War II, no word even existed for it. Subsequently, the Holocaust was considered taboo in all three countries in ways determined by their specific cultural and political realities. Despite the different contexts in which this came about, it is not an accident that all three countries have come to use the term "Holocaust." In the next chapter, we analyze how Holocaust remembrance in these three nations has changed over the course of time. We also look at how national memories, despite their different taboo structures, are marked by historical processes that transcend national contexts. We maintain that this process culminates in a form of anamnesis specific to second modernity—namely, cosmopolitan memory.

In studying the vicissitudes of respective taboos, we pose a question: How and when did the Holocaust hit a central nerve in the identity formation of these individual nations? We outline how global and national cultures of remembrance represent two inseparable sides of one and the same process—namely, glocalization. We conclude that this dual process of particularism and universalism has contributed to the de-contextualization of the Holocaust, transforming it into a potential symbol of global solidarity. At this point, it should be clear that we are not dealing with a linear or evolutionary approach that begins with national memory and ends with the global. The new form of memory does not dissolve the national completely. Rather, it exists alongside the national as a broader normative horizon. The transition from First to Second Modernity is thus analyzed within the context of changing forms of collective memory.

Part II

4

The Postwar Years

AFTER WORLD WAR II, people affected by the war wanted more than anything else a stable life, a steady job, and a nice family with clearly defined roles for men, women, and children. Clearly, these longings were defined in direct opposition to memories of the destruction wrought by the war. It was a time of new beginnings in which the relationship to one's past was determined by the needs and demands of the present. When a new line of work, a new type of self-image, and a new definition of state security and threats are to be identified, it is necessary to inquire into the role that the war played in the process. How is past suffering integrated into a concept of the future? Does it result in a new type of memory?

A glance at the postwar cultures of remembrance in West Germany, the United States, and Israel reveals national and cultural variations, but it also shows commonalities. For its own reasons, each country developed mechanisms of how not to talk about the past. This thoroughly "active" silencing is related, of course, to the type of modernization and political realities specific to the immediate postwar era. Postwar societies were indeed just that: Societies after war. And, of course, not everyone remained silent. From the outset, there were those who "thought Auschwitz." Indeed, the intellectual groundwork for cosmopolitan memory was laid during this era, but these reflections did not find expression on an institutional level.

Repression or Selective Memory?

The claim that nobody wanted to remember the Holocaust right after the war is supported not just by academic research, but also by public opinion. "Repression" and "trauma" are among the psychological terms used to analyze this "not remembering." In the final analysis, contemporary perceptions are being imposed on the past, and concepts belonging to different eras are blurred. This is the case not only in Germany, but also in other European countries (Judt 1993), Israel (Segev 1993), and the United States. Part of the silence was connected to lack of information at that time. What did people know, and when? But this was not the only problem. What people also lacked was a proper cognitive framework.

Contemporary forms of Holocaust remembrance provide that framework by naming it. There had been no proper name for the genocide of the Jews, as it was subsumed under the broader category of Crimes against Humanity. On a more basic level, the genocide was understood within the context of the war and, since there was no other way to understand wars, within national frameworks. For this reason, the destruction of European Jewry was hardly present as a topic in public forms of remembrance. But this certainly did not mean that people did not know about it at the time (Marrus 1998).

The contrast between what one knew right after the war and public perceptions—more specifically, its public expressions—is striking. This is especially apparent if one looks at the Nuremberg trials, which began in November 1945, shortly after the cease-fire. While the evidence presented was unequivocal, and many leading Nazis were convicted, the murder of the Jews played only a secondary role in the trials.[1] It was listed under the general heading "war crimes." That is a fairly graphic representation of how the Holocaust was originally conceived: as one in an almost endless list of Nazi crimes.

The same attitude is apparent in the films made by the British and American military about concentration-camp survivors, which were presented during the Nuremberg trials as evidence. Visual

---

1. The verdicts total 226 pages, of which only three deal with the annihilation of the Jews: see the Avalon Project, Yale Law School, available at: www.yale.edu/lawweb/avalon/imt/proc/judcont.htm.

representation of what was not yet called the Holocaust thus began as court documents. Even before the trials, images of the mounds of corpses and the mass graves were made public in many parts of the world (Douglas 1995). The same documentary footage, taken at Bergen-Belsen and Buchenwald and titled *The Nazi Concentration Camps*, was used as evidence at the Eichmann trial in Israel.

So it is clear that the Nazi crimes were never buried completely. The facts as well as the images were publicized immediately after the war. These images did not have the same effect then that they do now, however, when we talk about the Holocaust. For the Holocaust to be recognized as something unique, a discursive and political frame of reference needed to be put in place.

Memories of Anne Frank

There are various reasons for the relative absence of Holocaust remembrance in the official and public discourses of Germany, Israel, and the United States. While the perpetrator, victim, and victor nation had different memory structures to fall back on, they share mnemonic qualities. A good indicator of this is the reception of Anne Frank's diary. This icon is of interest because the transformations it has undergone over the years reflect changes in the memory cultures of First and Second Modernity. The basic trajectory begins with an emphasis on the universal, eventually includes national forms of memory, and finally, in Second Modernity, becomes a symbol of self-reflexive memory.

The different interpretations of Anne Frank's diary underscore the iconographic meaning of the Holocaust and the epochal transformations in cultures of remembrance. In many respects, the way that Anne Frank—or, rather, her diary—has been adapted for different media is a symbol of the Holocaust per se. The book has been translated into more than fifty languages and has sold millions of copies. It is often the first exposure children have to the Holocaust, which is one reason for its enormous influence. In addition, the diary is far removed from Judaism and Jewish culture, making it more accessible to a non-Jewish readership. But through what forms is this influence evident? What does the figure of Anne Frank represent? Or, more precisely, what meanings have been attached to her over the past fifty years, and what does this say about the changing nature of Holocaust memories?

At the end of World War II, Anne Frank did not yet personify the murder of the European Jews. At that time, there was an overall lack of awareness of the extent to which anti-Semitism had fuelled Nazi crimes, and her diary was pushed to the wayside. It was first published in 1947 in Holland, with only 1,500 copies printed in the first edition. In the immediate postwar era, memories of the Holocaust were above all characterized by universal—and, hence, not specifically Jewish—models of interpretation. In the United States, a general ethics prevailed that left little room for articulating the Jewish experience. World War II was not recognized as a specifically Jewish tragedy, and the victims were categorized by their political rather than ethnic and religious orientation. The Americans universalized the liberation to highlight the triumph of good over evil. This frame of reference was adopted during the Cold War to confirm the superiority of democracy over totalitarianism, or, again, of good over evil.

In Germany, by contrast, numerous politicians and other public figures recognized that Germany (but, notably, not the Germans) had to take responsibility for the concentration camps. They managed quite well, however, to distance themselves from what had actually happened. Making the distinction between "regular Germans" and "Nazis" and using the designation "crimes in the name of Germany" were useful in this respect. In addition, the Holocaust was explained as one component in the "European war." This is a tendency that reappeared in various guises in the revisionist histories of the 1980s. Knowledge about the Holocaust actually declined in the postwar years, which has to do with the fact that the war was perceived in literature and film as a conventional military conflict (Kushner 1997). In other words, it was not just a name for the Holocaust that was missing. No adequate conceptual framework existed for the reception of the diary of Anne Frank within the context of the Holocaust.

The Americanization of Anne Frank

By 1950, German and French audiences could read Anne Frank's diary in their own languages, but it gained real popularity because of a staged version in 1955. Thus, it was not until the mid-1950s that Anne Frank became a worldwide symbol of the Holocaust. In 1959, a Hollywood film based largely on the play was released.

The growth of the diary's popularity in the United States was closely tied to the 1955 theater production. In 1950, the Jewish American author Meyer Levin read the French translation of the diary and advised Anne's father, Otto Frank, who owned the copyright, to look for an American publisher. Shaken by what he had read, Levin asked Frank for the rights to adapt the material for the stage. His dramatization was not the theater piece that eventually lead to the overwhelming identification of Anne Frank with the Holocaust, however. Instead, Otto Frank chose a version written by two (non-Jewish) Hollywood scriptwriters, Frances Goodrich and Albert Hackett, that precisely answered his wish that his daughter's writing be made into something didactically useful. In 1955, the production by Goodrich and Hackett became a huge success, reflecting American sensibilities of that time.

Early versions of the Anne Frank story tended to downplay the Jewish component. A particular Jewish fate came to represent universal human suffering. Given the future-oriented sentiments of Americans at the time and the desire for universal symbols, the lives of the Franks, played out in a back-alley garret in Amsterdam, were rendered into a symbol of "humanity." This universalization reaches its apex at the play's conclusion. The famous line, "In spite of everything, I still really believe that people are really good at heart," does appear in Anne Frank's diary but in a completely different context. In the diary, it is something Anne says to give herself courage when she is in great despair. Goodrich and Hackett, however, use the line at the end of the final act, which had its desired effect: For audiences, who were told nothing about Anne Frank's fate at Auschwitz or her death at Bergen-Belsen, these optimistic last words symbolized the possibility of picking up the pieces and carrying on with life after the war.

This interpretation was meaningful far beyond the American context. The Goodrich and Hackett play became one of the first popularizations of the Holocaust on an international level. A document of European origin was thus Americanized and subsequently reintroduced in Europe in its modified form. We are not pointing here to the diary as a case of "cultural imperialism." While it is true that the American interpretation has played a major role in determining the media's treatment of the Holocaust, this by no means implies that reception of the Holocaust has been identical everywhere. Even though the American stage version was immensely popular, the underlying motives and circumstances that determined the production of meaning differed from country to country. The Americanization of Anne Frank's diary has not necessarily led to its homogenization. Rather, the diary has been reconfigured within the framework of local (national) contexts.

The universalization of Anne Frank after her murder allowed for a traumatic story to take on an innocuous form, the message being that everyone was in some respects a victim of World War II. The Germans and Japanese adopted the diary to represent the extreme confusion of the war. For the Japanese, Anne Frank was a figure who ushered in hope for the future rather than feelings of guilt about the past. The British reception of the work emerged in a different thematic context (Kushner 1997). The book was marketed as an example of the complex problems of adolescence and youth. Presented within the context of generational conflict, *Diary of a Young Girl* took on a completely different meaning.

When the diary was published in West Germany in 1950, the initial reaction was muted. Only 4,500 copies of the first German edition were printed. Nevertheless, one can safely say that this publication heralded the first reference to the Holocaust that did not involve cover-ups or out-and-out denial. In contrast to the Germans' negative reaction to the Nuremberg trials and to documentary films about the concentration camps, the book was a great success. Right after the war, the Allies' de-Nazification program included playing films that revealed the Nazi politics of annihilation. This practice was abandoned, however, in the face of growing opposition from the populace and the need to redefine priorities during the Cold War. In 1955, Anne Frank's diary appeared in paperback with the line, "I believe in the goodness of people," featured on the cover. This situated the Holocaust in a universal context, enabling Germans to reclaim their place in the family of nations.

The rather slanted German translation aided this process. Over the course of five years, eighteen editions, for a total of 700,000 copies, were published. By now, more than 2.5 million copies have been sold. The theater production opened in 1956 and was a great success, resulting in a type of Anne Frank cult. The media were devoted to her story, which was also incorporated into the school curriculum.

The positive reception of Anne Frank occurred as Germans were attempting to come to terms with their past. In this case, identifying with the suffering of the victims or confronting the murderous deeds of the Germans was less important than establishing a postwar identity and determining future ethical and political responsibilities. With this future-oriented vision, Germans adopted the American representation of the Holocaust in making the past part of their present reality. It was an act of exculpation, bolstered by the fact that, in the American version, Anne Frank focused on the positive in life instead of pointing the finger at her tormenters. Alvin Rosenfeld claims that the appeal of Anne Frank for German readers has to do with the "forgiving tone of the book, which seemed to suggest that the victims had pardoned their murderers" (Rosenfeld 1991: 265). In this way, Anne Frank's experience was universalized. In other words, it was ripped from its historical context and turned into an individualized text.

Political Reconciliation in Germany: Introducing the Past into the Present

Anne Frank is an example of political processes that can also be connected to democratization and political reconciliation. Can a newly constituted democracy afford to exclude, in one form or another, all those who supported the former regime? What is the function of memory in this case? Ethical issues concerning basic democratic values as well as practical aspects of running a government are at stake here. These political questions surfaced in 1945, at the end of the war, but they captured renewed attention under the heading "transitional justice" after the collapse of various dictatorships after 1989. From this, we can draw connections between the post–World War II era and today. After all, new democracies frequently rely on the same people who were around when the totalitarian regime was in power. Reconciliation with those who supported past dictatorships can be a necessary condition for democracies to be rebuilt. Different countries deal with this in different ways—from trials resulting in convictions

(Germany) to truth commissions with license to pardon (e.g., South Africa), secrecy, and cover-ups (e.g., the torture used by the French in Algeria). What they all have in common—at least, within the context of the democratization process—is the desire to reconstitute a political community. This was the pressing issue not just for German reconstruction after World War II, but also for post-communism debates regarding civil society in Central and Eastern Europe. In both examples, the political elite, who needed new myths to fall back on to give democracy a jump-start, had a selective memory. But it is precisely here that we notice a mutual interaction between particular and universal forms of memory. As Tony Judt (1993) notes, two different forms of memory determine the postwar period. On the one hand, the countries that had suffered under German occupation focused on what had been done to them; on the other, questions arose about degrees of collaboration and assistance in the persecution of Jews. Questions not only of victimhood but also of being perpetrators had to be asked.

In her book about the democratization of the Federal Republic of Germany before and after reunification, Anne Sa'adah (1998) outlines two different possibilities for democracies to be born. She assumes that a democracy has two priorities at its inception: to demonstrate an appropriate public mode of conduct that garners at least a minimum of respect for democratic procedures and institutions; and to internalize democratic values and norms. In light of this, Sa'adah identifies two further strategies. First, the state practices an "institutionalized strategy of reconciliation," which allows for initial complacency or passivity on the part of its citizens. Here, it is assumed that institutions are able to lay the groundwork for a democratic political culture, even in the absence of true convictions on the part of individuals. Second, a "cultural strategy" is set in motion that aims to broaden democratic sentiments and consciously overcome the legacy of the former regime. Similar discussions about "transitional justice" are taking place with respect to the former Eastern bloc countries, the post-apartheid regime in South Africa, and the newly formed democracies of Latin America.

Above and beyond the various solutions individual countries pursue, a common thread in this discussion is the relationship between personal guilt and the need to provide a basis for a future in which justice prevails (however that may be accomplished). On an empirical level, most successful democracies have been established by implementing institutional strategies (Sa'adah 1998).

Thus, we need to look not so much at what is behind the silence as at how that suppressed past has been articulated within a broader context. In light of this, one needs not only to distinguish between the institutional and cultural strategies but also to differentiate between established democracies and emerging democracies. "Cultural strategies tend to put victims first; institutional strategies tend to put order first" (Sa'adah 1998: 5). If one looks at postwar history, it becomes obvious that, in all three of the countries in question, silence about the Holocaust prevailed, and pervasive memorialization of the victims emerged only in the past two decades.

In what follows, we will show how "silence" has taken on particular forms according to each nation's relationship to the Holocaust. We will also show how silence has contributed not only to processes of democratization, but also to the development of universal tendencies that transcend national particularities. The framework for this supranational process was established in academic and government circles through the immense popularity of various modernization theories. The social sciences in Germany and in Israel were strongly influenced by Parsonian structural functionalism, with U.S. society serving as an implied reference model. This outlook was based on an idea of progress specific to First Modernity. According to these paradigms, West Germany and Israel became "normal" industrial countries. Consequently, their specific histories were considered—at least, within research circles—to be of little consequence and were subsumed under a universal logic of modernization. A similar dynamic is apparent in the political sphere, which was increasingly defined by the Cold War and its accompanying theories of totalitarianism.

At this point, it should be clear that public silence is not the equivalent of an inability to remember privately. In the postwar era, memories of the Holocaust were limited to the private sphere. They were, above all, preserved by the survivors. At the time, these victims were concerned primarily with blending into what were, for most of them, new and strange surroundings. Although they could not shed their past, they could keep it private. The privatization of Holocaust memories coincided with the public, future-oriented stance of the reconstruction phase of the 1950s, and this was not limited to West Germany, Israel, and the United States.

Karl Jaspers and Coming to Terms with the Past

Ignoring the Holocaust can be considered part and parcel of the United States' future-oriented ethos. One cannot make this claim about the Federal Republic of Germany. After the war, Germany had to tackle the problem of maintaining a positive national consciousness. How could the concept of nationhood be retained without being contaminated and marked by the Nazi era? One important way this was achieved was by bracketing any mention of the Holocaust in public political discourses (Dubiel 1999; Herf 1997; Olick 1993).

This is not to say that these tendencies did not meet with resistance. There were voices in Germany immediately after the war that tried to counter this silence, among them the philosopher Karl Jaspers. Jaspers recognized the postwar era (and the Nuremberg trials) as the beginning of a transnational world. That world needed to be based on a universal Kantian cosmopolitanism, a world without "Others" and without borders (Rabinbach 1997; Traverso 1999). In *The Question of German Guilt* (1961), Jaspers distinguishes among criminal, political, moral, and metaphysical guilt. In the case of moral guilt, the individual must come to terms with the breakdown of his or her conscience after the fact. This is a guilt that grew out of having decided to make one's conscience subservient to the state. It was clear to Jaspers that, in the short term, an open dialogue regarding the guilt of specific individuals would lead to great conflict. However, he considered this process necessary and constructive for the long term. As Jaspers envisioned it, the aim was more about making Germany part of a new cosmopolitan community than about focusing on the victims of National Socialism. His formulations grew out of an identification with the Jewish victims. He saw the Nuremberg trials as a first attempt to implement cosmopolitan laws against the sovereignty of the state. For him, the trials were more than simply justice imposed by the victors. They ushered in a new era. Thus, Jaspers wrote, "The powers initiating Nuremberg thereby attest their common aim of world government, by submitting to world order. They attest their willingness really to accept responsibility for mankind as the result of their victory—not just for their own countries. Such testimony must not be false testimony" (Jaspers 1961: 59).

Jaspers recognized this cosmopolitan potential within the legal realm, but he soon had to admit that the Cold War was preventing it from being realized on a broader level. This also explains Jaspers's critique of the Eichmann trial sixteen years later, in which he held that Israel did not have the right to speak in the name of all of Jewry (see Köhler and Saner 1985: 447). These trials were not simply about handing down guilty sentences, however. They were a historic moment in which the law addressed the murder of the Jews, even though it was recognized within the context of Nazi atrocities rather than as "the Holocaust" (Marrus 1998).

The Cold War was decisive in influencing perceptions of the genocide. In addition, the increasingly nationalized character of the event, which reached its high point during the 1961 Eichmann trial in Jerusalem, signaled a departure from the universal approach at Nuremberg. From this perspective, the Eichmann trial can be identified as the beginning of Jewish ethnic politics in the United States and of a national appropriation of the murders in Israel. In the immediate aftermath of the war, intellectuals such as Jaspers, who insisted on working through the past, remained in the minority. No institutional framework was in place yet. In an ironic twist, in the late 1940s and early 1950s, politicians used Jaspers's thesis to absolve former Nazis of guilt, as becomes clear when one reviews parliamentary debates of that time. Some members of Parliament borrowed Jaspers's distinctions to establish a hierarchy of guilt. According to an argument popular at that time, no legal punishment existed for metaphysical or moral guilt (Dubiel 1999). Beyond these claims of innocence, which were often personally motivated, this approach later allowed for "guilt" to become (un)touchable as a de-territorialized category.[2]

---

2. As we outline in more detail in chapter 5, the judges in the 1963 Auschwitz trials, which were held in Frankfurt, used similar lines of argumentation. Sentences, they claimed, could be imposed only for criminal acts.

Jaspers's insight that metaphysical and moral guilt had escaped the boundaries of the law also formed the basis of Arendt's claim that the Nazi crimes had exploded the conventional framework for criminal proceedings. This did not prevent Arendt from supporting the death sentence for Eichmann, something that is frequently overlooked in the critical and often polemical reactions to *Eichmann in Jerusalem*. Arendt ends by addressing Eichmann as a representative of evil per se:

> And as you supported and carried out a policy of not wanting to share the earth with the Jewish people and the people of a number of other nations—as though you and your superiors had any right to determine who should and who should not inhabit the world— we find that no one, that is, no member of the human race, can be expected to want to share the earth with you. This is the reason, and the only reason, you must hang. (Arendt 1992 [1963]: 279)

Radically new forms of evil should also be met with the appropriate punishment.

Since the 1960s, there has been a broad consensus among intellectuals in Germany that it is necessary to come to terms with the past. They had criticized the Federal Republic—and above all the political leaders—in its early years for failing to embrace a cultural strategy that would address the issue of guilt. This was interpreted as a symptom of the failure of democracy. Helmut Dubiel (1999), for instance, claims that Germany did not begin to develop a truly democratic culture until the 1970s, when the Holocaust victims were recognized and memorialized. In contrast, we claim that it is precisely the silence regarding the Jewish victims in public discourse that enabled Germany to become democratic in the first place.[3]

We are not challenging the claim that silence surrounding the topic of the Holocaust was pervasive. Rather, we are challenging the idea that this silence had negative consequences for an emerging democratic culture in Germany. It was precisely the denial of guilt that provided the cultural foundation for Germany to become democratic and, within certain limits, "normalize" itself. From this perspective, our interpretation places a higher value on the admittedly limited

---

3. In *The Germans*, Norbert Elias (1996) claimed that what has been described in the press as "negative nationalism" can turn into collective shame, which in turn can lead to an extremist nationalism. It is clear that Elias was influenced by reactionary tendencies that came to light in polemics against the Treaty of Versailles.

advantages of an institutional strategy than on the moralizing, but not necessarily feasible, cultural strategy aimed at tackling the Holocaust directly. Our position counters the basic consensus of the past three decades that demands a full reckoning concerning the Holocaust. The advantage of the institutional strategy is that it laid the groundwork for the Holocaust to escape its national and ethnic confines. In our present day, it is precisely the admission of guilt that has enabled Germany to become part of an international community with a shared value system.

Criticism or skepticism regarding Germany's politics of dealing with the past—a politics that is often ritualized and is fetishistically displayed as evidence of Germany's democratic sensibilities—is increasingly regarded as controversial. This is evident in the reaction to the work of Hermann Lübbe (1983). In his polemic against the New Left and its attempt to monopolize the politics of confronting German history, Lübbe observed: "In fighting the ideology and politics of National Socialism . . . the new German state had to be established. If the state had had to fight against the majority of German citizens, it never would have been established in the first place" (Lübbe 1983: 334). From this perspective, it is irrelevant whether or not "the citizenry of this republic was free of all remnants of National Socialism from the very start" (Lübbe 1983: 332). This was not a prerequisite for an effective cultural strategy. What was important was the way in which the burden of the past was dealt with on a political and institutional level:

> The moral and political climate cannot be gauged by the attitudes of individual subjects. It can be gauged by knowing what the binding moral and political standards are, standards that cannot be publicly challenged without isolating oneself morally and politically. If one analyzes the history of the founding of the Federal Republic of Germany from this perspective, it becomes clear that public recognition of the political and moral vanquishing of Nazi rule was a centerpiece in legitimating the new government. The same can be said about the drive. . . to design a constitution by understanding how the old constitution had enabled the Nazis to seize power. (Lübbe 1983: 332–33)

This differentiation between the individual psychology of mourning and a politically motivated public recognition remains controversial. It also played a role in post-reunification debates surrounding the "Stasi files," which were kept by the East German secret police and involved a broad net of civilian informants working for the state. Comparisons between this case and the postwar era are ubiquitous in the press. One need only think of all the talk about a double process of dealing with the past. One must distinguish between the fragile political order of postwar Germany, whose legitimacy was imposed on the Germans from the outside, and the later republic, which was secure in its democracy.

Selective Memory Regarding the Genocide

Whereas Dubiel and Lübbe differ in their assessments of postwar relations in the Federal Republic, they ultimately agree on the fact that there was a silence surrounding the German past. We want to examine this silence from another vantage point that situates Holocaust remembrance within a broader context. If one analyzes the form and function of Holocaust remembrance right after the war in Germany, one cannot talk about silence per se. Keeping silent was not the only strategy among the sweeping attempts to deny responsibility for the Holocaust. It is necessary to draw a distinction here between forgetting and selective memory. The Holocaust played an absolutely central role in the collective memory of the first decade after the war. No ritualized form of memorializing the Jewish victims existed (yet), however. Such forms became part of the official repertoire only during the 1970s, at the latest. During the postwar occupation period and the early years of the Federal Republic, the *Volk* (the popular term at that time) and the political elite were mainly concerned with remembering the Holocaust as a means for gauging their own suffering, situating it in a universal and comparative context.

The extent to which Holocaust remembrance in Germany has become a central historical reference point is apparent in the fact, among others, that the term "coming to terms with the past" (*Vergangenheitsbewältigung*) is used exclusively in reference to the Nazi era. Its use for rhetorical purposes is limited. Attempts to introduce it into discussions about the history of the German Democratic Republic (GDR), for instance, have been met with the argument that one cannot draw parallels between the Holocaust and East Germany.

In addition to statements that explicitly refer to the destruction of European Jewry, one must look at those that emphasize a universal context of victimhood. It is true that direct references to the Holocaust were avoided in the immediate postwar period (Dubiel 1999). This did not mean, however, that the Jews were not remembered during the founding of the Federal Republic. In many respects, the victims were accorded an important legitimating meaning (Bodemann 1996). Fundamentally, there were two interrelated reactions. Germany's official relations with the Jews and Israel were characterized by a philo-Semitism that took on social as well as official political dimensions. Frank Stern describes how the term "Jewish fellow citizens" was used to counter charges of anti-Semitism and how "praise of the Jewish contribution to German culture, science, and economy became a fixed topos of the political culture" (Stern 1992: 16). According to Stern, this attitude was not limited to contact between individuals:

> The closer it came to the founding of the German Federal Republic in those years, the more quickly this social-psychological factor was turned into an ideological and political instrument. Philo-Semitism became a means for moral legitimation. The entire complex of . . . so-called "restitution" belongs within this context of official philo-Semitic efforts in establishing the credibility of the Federal Republic and aiding in the drive toward integration into the West and state sovereignty. (Stern 1992: 17)

In many respects, this philo-Semitism is the flip side of anti-Semitism as an additional mechanism for distancing oneself from remembering the Holocaust. Seen in this light, philo-Semitism is not "a working through of the past in the sense of coming to terms with it on a spiritual and cultural level, but rather a pragmatic form of dealing with prejudices and social experience" (Stern 1992: 343). As for the bracketing of Holocaust memories, the philo-Semite generally falls back on notions of a German–Jewish symbiosis. This represents an idealized image of the past that has to do with the desire (on both sides) to identify a positive relationship. At the same time, this notion of symbiosis had absolutely no basis in the social reality of postwar Germany, where most of the Jewish inhabitants were Eastern European transplants. Furthermore, nobody was really left who conformed to this idealized stereotype (which even today does not deter politicians from claiming a positive relationship to Jews in Germany by pointing to the Jews' great cultural and other achievements of the past). Stern points out that this distancing carries with it a spatial quality: "Between the Third Reich and postwar Germany, a 'geography of genocide' arose in the German consciousness of its own past. The guilt that was discussed in the media after 1945 referred to the crimes perpetrated in the East, in the camps, by forces of destruction such as the SS" (Stern 1992: 237).

We are less concerned with the thorny question of instrumentalization than with how this mechanism turned the German persecution of the Jews into a taboo. The push to incorporate the Nazi past into a universal framework constitutes the flip side of this process. Minimizing the differences between various victim groups is one distancing technique. The so-called Week of Brotherhood, instituted in the late 1940s by the American occupation forces and supported primarily by Protestant groups in Germany, is probably the most glaring example of this type of universalizing. It was one way in which the specifically anti-Semitic nature of Nazi crimes became marginalized in public discourse.

Thus, discussions that focused specifically on the Holocaust remained the exception. This state of affairs contributed heavily to sweeping judgments in academic and public life about the silence and repression that surrounded the topic—judgments that have become entrenched since the 1960s. As Dubiel notes, "In the 1950s, the dominant tendency in Parliament was to remain absolutely silent about the Nazi past. Only legislative demands having to do with transferring power in the wake of the Third Reich created some chinks in the wall of shame and silent guilt" (Dubiel 1999: 14). Various distancing mechanisms were disseminated through the language of public discourses (Olick 1993). For one thing, Germans could push responsibility for the Holocaust onto a small group of Nazis who had committed "criminal acts in the name of Germany."

The choice of "collective guilt" terminology, which dominated the early debate about Germany's responsibility for the Nazi terror (Frei 1997), is particularly telling. Attributing the concept to the Western allies established yet another basis for comparison.[4] The concept of collective guilt was rendered absurd either by showing that not everyone was equally responsible, let alone guilty, or by using it to criticize some measures the Allies imposed on Germany.[5] By criticizing the Allied occupation, Germans sought to avoid responsibility for widespread support of the Nazi regime and the war itself. Furthermore, it absolved the political class from taking responsibility for the misery of the immediate postwar years.[6]

The German government as well as some journalists cloaked the accusation of collective guilt in formulations that ultimately left no one to blame. On the one hand, collective guilt was generalized to an absurd degree, ignoring the fact that, in reality, not all Germans participated in the genocide. On the other hand, the obvious exceptions (resistance fighters, political opponents, those who came to the aid of the persecuted) were held up to such an extent that the only remaining perpetrators were those who had been in Hitler's innermost circle. Thus, collective guilt was turned into a caricature, a rhetorical strategy that found special resonance during the occupation period between 1945 and 1948. The Germans often understood the measures implemented by the Allies as a form of collective punishment

4. By analyzing official speeches in the Federal Republic, Jeffrey Olick (1993) has shown that German politicians at no point accepted the idea of collective guilt.

5. In a recent study about failed de-Nazification and the rapid reinstatement of former Nazis to the civil service of the Federal Republic, Norbert Frei (1997) documented how the "collective guilt" thesis was articulated. Politicians frequently talked about how the Allies blamed Germans collectively, only to shift the attention away from those Nazis who were actually guilty of crimes. Pointing to the absurdity of collective guilt generated public indignation against these accusations, and subsequently individual crimes were also widely ignored.

6. Faulenbach (1993) has noted that this view was also reflected in early West German historiography, which tended to divide the reconstruction of the Federal Republic into two periods. It depicted the period after the war up to currency reform in 1948 as a bleak one, reserving all the achievements to the sovereign West Germany. When asked in November 1951 which period had been the worst for Germany in this century, 80 percent referred to the occupation years of 1945–48, while only 2 percent mentioned the time between 1933 and 1938 and only 8 percent thought that the war years between 1939 and 1945 were the worst. Conversely, when asked which period had been the best, 45 percent and 40 percent, respectively, referred to Imperial Germany and the Third Reich, with only 2 percent referring to the period after 1945 (Noelle and Neumann 1956).

and associated that punishment with the idea of collective guilt. (In fact, the charge of collective guilt was hardly ever mentioned. It was meaningless in a legal context, because the de-Nazification process focused on the individual person.) From a legal standpoint, collective punishment was as untenable as supposed collective guilt for the crimes committed under the Nazis. In his study of the failure of de-Nazification, Frei (1997) has shown how the theory of collective guilt was exploited. Politicians often grumbled about how the Allies supposedly considered all Germans culpable, in the process turning attention away from the real war criminals. The reaction to the charge of collective guilt was so vehement that even the most obvious criminals remained at large.

The implicit and often explicit comparative reference to the suffering of Germans thus constituted an important strategy for the reproduction of nationhood. It neutralized many of the constraints that prevented national identity from being reasserted in West Germany. In its comparison to communism, Nazism was part of the totalitarian experience; as such, it no longer seemed to be a uniquely German project. By pointing to the suffering that resulted from expulsion and the bombings of civilians, questions of moral responsibility were assuaged.

What is more, the response to the collective guilt theory had a disintegrative effect. Konrad Adenauer introduced discussion of the "negative consequences" of such ongoing allegations. Rejection of the charge of collective guilt, which marked the German–Allied relationship during the occupation, was repeated regularly at the highest levels of the new legislature. Nevertheless, such rejections were less a matter of defending the homeland (or even grappling with the issue of wrongdoing) than of ensuring that the progress of democratization would remain unimpeded by such accusations.

The Holocaust as a Measure for Personal Suffering

Silence was not the only response to the Holocaust after the war. The topic did surface within a pan-European context to provide a measure for individual suffering. This is apparent in parliamentary debates and other public statements that were formulated between 1949 and 1953. With the consolidation of the Federal Republic under its first chancellor, Adenauer, the crimes against the European Jews became an important component in the rehabilitation of Germany. Adenauer and most of his contemporaries sought to free the Holocaust from its specifically German context and resituate it within a general European one. Whereas the Holocaust has been presented as a symbol of German particularism over the past forty years, in the postwar era it was used as a negative example to support the creation of a "universal" community of peoples. Adenauer's inaugural speech as chancellor in 1949 is indicative of this trend. He calls for

> putting the past behind us, especially since de-Nazification has led to great misfortune and wrongdoing. . . . The war and the ensuing confusion in its aftermath have been such a hard test for so many. Consequently, one should approach some of the mistakes and misdemeanors that come with these experiments with a degree of understanding. . . . All this has been done, after all, for the sake of the betterment of the German people and to foster peace in Europe and throughout the world. (Adenauer 1949)

Thus, the memory of the Holocaust connected the Federal Republic to Europe and the West. As is evident from the examples we have used, memories of the Nazi past are useful primarily for reestablishing a perspective on the future that conforms to a universal framework. The political elite—above all, the Adenauer administration—was not so concerned with the repression of Holocaust memories. Rather, it sought to incorporate this chapter of German history into a general European context and to include the German people among the myriad victims of National Socialism. The formulation of a "European civil war," an idea that enjoyed widespread popularity at the time, was an important rhetorical tool toward these ends. By reducing the issue of responsibility for World War II to broad tensions between countries and regimes, the specificity of the Third Reich was lost. In the interwar period, chauvinism was a phenomenon common to all of Europe. From this perspective, Germany was not the only aggressor; it was simply one player in an extreme political situation in Europe. The focus thus shifts from German nationalism to a rabid form of nationalism that mushroomed during that particular era.

The basic outlines of this position are apparent if one looks at how fascism and totalitarianism came to be defined. In the 1960s, the term "fascism" referred to a spectrum of totalitarian regimes that were ordered into broad categories. German Nazism, Italian fascism, and Soviet communism were clumped together into one group. Interestingly, it was the book *Three Faces of Fascism* (1966) by the historian Ernst Nolte that set the academic tone at that time. Twenty years later, the term "fascism," as well as the comparison between Nazism and Stalinism, sparked the protracted, so-called Historians' Dispute, which centered on issues of the uniqueness of the Holocaust and whether it could be compared to other historical events.

Comparative Victimhood

One way to avoid responsibility and the negative consequences associated with remembering the Holocaust after the war was to equate German victims and victims of Germans. It is quite clear that the former dominated the political and public discussions of the young Federal Republic. Such a broad spectrum of victims was identified that one started to wonder who had kept the Nazi regime and its machinery of destruction running. German civilians were identified as victims (bombing victims, victims of the occupation, women forced to clean up the rubble, and so on) and as prisoners of war. Former Nazis were also among those transformed into victims, largely in the context of emerging Cold War politics. Much of the information about Nazi activities among West German functionaries came out of the GDR, which precipitated a public (and political) outcry. Accused Nazis were offered protection as victims of communist propaganda without investigation into their ties to National Socialism (Levy 2001).

After the war, Germany faced the question of how to salvage a positive sense of nationhood that was not tainted or defined by the memory of the Nazi experience. West Germany largely embraced a self-perception that stressed its own victimhood. Ethnic German expellees were the central social carriers of this self-victimization.[7]

7. They are descendants of Germans who had settled in Eastern Europe since the eighteenth century. After the war, the Potsdam Treaty sanctioned large population transfers, which led to the flight and expulsion of about 10 million ethnic Germans from Eastern Europe. They are commonly referred to as *Vertriebene* (expellees). Another 2 million followed between 1950 and 1988. They are referred to as *Aussiedler* (resettlers).

Numbering about 10 million, they were the largest group around which this discourse of suffering was established. Perceptions of ethnic Germans' suffering were sustained through social memories. Expellees' suffering was institutionalized through public commemorations, privately published autobiographies, broad nonpartisan support, union newsletters, and *Wiedergutmachung*, or "making good again," generally in the form of financial compensation.[8]

A few examples of how victimhood was inscribed into public memory underscore the ways in which an equivalence of suffering was established. The fate of expellees and German victims was frequently invoked to establish that Germans suffered no less from the war than those attacked by Germany. This was mostly intended to abrogate responsibility for the war crimes committed by Germans. Representatives of various political outlooks sought to capitalize on their opposition to Allied politics in general and did not hesitate to compare the deeds of the Nazis to the Allies' decisions in Potsdam that sanctioned the expulsion of ethnic Germans. The suffering of expellees was constructed around memories of often violent large-scale expulsions from states under Soviet influence. This was the beginning of the Cold War: The Allies as well as Adenauer perceived the expellees as a bulwark of anticommunism, and they were eager to exploit the memories of expulsion as a reminder of Soviet aggression.

The fate of the expellees was also employed to establish an equivalence of victimhood with Holocaust victims. This conflation of victimhood—grouping expellees and Nazi victims together—was ubiquitous and continued in the first years of the Federal Republic of Germany. To be sure, Jewish victims were also recalled, but, as Robert Moeller (1996) has shown, "Acknowledgment of Jewish victims of National Socialist crimes . . . also made it easier for the Bonn government to acknowledge German victims of the Red Army and postwar Communism. In the process, the fates of these two victim

8. The German term *Wiedergutmachung* has, in fact, become synonymous with restitution to Nazi victims, including reparations to the State of Israel as well as to persecuted Jewish individuals. The term, which literally means "to make good again," has pedagogic and redemptive connotations. In other languages, one speaks of restoration or indemnification, whereas *Wiedergutmachung* refers to German–Jewish relations and a set of restitutive efforts.

groups were frequently linked. . . . Victims were also joined by a language of 'millions,' a denomination associated with Jewish victims of National Socialism, prisoners of war in the USSR, and expellees" (Moeller 1996: 1017). Moeller shows how the presence of victims of Germans ultimately served to create the impression that all groups of victims were equal and part of a broader struggle: "German expellees became another category of victims driven from their historic homeland because of their 'ethnicity' (*Volkszugehörigkeit*); Jews persecuted by German were one group of victims among others" (Moeller 1996: 1019). The atrocities committed against the Jews provided simply one of many ways to measure the suffering of German expellees.

This form of nation-centered remembrance is typical of First Modernity. While it appears to be a thoroughly universal line of reasoning, it is in actuality nationally based, just as nationalism itself is a universalization of the particular. This kind of remembrance is not based on a global community of fate or on a global sense of responsibility in the face of globally shared risks. In his work on attempts to confront the past in Belgium, France, and Holland, Pieter Lagrou (1997) has shown how these states also have not provided a public space for the Jewish victims who were once deported from their territories. Instead, the main concern has been with those who represented the heroic opposition to military defeat and collaboration—namely, the resistance fighters, who have become part of an important founding myth for these states. Lagrou describes how this period of reconstruction was marked by living (i.e., social) memories, leaving little room for the dead. In this way, a patriotic image of the resistance was projected onto the national collectivity immediately after the war. The actions of a minority were thus extended to the majority of the population, and the term "resistance" came to include a broad spectrum of social practices, enabling the state to "nationalize" commemoration of political opposition on a broad scale. Memories of the Jewish victims, and specifically of the Holocaust, did not fit into this schema. Because the Jews were murdered not because of their convictions or actions but simply on the basis of their religious and ethnic heritage, they did not conform to heroic images cultivated through memories of World War II. As we will show, the consequences of involuntarily belonging to such a group is precisely what has made Holocaust memories a central metaphor at the end of the twentieth century and the beginning of the third millennium.

The Cold War functions as an important universalizing force. On a sociopolitical level, it de facto brought the de-Nazification process, which had been dragging on, to a close. In the ideological struggles against the East, the Federal Republic became an important partner in the Western alliance, and the ideal of reeducating the public took second place to the dictates of anticommunism, which were readily embraced by West Germany. Even though theories of totalitarianism were actively cultivated during the Cold War, it was not possible to extend those theories to corresponding memories of the victims of totalitarianism. Even if we regard the Nuremberg trials as an important moment in the development of cosmopolitan memory, this interpretation does not discount the fact that very specific scores were simultaneously being settled. For instance, Soviet judges presided over Nazi defendants at the trials, but Soviet crimes were never mentioned. On the contrary. The Soviet massacre of Polish officers at Katyn was blamed on the German army (Diner 1999: 234).

The Cold War and its effects did not actually determine this structure of memory, but the relationship between perpetrators and victims played an important role. Dan Diner (1999) explains the differences in commemorative rituals against the following backdrop: National Socialist crimes were simultaneously German crimes, and national memories of these transgressions were often connected to the Nazi era, so it was difficult to distinguish between the two. This extends to the German point of view as well as to perceptions from the outside. The crimes of the Soviet Union present a different case. The Soviet Union no longer exists, and the victims of this system were the Soviet people themselves. Diner argues that it is difficult to remember crimes that are not part of one's ethnic, or "long-term," memory (Diner 1999: 233–49). From this perspective, the victims— the Jews—thus were not a single, defined ethnic group. To put it bluntly, "The Jews were, for Christianity, the Other as such" (Diner 1999: 230). But what is at stake here, according to Diner, is more than simply ethnic memory. The attempts at comparison, the universalization of the Holocaust, seem to conform to the modus operandi

of the Christian tradition, whereas the insistence on singularity conforms to a Jewish outlook Diner's approach does not merely reflect
important differences between the two groups' cultural forms of
memory, however, but tends to essentialize them.

In contrast, we want to show how forms of remembrance become
displaced from their original group-specific (or religious) context and
are transformed into a widely disseminated set of common values. We
intend to outline the political and cultural conditions for secularization, universalization, and, finally, globalization from a sociological
perspective. Our understanding of globalization is not based exclusively on the Christian concept of universalism. Rather, it is based on
a future-oriented mixture of these conceptions. Consequently, the dichotomy between Christian and Jewish narratives in its present form
can no longer be sustained. This is so, among other things, because of
the increasingly diasporic nature of human existence in general and
the so-called Americanization of Holocaust remembrance, which we
will look at in greater detail later.

With the emergence of the Cold War, Nazism was increasingly
examined via a comparative approach to totalitarianism. From this
point of view, Nazism was not an exclusively German phenomenon
and could successfully be compared to Stalinism. This left little room
for understanding the Holocaust as a specifically German event. The
conceptual language of totalitarianism developed primarily in academic discourses, but it soon took hold in day-to-day politics and
language, as well. Dubiel (1999) describes the multiple functions
of these linguistic transfers for German collective memory. On the
one hand, the Nazi past could be obfuscated behind a firm rejection of totalitarianism; on the other, all public attention was directed toward a real, living form of totalitarianism—namely, communism. This camp mentality that pervaded international politics
also benefited Adenauer's program of integrating Germany into the
West.

Our attempt here has been to embed the non-remembering of
the Holocaust into a broader context of democratization. In light
of the institutional strategy implemented in the Federal Republic,
denying the uniqueness of the Holocaust and the specific responsibility of the Germans became necessary for democratization. From

this perspective, the selective public memory was neither a cynical nor a traumatic response to the overwhelming force of Holocaust memories (and of many Germans' guilt). Rather, it was a necessary strategy within the context of democratization and justice during a transitional period. At stake was the creation of the "other Germany" (a term that David Ben-Gurion, Israel's first prime minister, placed at Adenauer's "disposal" at the beginning of the 1950s). Such a process was necessary so that Europe as a concept and as a political reality could emerge from the rubble and from the crimes of World War II in Germany, as is shown by the central role Germany has played in Europe ever since.

Consuming the Nation

The postwar era defined itself through experiences of the war, which provided a unifying context. Many people had suffered deprivation during the war, for example; postwar consumer culture provided an antidote to that experience. Thus, "silence" went hand in hand with consumerism. Many critics regard the postwar period exclusively in terms of silence, repression, and apolitical consumerism. Anti-totalitarianism and the national economy were nothing but expedient means for creating a new identity. Alexander and Margarethe Mitscherlich's *The Inability to Mourn* (1975 [1967]) is highly relevant in this context. The Mitscherlichs claim that a great deal of indifference and apathy toward politics characterized West Germany in the 1960s and that this was caused by the stimulation that emerging consumption patterns were generating. They argue that the Germans submitted to the seductive powers of consumer culture to escape the memories of the Nazi years. Only consumerism on a grand scale could keep the Germans from confronting their pasts and facing up to their deeds.[9] The Mitscherlichs do acknowledge that "consumerism" can disassociate a collective from space and time; they emphasize, however, the idea that consumerism worked to depoliticize the Germans. Consumer culture, for them, was part of mass culture, and mass culture was not merely apolitical but, in fact, connected to fascism

---

9. For a detailed critique of this approach to consumerism, see Sznaider 1998a.

in some way. This premise was embraced at least in part by Catholic and conservative critics who shared the distaste for consumerism. What was needed was a new evil. After the Holocaust, the Jews could no longer be used as the symbol of footloose, morally bankrupt consumers and dealers. Hence, the United States—victor over Germany, symbol of the ultimate moral bankruptcy, and land of the "merry consumers"—took the place of the Jews. "Americanization" had become the new catchword.

Consumer culture is immanent in societies that enjoy widespread wealth, a specifically modern constellation. In current discussions, the nineteenth-century dichotomy between production–consumption and culture no longer holds. Instead, we have production–consumption versus politics–democracy. It is quite clear that mass culture and collective economic gains have been instrumental in shaping a specifically West German identity and contributed to the country's adoption of bourgeois values (Heineman 1996). Ludwig Erhard, the architect of Germany's "economic miracle" and later the country's chancellor, formulated this unequivocally. His slogan was "Prosperity for All!" For Erhard, consumption not only pointed to the end of the old German class structures; it also heralded the emergence of a new feeling of self-worth and freedom for the German people (Carter 1997). The possibility of relatively unlimited consumption also played a role in forming a West German identity that was distinct from that of the GDR. Forced limitations on consumption and long lines were considered typical of East Germany. The image of the rich West German relatives who mailed their poor siblings in the East jeans and coffee, symbols of consumer culture, became a cornerstone of West German identity.

The essential aspect of these processes is, above all, that they plug into a universal ethos that characterized the postwar period. This was a form of universalism that even had an effect on the Jewish self-image:

> Even in Germany, the Jewish victims considered themselves for a long time to be part of a larger society of people who had been persecuted. Here, changes in language are quite noticeable. Today we speak primarily of "victims" and "survivors." While it is true that the term "victim" was used from the very beginning, the more

popular term at the time was "persecuted," which also appeared in the names of their organizations: The Union of Individuals Persecuted on the Basis of Politics, Race, and Religion (Vereinigung der politisch, rassisch, religiös Verfolgten—PRV); The Union of Individuals Persecuted under the Nazi Regime (Vereinigung der Verfolgten des Naziregimes—VVN); The Alliance of Individuals Persecuted under the Nazi Regime (Bund der Verfolgten des Naziregimes—BVN). The names of these organizations also identify the common interests of all of those persecuted, regardless of their background. (Bodemann 2000)

The antifascist discourse of the left tended to emphasize what the victims had in common. Antifascism opened the door to understanding the Holocaust, as senseless and arbitrary as the extermination was, as a political act. Many of the Jewish survivors identified their fate with this antifascism, which also explains why so many Jews were sympathetic to the communist regime after the war.

Remembering the Holocaust in Israel

Ethnos or Demos: Jewish or Democratic State?

From the very beginning, Israel's handling of the Holocaust has been marked by ambivalence. On the one hand, the state legitimates itself in a negative manner through the Holocaust: Only a strong Israel can prevent another Holocaust. On the other hand, it sees itself as the legal and moral successor to the victims. Public treatment of the Holocaust changes, therefore, in accordance with the prevailing national self-image. This, in turn, is partly a product of the relationship between secular Zionism and the Jewish religion and the chiefly negative assessment of the diaspora. In addition, tension exists between the particular character of the Jewish state and the universal demands of a democratic society. Here, it is necessary to stress that we are not approaching particularism and universalism as essentially opposite in nature. Rather, we see the two as mutually defining qualities whose relationship to each other is mutable. There are universal religions (Christianity) and folk religions (Judaism). The former led to universal philosophy, to the Enlightenment and modernity, and by extension to the possibility of the universalization of the Holocaust.

In contrast, for the Jews, the Holocaust had to remain an exclusively ethnic problem. For Jews, universalizing the Holocaust means letting the most significant event in Jewish history become an accident in the march of history.

Territorial Identity and the Diaspora

The Jewish state was a product of the Zionist revolution. This was a revolution aimed at engendering a new Jewish individual on Jewish territory, which it accomplished by borrowing from ancient Jewish symbolism (Ravitzky 1996). In Israel, it is impossible to distinguish between ethnicity and religion. Zionism was never a universal ideology; it was always directed solely at one, specific ethnic-religious group. National symbols are simultaneously religious symbols. The "Land of Israel" is at once a secular homeland and sacred ground. Whereas modernity suppressed religion as an integrative tool in other regions, the Jewish nationalist movements had to give modernity more leeway. Without religious symbolism, it would hardly be possible for the Jewish state to legitimate itself or for its citizens to become integrated. This is not to say, however, that the relationship between the secular aims of Zionism and the incorporation of religious symbols is by any means static.

A second essential factor influencing the reception of the Holocaust in Israel involves negative representations of diaspora Jews during the nation's founding. Zionism was rooted in the ideological context of national independence movements. Theodor Herzl's *The Jewish State* (1989 [1896]) is an expression of this ideology, which dominated the nineteenth century in large parts of Europe. The Jewish variant is distinguished by its rejection of any assimilationist projects in the face of ongoing anti-Semitism. This is not only a matter of rejecting assimilation (in the sense of giving up Jewish religious ways). It also involves a negative assessment of a particular type of Jewish existence, which was the target of the Nazi death machine. A portion of the Zionist program harked back to the ideas of Max Nordau, a German Jewish Zionist who, in an effort to create the "new Jew," drew the opposition between the *Luftmensch* (impractical dreamer) of the diaspora and the *Muskeljude* (strong Jew) in Palestine (Nordau 1909). The "negation of the diaspora" became a catchphrase of

Zionist political thought (Boyarin and Boyarin 1993; Raz-Krakotzkin 1993).[10]

"Diaspora," as we have noted, is a term that came out of the Jewish tradition. In its current usage in the social sciences, it has been taken out of its original context and come to mean de-territoralization not only from one's material existence but also in terms of one's repertoires of memories. Diaspora should not be idealized as a normative state, as often happens today (for a summary of this trend, see Clifford 1994). In traditional Judaism, the concept of diaspora is many-sided insofar as it refers to a way of life imposed on a people as a punishment for their religious sins. In addition, it is a geopolitical concept that describes life outside the land of Israel in a non-Jewish land. At the same time, it is a cultural term that designates an existential state of alienation and rootlessness. This last element corresponds to the archetype that we discussed in chapter 3, where we pointed to the affinity between the Jewish experience and de-territorialized memory in the age of globalization. This type of memory is indicative of universalized forms of remembrance. Within the framework of a Zionism marked by a nationalist ethos, this rootlessness points, of course, to an inevitable lack in Jewish existence outside of Israel. The diasporic state is also viewed as something negative among other ethnic groups who have been forced to leave their homeland against their will. The term "diaspora" thus should be understood not only as an analytic category but also as connected to concrete memories of a very broad range of forced migrations.

---

10. This may also explain the relative lack of attention given to the diary of Anne Frank in Israel. The book was translated into Hebrew in 1953, and a new edition appears every few years. We also know that it has been identified as the most popular Holocaust book among young Israelis (Fargo 1989). Nevertheless, Anne Frank has never become an icon in Israel. Hardly any public places or streets are named after her, for instance. Because of its "non-Zionist" message, the book does not lend itself as a pedagogical tool. The types of issues that concerned non-Jews and for which Anne Frank could provide "help" were not relevant in Israel. The defining quality of the book, however, is its non-Zionist outlook. This makes the fact that it is so widely read on a private level despite this fact (or perhaps precisely because of it) all the more remarkable. We can only speculate that this will change after Steven Spielberg's film about Anne Frank is released and that she will subsequently become a global icon in Israel, as well.

Because they shed light simultaneously on the tension between diaspora and territorial sovereignty, the tensions between Jewish and Israeli remembrance provide a fascinating case when one examines the relationship between universal and particular memory. One may ask: What significance does all of this have for Jewish life inside and outside of Israel and for corresponding forms of Holocaust remembrance? Earlier, Jewish and national identities could not be brought into accord with each other. Although Zionism and the founding of the State of Israel did manage to combine these two tendencies for the Jews, the cosmopolitanism that is part of Jewish identity has not yet found expression. The Zionist left, as well as the right, is trapped in a concept of political existence based on territorialism. Seen in this light, Zionism is not just an emancipation movement that rejects assimilation; it is itself the ultimate assimilationist project. As is evident above all in its Central European variant, Zionism had a cultural affinity to the culture of non-Jewish society, which led to a distancing of the Eastern European Jewish habitus. Zionism has become a form of therapy against the pathogenic Eastern Jew, promising regeneration for the ostensibly "diseased" Jewish bodies and minds.

Heroes and Victims

Israel's postwar relationship to the Holocaust can be explained through this rejection of the Jewish diaspora, on the one hand, and the mythic image of Israel, on the other. Memories of the Holocaust perform two opposing functions in the Israeli context: The victims of the Holocaust conform to the image of the diaspora as passive; at the same time, the (Zionist) martyrs who distinguished themselves through their resistance to the Nazis are remembered. This self-image was prevalent in the first two decades after the war. In the Zionist ideology and practice of "real" Jews and in the process of reconstruction, the dichotomy between positive national memory and negative Jewish memory in the diaspora was sharpened to an even greater extent. The new sovereign form of politics was linked to agency, to the ability to make decisions independently. The Holocaust occurred precisely in a state of exile and could be traced back to the helplessness associated with this condition. This alleged passivity was not acceptable for a young, new nation. Politics took precedence, which found its expression in the new State of Israel through the centrality accorded to statehood (*mamlachtiut*, in Hebrew).

The State of Israel viewed the exilic existence as unproductive, ahistorical, and downright characteristic of a *"Luftmensch"* mentality. The slogan that Jews let themselves be led like "sheep to the slaughter" (which was probably taken up as early as 1942 by the partisan poet Abba Kovner, although it had already been used in reference to the pogroms in Eastern Europe) strongly influenced the stance taken by the young nation. For this type of political idiom expressed in speeches, history books, and newspaper articles, the Holocaust provided ultimate confirmation of how undesirable diaspora existence was. This was the case even though about 350,000 Jewish survivors had arrived in Israel by 1948, and this group formed nearly half the population of Israel. It is even more surprising considering that the events that later would be labeled the Holocaust did not play a large role in the first years of political independence. During the first decade after Israel's founding, religious groups undertook the collective work of remembrance. One of the first projects—bringing ashes to Israel from the Flossenburg concentration camp—was organized by an Israeli congregation. The interment took place on the "tenth of Tewet" on the mountain of Zion. The date marked Nebuchadnezzar's occupation of Jerusalem, and Zion was the burial site of King David, from whose house the Messiah would come— after the deliverance. Thus, "destruction and redemption" marked the religious parameters that would later also determine the nature of national remembrance (Friedlander and Seligman 1994; Liebman and Don-Yehiya 1983; Segev 1993).

This opposition between religion and nation-state, which finds expression in the antagonism between Jews ("returning" from exile) and Israelis, would explain, among other things, the "active silence" mentioned earlier. As in Germany—albeit manifesting itself in an opposite fashion—this silence was not absolute. In the first five years after the war, Holocaust victims were remembered with relatively little fanfare. The young Israeli state wished to distance itself from the diaspora Jews' history of suffering and their passive stance as victims. The Zionist elites cultivated this negative image of diaspora Jews to make the new life in Israel appear all the more positive. This tendency can be traced back to a heroic conception of history in which there is no place for passive victims. It was primarily those victims who had participated in the resistance who were commemorated. The uprising in the Warsaw ghetto became a paradigmatic case for remembering the Holocaust. Consequently, the Israeli state institutionalized memorials in which genocide and heroism were mentioned in the same breath. "Holocaust and Heroism Remembrance Day" commemorates the Holocaust victims, but it also focuses on Jewish resistance fighters in Palestine.

Through the end of the 1950s, the Holocaust was not acknowledged as a unique historical event in public consciousness or historical thought in Israel. As we have already mentioned, no unifying terminology even existed at that point. It was not until 1951 that a parliamentary resolution was passed for a national day of commemoration, to take place on the twenty-seventh day of the Hebrew month Nissan. Even in this case, the mixing of secular Zionism with religious symbolism is apparent. The date falls on the so-called Omer days, in which orthodox Jews commemorate the massacre of Jews during the crusades. What is more, the date falls between the end of Passover, when the Warsaw ghetto uprising is commemorated, and the Israeli Day of Independence. Every component of Israel's self-image at that time culminates in this period of commemoration: the eternal history of Jewish persecution; resistance against the Nazis; and the independent State of Israel. "Here" and "over there" were brought together into an incongruous unity. In 1953, Israeli legislators passed a law instating Holocaust and Heroism Remembrance Day and Yad Vashem, the country's central Holocaust memorial. It took six more years before the details of this national holiday were made legal (Don-Yehiya 1993). Places of entertainment are closed on Holocaust and Heroism Remembrance Day, and in the morning a siren sounds throughout the country for two minutes, signaling the start of a collective moment of silence.

Holocaust Remembrance from a Political and Moral Perspective

In examining this period, one dominant national discourse of remembrance can certainly be identified. This is not to say, however, that we are dealing with a single hegemonic project. Silence was not the only response in Israel; nor was there a dearth of critical voices demanding an official rhetoric of commemoration. At that time, there was no consensus surrounding the Holocaust, and it certainly was not a consensus-building event. On the contrary, a string of political scandals surfaced in which Holocaust memories became a central focus in partisan squabbles. Interestingly, Yad Vashem was erected at precisely the same time that negotiations with Germany over restitution were taking place. Those negotiations led to fierce public conflicts.

Two opposing positions faced off during this period. One was driven by national interests; the other, by the desire to recognize the survivors on a symbolic level. The state's conception of national interest prevailed, a fact that most of the survivors accepted (although the Herut Party led by Menachem Begin did not). Ultimately, most of Israel's new citizens were concerned with leaving their past behind and opening a new chapter in their lives. To a certain extent, donning a new identification with Israel at that time also entailed shedding a part of one's past. And, as was the case in the "negation of the diaspora," the interests of the state needed to be articulated in the "here and now," whereas survivors' memories were situated in a geographic and historic that was "beyond" the expediencies of the present. The realpolitik of the Zionists was pitted against the moral demands of their critics. Here, a clear preference for an institutional strategy is apparent, winning out over a cultural strategy in the debates surrounding restitution. The cultural approach is based on memories oriented toward the past, while the institutional strategy takes up memories for the purpose of establishing a future-oriented politics. "Now we are a sovereign state. A state does not get wrapped up in mysticism; it must concern itself with politics," Ben-Gurion said just as Israel was about to establish diplomatic relations with Germany (Weitz 2000). Here, "non-remembrance" of the Holocaust (within the context of reparations), part of the realpolitik practiced by "Jews in their sovereign state," was distinguished from ghetto Judaism, which would not forget and could not "forgive" (Protocols of the Israeli Cabinet, 10 October 1950, as cited in Weitz 2000: 260).

Nevertheless, it would be wrong to claim that the state had a monopoly over remembrance forms. Pressure also was exerted at a grassroots level. As mentioned, the population of Israel at that time included 350,000 people who had come from Nazi-occupied Europe. In contrast to Germany and the United States, this constitutes a type of "critical mass." People combed newspaper listings for missing relatives, and an Israeli radio station helped people search for families and friends. From the outset, official silence ran up against private testimonies of pain and loss. Thus, in some ways the official silence was exactly the same as that practiced by other nations. Nevertheless, Israel was a unique case. For one thing, it never simply clumped the Holocaust together with other Nazi crimes. What is more, because the Holocaust affected a majority of the population directly or indirectly, it was part of the national experience even before it became publicly articulated. But even in Israel, consciousness about Holocaust remembrance was only truly possible once it was given an appropriate political-cultural framework. During the founding of Israel, such a framework could not be imagined for the reasons mentioned earlier. Thus, almost nothing was initiated by the state in the first decades after the war to commemorate the Holocaust. The relative silence at that time, as well as the current sacralization of Holocaust memories, are expressions of Israel's self-image and of its position in the world.

Holocaust Remembrance in 1950s America

The United States was neither a perpetrator nor a victim of the Holocaust. It embodied the role of "liberator." Consequently, what dominated the U.S. postwar commemoration was the universalist perspective, which left little room for focusing on the fate of the Jews. Americans cultivated an image of the Holocaust that highlighted the diversity of the victims. As in the other cases, this is not simply a product of repression. Rather, America's tendency to universalize is an expression of its self-proclaimed mission to act as defender of the free world. This stance, together with the concrete circumstances surrounding the Cold War, influenced the American formula for remembering the Holocaust.

Two political strategies determined the United States' universal perspective in the first decade after the war. First, the United Nations

"eliminatory form of anti-Semitism." There was no space in postwar America to cultivate this particularistic approach. Instead of examining the nature of anti-Semitism and national–cultural distinctions, people studied the psychological makeup of prejudice in general.[11] In the final analysis, the Holocaust was used as a cautionary example of the consequences of "bystanderism" (Zelizer 1998). The importance of civil acts of courage and antiracism were the lessons drawn from the Holocaust. In this fashion, the Holocaust was incorporated into a universal framework that was dominant in America.

Other political and social circumstances contributed to this universalizing process. Postwar American society, like European societies, was caught up in a transition in which economic growth, and the consumer culture that went with it, were taking center stage. The view was future-oriented, leaving no room for examining the immediate past. The facts that, with the exception of Pearl Harbor, there had been no fighting on American soil also played a role in the way memories of the war were constructed. The American public had followed the fighting in the Pacific much more closely than the events taking place in Europe.

This geographic orientation was maintained after the war. The central lesson of the war remained Hiroshima. According to Novick, the Holocaust represented a bygone epoch; Hiroshima was politically much more relevant to the United States. It served as an emblem of the potential for destruction in the present and for the danger of a possible nuclear war in the future (Novick 1999). This future-oriented memory resonated with the euphoric attitude that permeated American society at that time. For instance, within this context, the role of suffering, which is considered so important today, took on a negative meaning. In the past four decades, the most diverse groups have embraced the status of victim in establishing a moral and political

---

11. The best-known example of this approach is the study undertaken by Theodor Adorno and his American colleagues, *The Authoritarian Personality* (1950). The specific cultural elements that were mentioned in that study were subsequently neutralized by Stanley Milgram's research on conformity in the 1970s (Milgram 1973). As a social psychologist working within a behaviorist framework, Milgram presented clear-cut findings: Given the right circumstances, everybody has the potential to turn into an Eichmann—or, in Milgram's more specific setting, to administer painful and even deadly electric shocks.

basis—not to mention a sense of identity—for achieving social and, frequently, legal recognition. In contrast, the victim label tended to be shunned in the 1940s and 1950s. The helplessness associated with it evoked a mixture of sympathy and resentment (Novick 1999). Consequently, people focused on the survivors and their ability to put their horrible experiences behind them.

This dominant orientation to the future is apparent in American-Jewish reactions to the Holocaust as well. Although they were aware of the fate of European Jews and did an enormous amount in providing the survivors with aid, they were (perhaps for that very reason) intent on distancing themselves from the victim identity. The latter symbolized the "Old World" that American Jews, with their increasing integration into the "New World," wanted to leave behind. There was therefore no interest at the time in erecting memorials, since these would have been interpreted as commemorating the weakness and helplessness of the Jewish people. On the other hand, one dutifully honored the Jewish soldiers in the American military and the success of ongoing assimilation into American society. The approximately 100,000 Holocaust survivors who immigrated to America after the war also adopted this future-oriented attitude. In the last thirty years, we have tended to focus on the permanent trauma that survivors suffered. In earlier years, these very same survivors were praised for their ability to forget the past and move on.

Holocaust remembrance was thus infused with a universal message. This type of universalism was not yet the same as the epoch-transcending German images of today. It was not regarded as a timeless measure of good and evil so much as a representation of an earlier era associated with World War II. In the years immediately after the war, reconstruction, new beginnings, and optimism, all geared toward the reconstruction of the state, took on nation-transcending features. Another name for this is modernization.

Nevertheless, the Cold War split Europe into opposing camps. Those nations in particular who had been affected by World War II were forced to choose sides. The friend-or-foe dichotomy also permeated historical memory and silence. However, gaps were gradually emerging in this perspective, which were magnified with the emergence of a new type of Holocaust remembrance. At that time, national cultures integrated Holocaust remembrance into their own narratives, which, paradoxically, would later provide the foundation for the cosmopolitanization of memory. But we have not reached this point in our analysis yet. In Germany, the Holocaust provided a means for the left to examine its own history from a distanced, critical perspective and, above all, to discredit the national perspective. In Israel, the Holocaust became a symbol for insecurity and the need to maintain a strong, militarized state. In the United States, it provided the basis for a newly emerging ethnic politics. This ethnic and national context laid the foundations for later developments, which we will take up in the following chapters.

5

Debates and Reflections

The Centrality of Jewish Holocaust Victims

THE 1960S MARKED a turning point in the reception and institutionalization of Holocaust memories. From the 1960s to the 1980s, the iconographic meaning of the Holocaust was established within the framework of various political and cultural events. In Israel and the United States, the Jewish victims were increasingly pushed into the limelight. In contrast to the postwar era, the process was no longer uniform among the three countries in terms of their marginalization of victimhood. Different sets of conditions and assumptions were now at play in directing public attention to the Holocaust.

A series of highly publicized trials in the 1960s formed a crucial background component in this historical shift. The centerpiece was the Eichmann trial in Jerusalem, which in many respects was staged as a major media event and, for many people, constituted the first comprehensive introduction to the topic. With the media coverage of the trial, the Holocaust escaped the boundaries of individual experience, presenting itself to a broad, new public. The generational aspect is particularly significant, since the Eichmann trial was as essential part of the political socialization of a large segment of the postwar generation. As Dan Diner (1999: 70) points out, historical discourses have a tendency to follow legal ones. He suggests that one can discover these discourses through a variety of historiographical approaches. They include the intentionalist approach, which stresses the anti-Semitic intentions of the perpetrators, and the functionalist approach, which focuses more on the bureaucratic practices associated with the extermination than on the crimes themselves. These approaches constitute renewed attempts to assign or repudiate guilt. The narratives, which we have come to recognize through representations of court trials, also provide a foundation for examining other issues from a political or moral perspective (Frei et al. 2000).

In the ensuing overview of the 1960s and 1970s, we shed light on three central developments:

1. Within the sphere of personal experience, there was a generational shift from social to historical memory. The war generation, whose perspective was shaped by firsthand experience, was increasingly forced to contend with the postwar generation, whose understanding of the Holocaust was by necessity historical. The postwar generation's image of the Holocaust is determined primarily by the social and political conflicts of the time and the approaches to the Holocaust that grew out of them.
2. Scholarly research into the topic began to change, albeit slowly at first. Historiographical reflexivity, a hallmark of contemporary research methods, is based on diversity. Hence, the debates took place between historians who fought over the "correct" interpretation of the national narrative.
3. The broadcast of the *Holocaust* television series marked a major shift in the media's representation of the Holocaust and its Americanization. This event challenged the traditional role of historians as producers of meaning and contested the accepted hierarchy between experts and lay people. The media representations and their creators emerged at this time as a new type of expert.

From German Victims to Victims of Germans: The *Sonderweg* Debate

In Germany, two factors in particular were responsible for increased public attention to the Holocaust and the changing political discourse: first, the widely publicized legal trials and, beginning in 1960, the debates surrounding a possible statute of limitations for Nazi crimes; and second, the postwar generation's confrontation with their parents' repressed Nazi past. It was during this period that the broader public was first made aware of the full extent of the extermination. Apart from a few state-sponsored official rituals, the task of preserving Holocaust memories had primarily been left to the survivors. For the most part, the survivors had shared their memories of the victims only among themselves. Thus, for instance, it was not until the end of the 1950s that survivors' demands for support in the building and upkeep of memorials were met. The installation and expansion of memorials in the former concentration camps of Dachau, Neuengamme, and Bergen-Belsen did not take place until the mid-1960s (Reichel 1995).

The Eichmann trial and, above all, the 1963 Auschwitz trial in Frankfurt were important catalysts in transforming the culture of remembrance. The Auschwitz trial lasted two years and covered the cases of twenty-two people who had worked at the camp. Between December 1963 and August 1965, nearly 400 witnesses were called to testify (Reichel 2001: 158–81). The media provided daily coverage of the trial and detailed testimony. In many respects, this was Germany's most comprehensive confrontation with the Holocaust, extending to the first postwar generation, for whom the legal processes surrounding Nazi crimes represented a defining political experience.

This event helped cultivate a new attitude toward the victims. Whereas in the first decade after the war most of the attention was directed toward German suffering, the focus was now on the victims of the Germans. The postwar generation was primarily responsible for this shift in perspective. However, they were concerned not so much with finding the appropriate form of remembrance for the Jews as with confronting their parents' culture of denial. More so than in any other country, the transformation of collective memory images in Germany was fraught with generational conflict. Large segments of the New Left adopted theories of fascism that regarded Nazism as the henchman of capitalism. This approach left little room for conceiving of the fate of the Jews. In contrast to their parents, the young generation acknowledged German culpability but still was not able to face the concrete experiences of the Jewish victims.

Peter Weiss's play *The Investigation*, which was based on court transcripts of the Auschwitz trial, reveals much about the prevailing attitude of the time. In October 1965, two months after the end of the trial, the play was staged simultaneously in sixteen theaters throughout East and West Germany and was later televised. For the '68 generation, this dramatic presentation was in many respects the chief carrier for remembering the Holocaust. Weiss, who was Jewish and had fled Germany with his family in 1934, represented the trial within the context of a Marxist theory of fascism popular at the time. According to his interpretation, the Federal Republic's capitalist system was marked by the persistence of fascism. The fact that many of the defendants in the Auschwitz trial managed to integrate themselves seamlessly into West German society was considered evidence of the link between fascism and capitalism. From this perspective, the Federal Republic was a successor to the Third Reich not only on a legal level but also on a political and cultural level:

> The investigation stipulates an unmediated causal nexus between capitalism and Auschwitz. The extermination of the Jews is presented and interpreted as an extreme form of capitalist exploitation. . . . Weiss subsumes the death of six million Jews to a universal Marxist critique of capitalism. (Huyssen 1980: 133)

In addition, Weiss's drama hardly allows any emotional identification with the victims, which the *Holocaust* TV series of the 1980s does. At first glance, this appears to be an example of a decontextualized universalism. In reality, however, it is a leftist version of obfuscation. In addressing this tendency, Diner (1999) speaks of a universalism that serves to deny guilt.

Whatever little identification the New Left harbored for the Jewish victims dissipated after the Six Day War in 1967. Former victims (Israelis) became the aggressors, and Palestinians joined the ranks of victims of Western imperialism. This reversal in many respects was a product of internal political conflicts. Coverage of the Six Day War in the Springer press,[1] the archenemy of the New Left, led to overwhelming support by the right-wing press for the Israeli state. An anti-Israel stance, along with the denunciation of Springer's

---

1. At the time, the Springer publishing house, owned by the anticommunist and conservative Axel Springer, accounted for almost half of the newspaper circulation in West Germany.

nationalist position, was part of the standing repertoire of the left. Thus, coming to terms with the past was not associated with Holocaust memories in the way that it was in the 1980s. Informed by Marxist theory, the left wanted primarily to expose the persistent authoritarianism in German history. This rejection of nationalist traditions provided a framework for redefining the notion of victimhood. The '68 generation criticized any attempts to blur the distinction between German and non-German groups of victims and looked at the popular image of the German victim as a relic of an outdated nationalism. This was why, in those days, any kind of compassion toward the suffering of Germans during and after World War II was regarded as implying a neglect of the victims of the Holocaust. This charge has recently been revived in several publications that deal with the expulsions and the Allied bombing of German cities (Friedrich 2002; Kettenacker 2003). However, between the late 1960s and the early 1990s, the majority of German cultural and political elites largely dismissed the memory of German victimization as a discredited form of nationalism.

Paradoxically, despite its universal orientation, the New Left is responsible for the re-nationalizing of German political culture. During the peace movement of the late 1970s in particular, it stressed "national identity" when addressing issues regarding the West, Germany's role in NATO, the possibility of maintaining neutrality, and broad anti-American sentiments. Debates about the national question and the "correct" way to remember the Holocaust became intertwined. The main emerging concern was Germany's understanding of itself as a nation.

Thus, arguments about the "right" way to understand the Holocaust played an important role in the development of a new political culture in Germany. What leaps to mind are the controversies that marked the 1980s (e.g., Ronald Reagan and Helmut Kohl's symbolic handshake at the cemetery at Bitburg; the so-called Historians' Dispute of that era) and the 1990s (Daniel Goldhagen's *Hitler's Willing Executioners*, the German exhibition "War of Annihilation: Crimes of the Wehrmacht"). These events can be explained only within the context of earlier developments—specifically, the new historical approach that emerged in the 1960s. The so-called *Sonderweg* (special path) thesis is the central concept that dominates historiographical debates in Germany (see Berger 1997; Iggers 1997).

A brief outline of this thesis will serve to underscore how questions of uniqueness and sameness and of continuity and discontintuity become politicized under various circumstances. The concept of the *Sonderweg* dates back to the nineteenth century and originally had a positive connotation. An emphasis on the uniqueness of the German nation crystallized in the mythological conception of a superior German *Volk*, whose culture was distinguished from that of other civilizations in many important respects. With rising nationalism, many of the attributes that had been stressed as part of a *Kulturnation* became part of an increasingly ethnocentric ideology and ultimately culminated in the racist excesses of the Nazi regime.[2] According to the *Sonderweg* thesis, Germany was not part of enlightened Western civilization. The West's universal-global orientation is, then, the polar opposite of the *Sonderweg* (Berger 1997).

In the 1970s, the historian Fritz Fischer criticized the defensive posture of his German colleagues—specifically, their insistence on seeing Nazism as an aberration in German history and their refusal to draw connections between it and earlier traditions. In his 1961 book *Griff nach der Weltmacht* (published in English as *Germany's Aims in the First World War* [1967]), he argued that the German government and military leadership were responsible for the outbreak of World War I, exposing the uninterrupted dominance of the same ruling elite into the Nazi period.

In a recent study on West German historians and their relationship to the Holocaust, Nicolas Berg (2003) argues that German historians were by and large unconcerned with the fate of Jewish victims. World War II and the Nazi state were all about Germany and the catastrophe it went through. Paradigmatic for this approach is *The*

---

2. In its formative phase, the German concept of nation centered on the *Volk*, signifying organic relationships among a people rather than a political organization. The centrality of cultural cohesion responded to the fragmentation of the German states between 1815 and 1871. After the unification of Germany, a new, state-centered conception of nationhood was introduced. Ever since, German politics have been shaped by tensions between ethno-national and state-national conceptions—between the *Kulturnation* and the *Staatsnation*.

German Catastrophe (1963 [1946]) by Friedrich Meinecke, Germany's most prominent historian. His study provides a prototype for the kind of approach that Fischer criticizes. The title of Meinecke's book is revealing: "Catastrophe" suggests that humans are no longer in control of their political decisions and carries an air of inevitability. In contrast, Fischer draws out the similarities and continuities between Imperial Germany and the Nazi regime. In the seething atmosphere of the universities, Fischer provided a credo for an entire generation of young historians (Berger 1997), a group that later became known as the "Bielefeld School." Their research was devoted to uncovering links between the military, undemocratic traditions of Imperial Germany and the authoritarian, murderous system of the Nazi era. According to this line of thinking, the *Sonderweg* had cut Germany off from the rational, Western history of civilization. Norbert Elias (1996) claims that the path from an aristocratic to a fascist society was so smooth in Germany because the middle class was never in a position to transform its economic dominance into a cultural one. Whether viewed from a positive or a negative perspective, the debate about the German *Sonderweg* forces one to focus on the nation-state. The various interpretations spawned by this debate continue to determine the relationship between particular and universal forms of Holocaust remembrance to this day.

The Transformation of Official Remembrance

In the 1970s, the Holocaust became an integral component of official German memory culture (Dubiel 1999: 129–75). To be sure, state-sponsored remembrance is not identical to the political culture of a nation. Nevertheless, official discourse is a dominant factor in the creation and institutionalization of a value system. With their privileged access to the media, the political classes determine the public agenda and lay out the criteria for remembering, thereby sanctioning the legitimate practices of remembrance.

For Willy Brandt, who became Germany's chancellor in 1969, the Holocaust became a litmus test for the new democratic self-image of the Federal Republic. Germany's acceptance of collective responsibility for the Holocaust has been central to every administration's official and symbolic repertoire since then (Herf 1997; Olick 1993). The celebrated moment in 1970 when Brandt kneeled in front of the Memorial for the Dead at the Warsaw ghetto, as well as the admission of German crimes against Poles and Jews that went along with this symbolic act, overshadowed the memories of the Germans' own suffering. In the immediate aftermath of the war, any attempt to understand the Holocaust from a moral perspective had been viewed as a barrier to the democratization process. In the Brandt era, however, such memories were considered essential in building a strong democracy. His campaign slogan, "Mehr Demokratie Wagen (Dare More Democracy)," articulates this transformation from an institutional to a cultural strategy very well.

Heated debates surrounding the statute of limitations for Nazi crimes provided the legal and political context for this transformation. In 1960, what would have been the normal statute of limitations for murder threatened to put an end to the prosecution of Nazi criminals. To prevent thousands of criminals from escaping conviction and, above all, from avoiding punishment, intensive parliamentary debates took place in 1960, 1965, 1969, and 1979 that brought the crimes perpetrated by the Nazis into the public limelight. However, they also exposed the legal community's failure to convict Nazis in the 1950s (Frei 1997). Thus, the protests against instating the statute of limitations were aimed not only at the old Nazis, but also at a politics of forgetting and the selective memory that reigned during the postwar years. The Social Democratic Party (SPD) supported extending the statute of limitations by using 1949 rather than 1945 as the beginning date for calculating the statute, but this solution was rejected in 1960 by the Adenauer administration and its coalition partner, the Free Democratic Party (FDP), which had yet to shed its National Socialist leanings. The second debate, which took place in 1965, marked a decisive shift in political and ethical tone (Dubiel 1999: 103–10). West Germans had begun to glean many more details about the genocide, partly because of the public attention that the first series of debates had stirred up, and even more because of the Eichmann and the Auschwitz trials. This had an effect on even the moderate segments of the Christian Democratic Union (CDU). In opposition to Fritz Schäfer, the minister of justice at the time,

Chancellor Ludwig Erhard declared in 1965 that it was not inconceivable that more crimes would be brought to light twenty years after the end of the war.

Generational shifts played a big role in this case, as well. Helmut Dubiel maintains that "the parliamentary debates of the 1970s concerning the past history of the dictatorship and the future of the democracy were nothing but a product of a generational conflict" (Dubiel 1999: 132). Erhard and a large segment of his coalition actually intended to preserve the existing statute of limitations, a position that ran counter to that of a young member of the CDU named Ernst Benda. His principal achievement was to place issues of constitutionality at the very political and ethical core of the debates. This approach led to a parliamentary majority vote in favor of extending the statute in 1965 as well as in 1969.

Subsequently, in 1970 the first official parliamentary commemoration of the end of World War II took place. Twenty-five years after the war's end, political orientations still determined whom one considered worthy of commemorating. The first memorial ceremony held on 8 May signaled the institutionalization of an official culture of remembrance that was based on the realization, in the words of Chancellor Brandt, that "a people must be prepared to face their own history with eyes wide open; for only he who remembers what has happened will be able to understand the present and to have an overview of what may happen in the future. This holds especially true for the younger generation. It was not involved in what came to an end that day . . . nevertheless, no one is free from history" (Brandt 1970). The 8 May ceremony and the image of a responsible "moral nation" (Olick 1993) were to become a standard formula for Germany's politics of remembrance in the years to come. Remembering the Holocaust—and, more specifically, taking note of the centrality of this memory—constituted the very core of Germany's political culture and its self-image as a nation.

The 1979 debate over the statute of limitations is evidence of how much Germany's political and cultural life had changed in the public politics of memory because of the generational shift. This time around, the debate was not about whether to extend the statute but about whether the statute should be abolished altogether for crimes committed during the Nazi era. The members of the Bundestag (Parliament) who supported such a decision were less concerned with legally apprehending former Nazis than, by confronting these crimes in a judicial context, with dealing publicly with the legacy of National Socialism on a political and moral level (Dubiel 1999: 161).

In summary, the debates over the statute of limitations can be seen as an expression of the social conditions that were necessary for a culture of remembrance to flourish. They also contributed significantly to the institutionalization of the injunction to remember on an official level.

Eichmann in Jerusalem: The Relationship between Universalist and Particularist Orientations

In Israel, as well as in Germany and the United States, the Eichmann trial was an important milestone in the history of Holocaust remembrance. The trial—or, more specifically, its media coverage—sharpened the public's awareness of the Holocaust. In Israel, the trial was proof of Israeli sovereignty. In 1960, Eichmann was captured in Argentina by the Israeli Secret Service and taken to Israel, where the trial was conducted in Hebrew. Whereas the Allies had been the primary force behind the Nuremberg trials, the State of Israel was in control now. The Jewish state would not and could not turn the trial into a cosmopolitan event. "I do not stand before you alone," declared the state's prosecutor, Gideon Hausner. "With me stand 6 million accusers." At the same time that Germany was admitting its guilt as a nation, via a critique of the *Sonderweg* theory, and thereby joining the "modern world," the Eichmann trial was contributing toward the labeling of "powerless" or "sovereign-less" Jews as a "victim nation" for whom a powerful and sovereign Israel was the solution.

A law passed by the Israeli Parliament in 1950 declaring the death penalty for Nazis and Nazi collaborators provided the legal foundation for the trial. The case was fraught with legal and ethical problems. Strangely enough, Karl Jaspers, a staunch supporter of the Nuremberg trials, was one of its chief detractors. His position is outlined in his correspondence with Hannah Arendt, in which he maintained that Israel was not legally entitled to try Eichmann. In a letter dated 12 December 1960, a few months before the start of the trial, Jaspers noted:

> Israel didn't even exist when the murders were committed. Israel is not the Jewish people. . . . The Jewish people are more than the state of Israel, not identical with it. If Israel were lost, the Jewish people would still not be lost. Israel does not have the right to speak for the Jewish people as a whole. (Köhler and Saner 1985: 410–11)

In arguing that Israel was only one component of the Jewish diaspora, Jaspers discounted the claims of Israel as a sovereign nation that David Ben-Gurion and the ruling parties had attempted to articulate. The aim was to make Israel a mouthpiece for all of Judaism and to declare its sovereignty, thereby providing a political legacy for the murdered Jews. Hannah Arendt accepted this point in her reply to Jaspers, which is surprising in light of the subsequent scandal unleashed by her book about the trial. In a letter dated 23 December 1960, she wrote:

> Israel may not have the right to speak for the Jews of the world. Although I would like to know who really does have the right to speak for the Jews qua Jews in a political sense. Certainly, many Jews don't want to be represented as Jews or only want to be in a religious sense. So Israel has no right to speak for them. But what about the others? Israel is the only political entity we have. . . . But in any case Israel has the right to speak for the victims, because the large majority of them (300,000) are living in Israel now as citizens. (Köhler and Saner 1985: 415)

In assessing the Eichmann case, Arendt's "rooted cosmopolitanism," which should not be confused with universalism, clashed with Jasper's universal cosmopolitanism. The political purpose of the trial was to use it as a didactic media event, as proof of Israel's legitimacy, and as a justification for possible armed conflicts with the Arabs, who were frequently characterized as a new incarnation of Nazis. In the 1950s, official Holocaust remembrance had been muted in Israel, focusing almost exclusively on the heroism of the resistance; now, the trial shifted the focus to the victims. Although the didactic mission was a success, the structure of the trial, which included a long series of eyewitness testimonies, yielded some unexpected results. Because of the trial, the private memories of many survivors were made public for the first time. The country tuned in to the radio daily (the trial was a radio event for most Israelis, as there was no television in Israel at the time). They listened in on the testimony of the survivors, who laid bare their private accounts of suffering (see Segev 1993). This in turn ignited discussions within families who had refrained from talking about their experiences until that point. Thus, while newspapers published articles proudly extolling the strength of Israel, and the state hoped that the trial would help foster increased loyalty among its citizens, the effects in some segments of Israeli society were quite different. The witnesses' testimony was not about heroism and resistance; it dealt with weakness, death, and vulnerability. The memories flooded out, and no state was in a position to contain them. The image that eventually became symbolic of the trial was that of the author Yehiel Dinur—better known as "Ka-Zetnik," who coined the term "Planet Auschwitz"—breaking down on the witness stand. In his early works, Dinur identified the State of Israel as the single essential answer to Planet Auschwitz.[3]

In this way, the Holocaust was transformed from a shameful symbol of weakness into a sacred memory that State Prosecutor Hausner brought to light as part of a historical lineage. The event took its place as yet another example in archetypal Jewish history. It was a new act in the old drama in which the enemies of the Jewish people had tried to eradicate them and had failed. Through the Eichmann trial, Israel became more Jewish than its founding fathers had originally planned, reinforcing tensions between Israeliness and Jewishness. National pride had to compete with a transnational Jewish culture. The initial revolutionary impulse, which sought to break away from its Jewish roots by embracing radical nationalism, gradually began to subside. The attempt at a new political beginning, in which premodern Judaism was to be transformed into a "normal" modern Jewish identity, was thwarted by the past. The simultaneous individualization and sacralization of the Holocaust, both products of

3. Dinur later modified his position to become an advocate of the universalization of the Holocaust. This went unnoticed by the Ministry of Education, since Dinur's books continued to be part of the compulsory learning material on the Holocaust. Dinur's case is yet another example of how a universal understanding can emerge out of the particular (for more on Dinur, see Bartov 1997).

the Eichmann trial, mark the beginning of the de-territorialization of memory. In addition, Israel felt it necessary to acquaint the large influx of Jewish emigrants from the Middle East and North Africa, who had no personal connection to the Holocaust, with the fate of European Jewry. Their own experience of a world turned upside down was of Arab countries in which they had lived for centuries suddenly turning anti-Semitic. This became the bridge between the two points of view, because for European Jews the story of the Holocaust, even when it was being played down, had always been a story of anti-Semitism. Now, by being mapped onto the Arab–Israeli conflict, the Holocaust became a way to bridge two divergent world views: Both groups were the victims of world anti-Semitism, which had come to a climax, then had been solved, with the creation of the State of Israel.

Thus, anti-Semitism became synonymous with criticism of Israel. But it was arguably the 1967 war that transformed such gestures into a permanent state ideology. In part it made the transformation possible, for only after the war did Israel begin to think of itself as a state that would endure. Perhaps this is what made it possible for the Jewish people to endure contemplation of the horror, which would have been demoralizing when they thought the state might be destroyed at any moment. In part, it also made such contemplation necessary. Although the country's original founders had desired above all for Israel to be a normal state like any other, retaining the Occupied Territories gained in the 1967 war made it just as necessary for Israel to be treated as an exception. The war made Israel into an occupying power. All parties to the conflict realized that the balance of power had changed, that Israel was not going to be pushed into the sea anytime soon. And it is no accident that, immediately thereafter, the battle was transposed to the diplomatic arena. In 1974, Yasir Arafat addressed the United Nations Assembly. In 1975, the Palestine Liberation Organization received observer status. In the same year, the United Nations overwhelmingly passed a resolution stating that Zionism was a form of racism.

In light of these events, the Eichmann trial fulfilled an important political and ideological function. This function was further bolstered through the 1967 and 1973 wars and Israel's occupation of Arab territories.

Eichmann in America

In the United States, television helped turn the Eichmann trial into a media event. The American approach was quite different from the Israeli approach, however. During the course of the trial, which took place sixteen years after the war had ended, the destruction of European Jewry was transformed into the "Holocaust." In other words, the American public stopped regarding the Holocaust as just an aspect of World War II and began to recognize it as a unique event with its own proper name and its own set of experiences and memories.

As the first major media event, the coverage of the trial was produced locally, but its reception was global. As is often the case with media events of such proportions, the local producers lost control over their product. A change took place in the culture of remembrance that had less to do with media manipulation than with the relationship of the local to the global, with the needs of the particular viewer and the historical context in which reception takes place. For many American Jews, this meant a reinterpretation of the Holocaust from the earlier universal understanding to an ethnically based one, thereby integrating the event into their own history. In its attempt to make itself the exclusive carrier of Holocaust memories, Israel had tried to do something similar with the Eichmann trial. In America, however, particular memories were not national, but ethnic. And those memories could be mobilized to rally support for Israel on a political level. The so-called Lessons of the Holocaust were thus often transferred onto Israel (Novick 1999). "Never again" was a slogan that linked the ethnic memory of the Holocaust to Jews as well as to Israel. As in Israel, the wars of 1967 and 1973 strengthened this ethnic form of identity politics in the United States, although other issues soon entered the American scene. There was simply no escaping the ideology of universalism in America. When one speaks of the "Americanization of the Holocaust," one is actually referring to this process of universalization. The American television viewer was constantly confronted with universal moral pronouncements, for U.S. commentators had no other way to interpret the trial. Even though the trial was conducted in Hebrew, its translation into English led to its Americanization and universalization (Shandler 1999). This foreshadows global media events surrounding the Holocaust. They were often produced in English and then translated for local settings. In the United States, the Eichmann trial led to an understanding of the Holocaust as the history of German evildoers and Jewish victims, on the one hand, and on the other, of evil and its paradigmatic victims—namely, the Jews.

It is thus no coincidence that, in *Eichmann in Jerusalem*, the cosmopolitan observer Hannah Arendt, a German Jewish woman living in the United States, interpreted the Holocaust as a "crime against humanity, perpetrated upon the body of the Jewish people" and insisted that "only the choice of victims, not the nature of the crime, could be derived from the long history of Jew-hatred and anti-Semitism" (Arendt 1992: 269). Arendt really was one of the first to employ social-science techniques to study the Holocaust. As early as 1950, she introduced her thesis of the "senselessness" of the Holocaust in a short published study: The Holocaust was senseless, she claimed, in that it could not be comprehended using modes of utilitarian reasoning (Arendt 1950). This monstrous senselessness was one reason that no appropriate punishment was left for the crimes committed during the Holocaust. After her book about the Eichmann trial, Arendt came under heavy attack for this statement, even though she had made it very clear that she had no reservations about calling for the death penalty in his case.

Arendt was less comfortable with the idea of the Holocaust as a deed typical of Germany than as a product of modern "totalitarianism." However, she was never able to accept the so-called negative dialectic of Enlightenment as an explanation, either. She felt a strong connection to the Enlightenment and considered National Socialism a failure of the Enlightenment, of critical modernism, and of moral judgment. Arendt's position remains difficult to categorize. The distinction between universalism and particularism never really made sense to her. In principle, she connected the two—the yearning for territorial independence, on the one hand, and the universal message of the diaspora, on the other. In other words, the Jews were at once cosmopolitans and a particular ethnic group—a tension but not a contradiction in terms. Israel wanted to provide the Jews with a home, but Arendt did not have much use for such a concrete notion of homeland. For her, the United States came closest to providing a Jewish existence that was open to the world. From Arendt's perspective, the "Americanization of the Holocaust" was a universalism that was embedded in the Jewish experience, which was the closest thing to a cosmopolitan view of the events. While this position was considered scandalous when her book appeared, it is widely accepted today.

Eichmann in Germany

In Germany, the Eichmann trial, like the Auschwitz trials of 1963–68, was met with ambivalence. To be sure, the trials heightened public awareness of the Holocaust. Despite this fact—or, perhaps, precisely because of it—the majority of the population had a negative reaction to the trials. To be sure, reactions varied greatly depending on the viewer's age and political leanings. The older (war) generation and many others reacted to their past with silence or repression or by publicly professing their philo-Semitism. The younger generation was much more open to dealing with the Nazi crimes of the past. This led, on the one hand, to a greater willingness to confront the Nazis and, on the other hand, to a tendency among the left and the New Left of the postwar generation to make the Holocaust fit their own agendas. Thus, Arendt's "banality of evil" thesis was quickly co-opted into the existing narratives of fascism and antifascism. In the narrative of antifascism, the Holocaust was not treated as a unique event but as a symbol of oppression and victimization. Once it was universalized and freed from issues of personal responsibility, the Holocaust could be used to promote understanding and tolerance. Above all, leftist postwar literary groups such as Group 47, which called for reeducation of the Germans, embraced this view. Here, Nazism served as a universal metaphor for suffering, whereby the fate of the Jews was by and large forgotten (Schlant 1999). This literature formed the basis of the dominant brand of antifascism from 1967 on, one that obscured the Jewish question and further marginalized remembrance of the Holocaust. Seen in this light, antifascism since the 1960s has fulfilled a function similar to the totalitarianism theory that was adopted at the beginning of the Cold War—namely, to situate the events within a framework of authoritarian regimes.

In summary, one can affirm that the Eichmann trial was an important catalyst in all three countries for raising awareness and knowledge about the Holocaust. Public and political discourse surrounding the trial provided a basis for nationally based interpretations and bolstered demands to see the Holocaust as part of a broader phenomenon—namely, fascism. The changing reception of Arendt's *Eichmann in Jerusalem* is evidence of the shift in balance between particularism and universalism. In the past decade especially, the question of the "banality of evil" has again dominated discussions about the possibilities of universalizing the Holocaust. This discussion is no longer confined to the antifascist narrative. In contrast to the way in which the topic was dealt with in Germany, Israel, and the United States in the 1960s and 1970s, it is now part of mainstream political repertoires. In the earlier era, discussions of the Holocaust were generally determined by internal developments in the three countries, despite apparent similarities.

America Discovers the Holocaust

One actually would not have expected the term "Holocaust," as it is used today to refer to the murder of the Jews, to become common currency in the United States. After the war, America waved the banner of universalism, placing itself at the spearhead of Enlightenment in defending Europe from the grip of the Soviets. This was the credo of the Cold War. Most American Jews, including the 100,000 survivors of the concentration camps who came to the United States after the war, supported American foreign policy. Americans for the most part were ignorant of what Europe had gone through to rebuild itself after the war. American political culture was overwhelmingly optimistic at the time. While Europe lay in ruins, the United States was new, young, and powerful, which was an important factor in determining the different types of memories that defined the two cultures. America was "free of pain" and thus able to uphold a universal type of memory. Americans did not see themselves as victims of air raids, occupation, and division as the Germans did; nor were they part of the Jewish collective of victims. America was a witness to these events and, as such, was able to hold a privileged position.

A sacralization of memory based on the experience of pain and suffering was unthinkable in 1950s America. Not even the atom bomb could shake this sense of moral superiority.

All this began to change in the 1960s, when the prevailing optimism began to wane. The Vietnam war; the assassination of President John F. Kennedy, who had symbolized young, optimistic America as nobody else had; the subsequent assassinations of Robert Kennedy, Martin Luther King, Jr., and Malcolm X; the Civil Rights Movement—these and many other factors contributed to the emerging tale of American suffering. This might not have been the case for all Americans, but it certainly was for minorities and ethnic groups. The new catchwords were racism and discrimination, under which the Holocaust fell, as well.

Relations between the African American and Jewish population are revealing in this respect. Their troubled relationship is based in large part on their individual conceptions of suffering, which they attempt to integrate into their own histories. Although these conceptions of suffering were forged outside official national discourse—indeed, often in opposition to it—the state frequently served as a source to turn to in times of need. These two groups were not equal in status, however. The African American community witnessed a decline in its socioeconomic status and the disintegration of its social structure, while the majority of Jews became integrated into the American mainstream. For the Jewish population, America's Enlightenment legacy was not just an empty promise; it was very real. In the United States, Jews could live as Jews *and* as American citizens without sacrificing their historical identity. They had won the right to do this through their material and ideal success, which was not the case for African Americans, who continued to suffer from racial discrimination.

Nevertheless, memories of suffering are not just affected by the social reality of the present. Black politicians borrowed themes from Jewish history, which Jews in turn "demanded back" from them. Connections were drawn between black slavery and Jewish slavery in Egypt, turning Moses into a more significant figure than Jesus. Many themes of black gospel songs, such as "Let My People Go," are derived from the history of Jewish suffering. Other connections include the Black Nationalist Movement, which drew heavily on Zionism

(Gilroy 2000), as well as the Civil Rights Movement, which was important for both blacks and Jews. As Jewish groups were opening up about their own history of suffering by raising awareness of the Holocaust, some members of the black community wanted to refer to the "Middle Passage," the transportation of black slaves across the Atlantic from the sixteenth to the nineteenth century that claimed millions of lives, and other instances of suffering as the "Black Holocaust." Though the diaspora experience is not the same, it is difficult to conceive one without the other. That is, when ethnic groups compete for sympathy and support, they learn things from each other. Hence, "racism" became a catchword in America for talking about the Holocaust, whereas the themes of fascism and anti-Semitism dominated discussions in Germany and Israel.

There is a subtle but crucial difference between the Holocaust as history's worst act of racism and the Holocaust as the culmination of the history of anti-Semitism (as it is understood in Israel). Anti-Semitism happens only to the Jews; racism can happen to anyone. In Israel, the question was always "Why us?" In America, the question in the same debate was "Why should we care?" And the answer was: Because it could happen to anyone—a very good answer to the question of "Why care?" but a very unsatisfying answer to the question "Why us?" Universalization grew out of the needs of the rhetorical context.

An additional reason is the fact that race is the central trauma of American history. Racism was also the central model of politics in the late 1960s and early 1970s, when the Holocaust entered American political discourse. Peter Novick (1999) has highlighted the irony in American Jews' beginning to claim that they were the most victimized group in history precisely as quotas against them were finally lifted and they began to assimilate into the elite. To this can be added the irony that Israel began to claim its victim status after the 1967 and 1973 wars, precisely as it was establishing that it was strong enough militarily to survive. But these are not ironies so much as counter-reactions. It was precisely Israel's victories on the battlefield that transposed the battle into a diplomatic one. In a similar manner, it was the success of American Jews that put a strain on their political alliance with African Americans. It became clear in both contexts that the Holocaust was the ultimate riposte to an accusation of racism. But as Jews are only a tiny part of the U.S. population, the meaning of the Holocaust in America was not its meaning for the Jews but, rather, the meaning that arose out of the interaction in the public debate—the meaning that answered the questions, "Why should we care?" and "Why should we remember?" That was the answer that resonated with racism.

The growing solidarity that American Jews felt for the State of Israel also proved to be an important factor in this process. The U.S. Constitution enables ethnic groups to show solidarity not just to the state but also to the "Old Country." This pertains not only to African Americans but also to the Irish, the Italians, and other groups. For Jews in America, Israel provided yet another point of reference precisely when anti-Semitism no longer posed a significant barrier to their success.

As in Germany, leftist strategies in America contributed to nationalization. The American left rejected anticommunist intervention, a pressing topic given the developments in Vietnam and Cambodia. In the late 1960s and early '70s in America, that meant defending anticommunist interventions around the world, starting foremost with the Vietnam war. But this was not at first obvious. In fact, in retrospect the opposite seems to be the more natural position: if the Holocaust was something that could happen to anyone, and the lesson was that people should not just stand by and let it happen, then was it not the duty of the United States to stop genocide everywhere? Was the United States not actually committing genocide from the air? And were not many of its client states doing so on the ground? In this respect, Jewish ethnic politics found itself in accord with American foreign policy. If the "lessons" of the Holocaust were meant to prevent further genocide, then Americans were guilty of perpetrating a new Holocaust through their global activities. However, if one interpreted the Holocaust as "unique," then one could never compare it to U.S. politics. Thus, American politics lent credence to the theory of the "uniqueness" of the Holocaust, a view that Israel supported without question. Comparing the Holocaust to other cases of genocide was tantamount to denying it, trivializing it, or engaging in racism. Because of the "uniqueness" doctrine,

Jewish American organizations had become players in the Cold War (Novick 1999).

Holocaust as Media Event

The "global broadcast" of the Holocaust reached its apex with the 1978 American miniseries *Holocaust*, another milestone in the media's representation of the event. Eichmann and issues of crime and evil were pushed out of the center of the drama to be replaced by the fictional story of the Weiss family, who represented typical, cosmopolitan European Jews. In the United States as well as in Germany, the *Holocaust* miniseries became a number-one topic of public discussion. In America, more than 100 million viewers tuned in on four consecutive evenings of broadcast, from 16 to 19 April 1978 (Shandler 1999: 155–78).

The miniseries' first installment aired on a Sunday, which was later dubbed "Holocaust Sunday." The choice of Sunday in and of itself points to a universalization—and hence, an Americanization and a Christianizing—of the event. This was further underscored by the portrayal of the Weiss family as "cosmopolitan," an association that was strengthened when non-Jewish clergy took up the topic of the Holocaust in sermons (Wuthnow 1987: 125). The American sociologist Robert Wuthnow has identified a connection between the uncertainty stemming from the Vietnam war and the Watergate scandal and the need for a public ritual involving clear-cut moral issues. He focuses on how the Holocaust is transposed onto present or future situations in which states act unethically. Wuthnow interprets the U.S. reaction to the *Holocaust* miniseries as an attempt by viewers to orient themselves in a world fraught with uncertainty. It was not so much the "history" of the Holocaust that interested them as the Holocaust as a symbol of present evil (Wuthnow 1987: 124–32).

The miniseries unleashed many of the issues that became pronounced in later debates surrounding Spielberg's *Schindler's List* and Goldhagen's *Hitler's Willing Executioners*, such as the mixing of fiction and nonfiction. Questions about the "limits of representation" of the Holocaust arose immediately after the first night's broadcast, when Elie Wiesel published an article in the *New York Times* decrying the program's "trivialization" of the event, which sparked a debate that continues to this day. The ethnic politics of Jewish Americans had reached a critical point of no return. The process of universalization had begun, followed by the Holocaust's induction into museum culture. It was easy for Americans to identify with the fictional Weisses; in this sense, they *were* Americans or Jewish Americans. The miniseries also introduced the viewers to the main sites of and actors in the Holocaust: the Warsaw ghetto; the Auschwitz and Dachau concentrations camps; the partisans; and so on. They all became part of the American, and thus the global, media landscape.

German Reception

The *Holocaust* series spawned the use of the term "Holocaust," a Greek word that means "burnt offering," which had become Americanized. This designation replaced others such as the "Final Solution," created by the Nazis, and the "destruction of the Jews." The word "Holocaust" provided a frame of reference for talking and thinking about the event without having to define it. The series became a media success in Germany.[4] This was evident in the incredibly high viewer ratings (40 percent, or about 15 million viewers), which seemed even more astonishing considering that the series was relegated to a less popular station because of raging political debates between parties on the left and right. But it was not the numbers alone that caused the media sensation. Thousands of phone calls and letters came pouring in to the WDR, the station that sponsored the series. Newspapers were flooded with letters from readers, and informational brochures were snapped up as fast as they were printed. During the entire week of the broadcast, the series and the Holocaust were the topic of conversations in schools, in offices, and at home. The main focus was on Germany's past failures in coming to terms with its past.

It is very clear that the success of the series and its influence on the younger generation has played a big role in making the Holocaust central to debates about German identity since the end of the 1970s

---

4. For articles that appeared almost simultaneously in response to the series, see the special edition *New German Critique* 19 (1980).

(Reichel 1995). Its immediate effect was evident in public reaction to debates in the Bundestag concerning lifting the statute of limitations for National Socialist crimes. The percentage of citizens who supported lifting the statute of limitations rose from 23 percent in 1968 to 40 percent in 1979, while those who supported maintaining the statute fell from 67 percent to 47 percent. Differences were even more striking between specific age groups. Among 16–29-year-olds, 38 percent favored lifting the statute, compared with 31 percent of the 45 and older group, 57 percent of whom called for the end of all criminal proceedings (Noelle-Neumann and Neumann 1981: 194). Since this time, the Holocaust has been the Gordian knot for all controversies surrounding German national identity. The right complained about the restrictive consequences of the series on the nation's identity; the left welcomed those consequences as a sign of an enlightened, universal society that needed to orient itself on post-national values.

Holocaust *in Israel*

The *Holocaust* miniseries was broadcast in Israel in 1978. It drew many viewers—because of the topic, of course, but also because Israel had only one television station at the time. Like many foreign representations of the Holocaust, however, *Holocaust* received only polite attention (as was the case with Goldhagen's book twenty years later). It is possible that the series was "too American" and the Weiss family "too un-Jewish" for many Israelis. While these were precisely the elements that drew viewers in Germany and America and enabled them to identify with the protagonists, they prevented many Israelis from considering the series meaningful. In Israel, one did not need to present Jews as "good citizens" to garner sympathy. Nevertheless, a study showed that most of the viewers were moved emotionally by the series (Levinson 1981). What is striking in the Israeli case is that the series did not lead to any public debates.

Holocaust as History Politics

The institutionalization of Holocaust memories since the beginning of the 1980s has been accompanied by a rise in controversies surrounding its historical interpretation and their political significance. In what ways have these debates contributed to a reformulation of memory? What happens to remembrance when it is no longer simply an awakening of memory but finds itself the subject of debate? In what follows, we analyze individual phases that illuminate the state of tension between universal and particular forms of remembrance, as well as an emerging self-reflexive memory.

Historiographical developments play a key role in determining how collective memory is structured. Historians maintain legitimacy by guarding their status as experts in matters pertaining to national identity. They link the present to the past, establish continuities, and work to legitimate repertoires of remembrance to which the national collective can turn to create a self-identity. Experts give rise to counter-experts, however. What is more, the experts no longer debate in the halls of academe; they now have a public that either applauds or boos them. This is why "pundit debates" now serve as entertainment and expert opinions no longer go unchallenged. Historiographical debates not only interpret anew the raw historical data; they also thematize methodological issues as ethical questions. As a consequence, questions regarding legitimate versions of the past become central to the political reality of the present. Memory itself becomes the subject of discussion—it reflects on itself. Memory becomes the reflection on reflection, which does not, of course, mean that it loses its power to form connections to the past. When this double reflection becomes a site of struggle for honor and glory, it is not surprising that alternative models are sought. At this point, popular culture provides fresh ground for disciplinary thought. The battle is over time itself. The future no longer emerges seamlessly from the present, which grows out of the past. Since no one knows what the future will look like, there is nothing left to do except fight over how it will be formed. What exactly was the subject of the debate? In terms of the Holocaust, the main issue was whether it was possible to compare the pasts of different nations. At first glance, this question seems to be a neutral one concerning methodology. Debates about whether a historical event is unique or whether it can be compared to others are also linked to the opposing positions of universal versus individualist models of identity and their corresponding theories of memory. Usually, the debate centers on the political and moral quality of the comparison.

A quick glance at the revisionist debates in Germany and Israel will illuminate the extent to which the relationship between comparison and uniqueness determines a nation's image of itself. The issue is somewhat different in the United States, however. There, ethnic politics rather than individual experts is the driving force behind questions of collective identity. For Israel and Germany, the Holocaust is a constitutive element of self-image, whether through an affirming memory of it or through its negation.

History Politics in Germany and Israel

Public memory in general and Holocaust memories in particular emerged as a central topic when Helmut Kohl was Germany's chancellor at the beginning of the 1980s. A number of important anniversaries and events contributed to this, including the fortieth anniversary of the end of the war in 1985 and President Richard von Weizsäcker's speech on the fortieth anniversary of the founding of the Federal Republic, in which he spoke about Germany's obligations with respect to a politics of memory.[5] Kohl tried to create a positive national feeling by issuing a series of commemorative state acts. His identity politics was based on a politics of history. From that time on, memories of the past became an important source of national pride. In the oft-cited words of Kohl's adviser, the historian Michael Stürmer, "In a land without history, the future belongs to those who convey memories and provide concepts" (Stürmer 1986).

From this perspective, Germany's identity problems were above all a result of the constrictions caused by Holocaust remembrance. Consequently, for Germany's self-image to improve, the Holocaust had to be downplayed. Conservative historians refused to accept the Holocaust as something unique or exclusively German. Ernst Nolte supported this view in 1986, which led to the *Historikerstreit* (Historians' Dispute), a public event that was played out in Germany's national press. Nolte maintained that one should place the wartime politics of the Nazis in a comparative context, side by side with

---

5. For a more detailed study of these historiographical debates, see Maier 1988.

Stalinism. During the postwar period and the Cold War through the 1970s, such comparisons were commonplace (as is evident in Nolte's *Three Faces of Fascism* [1966]). In the 1980s, however, they sparked a heated debate in which Jürgen Habermas criticized Nolte for his reactionary politics. What began as an academic dispute over historiographical methodology turned into a questioning of the central role played by the Holocaust in determining Germany's national self-understanding. Historians using a comparative approach placed the Holocaust within the context of a "European civil war," and the German role was downplayed, because other groups were also culpable.

Revisionist historians in Germany were politically conservative, seeking to distribute guilt "fairly" among all responsible parties. Critics of Holocaust remembrance in Israel, by contrast, tended to be left-leaning historians. The so-called new historians—often referred to with the catchall term "post-Zionist" (the Israeli version of postnationalism)—provided new data and interpretive tools for approaching some of the national myths about the founding of Israel (Morris 1987; Pappe 1994; Shafir 1989). For Israelis, the aim was to get away from the focus on themselves as the sole and unique victims and to admit to their own historical guilt. This involved, most importantly, a critique of Zionist historians and their eagerness to produce a "Zionist narrative of history." As in Germany, what began as a historiographical debate in Israel turned into a public discussion about the status and future of national identity. Questions regarding uniqueness versus comparability were implicit in this debate (Levy 1999). The revisionists criticized the historical establishment for refusing to place Zionism within a comparative context, thereby turning a blind eye to injustices against the Palestinians as well as to the colonialist practices of Zionists. The result of this critique was a blurring of the line between aggressor and victim. Everyone could be seen as either one or the other.

A similar critique was launched in reevaluating the way in which the Holocaust was remembered (Zertal 1998). Tom Segev's *The Seventh Million* (1993), which first appeared in 1991, is perhaps the best-known example of this reevaluation. His critique is aimed above all at the Zionist leaders, who, he says, were more concerned, first, with colonizing Palestine than with saving the Jews in Europe during the Holocaust, and later, with fashioning historical images of heroism rather than commemorating the fate of victims. Further, he claims, beginning in the 1970s the Zionists had instrumentalized memories of the Holocaust for political purposes—specifically, within the context of the Jewish–Arab conflict.

Again, the issue revolved less around presenting historical facts than critiquing a political leadership that had used the Holocaust to build its case that Zionism was the only option for ensuring a "normal" Jewish existence. Not everything about the new historians was new—in terms of method or content. Anti-Zionist intellectuals of the 1960s had already formulated many of the same arguments. In contrast to the marginalized and delegitimized position of the anti-Zionist intellectuals, however, the revisionists of the 1980s were considered part of an accepted discourse that played a central role in the academic world as well as in the popular press. Even state-run television borrowed from aspects of the revisionist position in a much discussed documentary series commemorating the fiftieth anniversary of the founding of Israel. These historiographical controversies are more symptoms than sources of a trend toward increasing pluralization in the Israeli landscape of remembrance. From this perspective, the debates surrounding the Holocaust are part of a sociopolitical and cultural process whereby the state, whose authority was once unquestioned, must face the challenges voiced by a burgeoning civil society.

The gulf between Germany and Israel is widening. As resentment against Germany fades, Europe is also distancing itself from Israel—and vice versa. This does not necessarily mean that Israel is succumbing to provincialism. In fact, the opposite can be said to be true: the globalization of Israel goes hand in hand with its return to a more ethnically determined society and with its turn away from Europe. Germany and even Europe have always been a problem for Israel, and they still are—less as clearly defined territorial entities than as abstractions that are not easily understood in concrete terms. As noted earlier, Zionism is a European ideology; it developed as a response to anti-Semitism in Europe. In the nineteenth and twentieth centuries, the Jew—who at certain points was perhaps the European par excellence—was declared the enemy of Europe. In turn, Zionism presented the non-Jewish society of Europe as the enemy of the

Jews. The Jewish state was not founded in Europe, however, but in the Middle East. Because of this, Europe became a complex mirror for Israel: One came from Europe but was not European; one had origins in Europe but nevertheless denounced Europe. The goal was to create something non-European, on the one hand, even though, on the other, Europe provided a civilization that was used to distancing itself from the "Oriental" reality of the Middle East. Even today, the ubiquity of Europe in Israel and its simultaneous negation defines the relationship of many Israelis to the non-Jewish reality around them.

The relationship to Germany is even more complicated: This is where Europe becomes localized and the reasons for Israel's ambivalence can be confirmed, since Germany was the driving force that led to the annihilation of the Jews throughout Europe. After the war, Germany repeatedly came into the limelight—during the restitution process, the establishment of diplomatic relationships, the Eichmann trial, and, finally, the Gulf War. In a certain sense, Germany is omnipresent in Israel: The images and emotions associated with it can well up in the collective memory at any time. At the same time, it seems that this omnipresence is waning and becoming more diffuse year by year. As long as there is no concrete occasion for reviving the images and complexes, it is being replaced by widespread indifference, which necessarily has repercussions for the politics of remembrance.

This is the necessary context for understanding the new historians and the new intellectual movement of post-Zionism, which, in academic and journalistic studies, express their discomfort with dominant modes of remembrance (Pappe 1994; Silberstein 1999). Western-oriented universalists are breaking away from the Israeli collective by calling its tradition into question.

What are the goals of post-Zionism? Its major theme is Western modernity, which is seen as dominant, progressive, forward-looking, and praiseworthy. Identity-building myths are being destroyed, as, for instance, the "glorious" wars of the past are being exposed as wars of colonialism and domination. National myths are analyzed as myths and thereby robbed of their power. Post-Zionist intellectuals play an important role in the creation of a new tradition. Their studies of Israeli history and society bring together theoretical reflections on consumerism, peace, and new post-nationalist identity. The "fate-oriented historiography" that sees the Jewish state as the pinnacle of development after thousands of years of ongoing suffering is being replaced by a "contingency-oriented historiography." That historiography is not teleological, and with the help of such universal concepts as modernization, it situates itself within general contexts (Diner 1995). The new historiography is also part and parcel of a new conception of the national citizen, which is to take the place of the old, ethnically determined idea of what it means to be Israeli. Post-Zionists are searching for a new post-traditional identity, an Israeli version of constitutional patriotism. Solidarity is achieved through participation rather than through membership (Habermas 2001).

Thus, in both Israel and Germany methodological questions of uniqueness and comparability are closely linked to universalism and particularism. Once more, we need to stress that, simply because public debates are often structured by dichotomies, particularism and universalism do not have to be mutually exclusive. On the contrary, the two are interdependent and together instigate social change. One must distinguish between the demands of the protagonists and our analytic use of the terms. In both countries, tension exists between the need to critique past failures in developing an institutional strategy and the need to address present injustices by developing a cultural strategy. Specifically, in Israel the concern is less with the proper representation of Holocaust victims after the war than with the way in which this lack of attention to the victims acts as a gauge in assessing the unjust treatment of Palestinians in the present and the past. In West and East Germany, the cultural strategy exists under reversed conditions. For the Federal Republic, a belated coming to terms with the Nazi past opened the door to confronting current issues of the Stasi past in East Germany. Vigorous insistence on a complete de-Stasification compensated for earlier failures in de-Nazification. This impulse to subscribe to a cultural strategy was also part of the initiatives that the Bürgerforum (citizen's forum), the leading East German civil-rights group, was pushing. However, this approach was perceived by most East Germans in the context of ongoing antagonistic relations with West Germans and was thus delegitimized as yet another measure West Germany imposed on them (Sa'adah 1998).

The revisionists in Germany and Israel come from completely different political camps. In Germany, they have emerged primarily from the conservative right, with an eye toward renationalizing the collective identity. In Israel, they principally come out of the left and are attempting to secure a post-Zionist position. Assertions of the uniqueness of the Holocaust are often understood as supporting a Zionist narrative, whereas a comparativist approach provides the basis for a critical, myth-breaking discourse. In Germany, the opposite is true. Those who seek to situate the Holocaust in a comparative context tend to see claims of uniqueness as hampering progress toward building a strong national identity. The revisionist right tries to rectify this situation by placing Germany in a comparative context that at least partly revives the rhetoric of the Cold War, as is the case in recent debates on German victims of expulsion and Allied bombings. Seen in this light, it becomes evident that the motivation for stressing the totalitarian character of the Soviet Union is actually to obscure the unique nature of the Holocaust, and thus of Germany. What lies behind the comparison is a desire to rehabilitate a discredited nation.

The connections that are made between past and present differ from country to country. In Israel, the new historians "relativize" the past on the basis of present exigencies that have to do above all with the fate of the Palestinians. They stress the fact that the seeds of oppression were already laid in the early years when the State of Israel was founded. In Germany, both the right and the left continue to search for appropriate models to secure a clear distinction between the Nazi past and contemporary German identity. For the right, Nazism must be considered an anomaly to maintain that German history does have an unsullied element to it. The left, in contrast, is searching for a past that will yield universalist conceptions, thereby acting as a moral corrective to ethnocentric forms of collective identity.

While the intentions of these groups are very different—and, indeed, are often at odds with one another—they have all worked to catapult remembrance out of its original place in historical and national time lines. In addition, the ongoing problematization of Holocaust remembrance has led to the public thematization of the importance of collective memory in determining identity. During Kohl's third term in office, in 1987, his interpretation of history became a topic of debate in a number of controversies. In the wake of numerous events, public awareness of history's political significance, as well as a concomitant politics of the past, has grown since the mid-1980s. Besides the Historians' Dispute, this reflexive relationship to memory has been sustained by the debates surrounding the German Historical Museum in Berlin and the Foundation Haus der Geschichte in Bonn, which both involved controversies over appropriate ways of representing National Socialism.[6] The main focus was on the underlying narrative of the exhibits—namely, whether a continuity with the past or a new beginning was implied. In Israel, actual historical data was quickly overshadowed by meta-historical discourses. The politics of remembrance increasingly concerned itself with problematizing the history of Israel.

Which national past (or pasts) is relevant? Whose past is it? We are not so much concerned with the details of any particular controversy here as with the consequences these debates carry for the development of reflexive forms of remembrance. Without a doubt, groups that questioned official practices of remembrance existed even in earlier times. Nevertheless, the nation's claims to supremacy have been challenged in Second Modernity—and to an unprecedented degree in the past twenty years. Most European countries, as well as other nations, have incorporated a critique of their own politics in relation to past injustices in their official repertoires of remembrance (Bosworth 1993; Rousso 1991). Within this context, Germany is a paradigm of the "de-heroized" and "skeptical" nation (Rüsen 1982). This transformation provides more space to cultivate an increasingly cosmopolitan type of collective remembrance. Even though their importance has diminished, historians still play a significant role in this process. Their contribution to the building of nation-states in the late nineteenth and early twentieth centuries is well documented (Hobsbawm 1996). The gradual transition from First to Second Modernity involves not only the weakening of the "national container" (Beck 1997, 2000) but also the waning of the formerly

6. The heated nature of these debates has also been evident in the lingering controversies surrounding the Holocaust memorial in Berlin.

dominant social and cultural-political function of historians. Overall, collective memories are no longer determined solely by narratives sanctioned by the state or by historians.

Reflexive memories in second modernity are characterized by a pluralization of pasts that emerge from a variety of groups. Revisionists in Germany have attempted to reinstate the nation at the center of identity-forming memories. Political traditions, from Bismarck to the Weimar Republic, provide models for collective self-understanding. Since reunification, the old Federal Republic itself has become part of history.

The Israeli scenario illustrates a pluralization whereby the dominant "Zionist master narrative" is rejected. In its stead, a plurality of Jewish, non-Jewish, secular, and religious perspectives vie to determine the relevance and usefulness of various collective memories. In the process, historical experts lose their privileged status. Historical disputes have unforeseen consequences that can even marginalize the historians themselves as new spaces open up to the public, making room for the "mass culture" that many historians abhor. This new space of remembrance can become the cosmopolitan form of memory. The dichotomy between universalism and particularism is "overcome" in this space and no longer makes any sense. Related questions about the uniqueness and comparability of the Holocaust may lose their significance, as well. The Holocaust, as a unique event, can be compared to others. The particular victimization experienced by the Jews can be universalized. These developments again are introduced via the United States and eventually reach Europe as well as Israel.

Part III

6

The Holocaust between
Representation and
Institutionalization

The "Universalization" of Evil

IN CHAPTER 5, we examined how the particular and universal coexist in Second Modernity as mutually determining forces rather than as polar opposites. In this chapter, we will look at the effects of globalization on cosmopolitan forms of memory. In his analysis of the transition from first to second modernity, Pierre Nora claims that there has been a departure from authentic memory *milieux* to less authentic places (*lieux*) of remembrance (Nora 1996). In contrast, we approach this process as a transition from communicative to cultural memory—or, rather, as a form of memory that is initially connected to a specific group but whose ties to that original source are eventually loosened. Cosmopolitan memory denotes the mutual interaction between global and local memories. More precisely, it involves a tension between national memories and memories that emerge from a global context to permeate the national framework without nullifying it.

In the wake of the Cold War, the lessons of the Holocaust provided a moral compass. Removed from its original national and ethnic context, the Holocaust—or, specifically, the memory of the Holocaust—was compared to other events. This led to the creation of moral guideposts that were used, among other ways, to legitimate political and military interventions. This is not to say, however, that all of this unfolded in a linear fashion. On the contrary, what we are dealing with is a highly contested terrain on which various groups attempt to claim the memories of the Holocaust as their own.

Often the "uniqueness" of the Holocaust means that it could and should not be compared to other events. The "Thou Shall Not Compare" argument created a separate field of study that attempts to merge science and morality (Katz 1993). Conservative historians in Germany pushed comparison for reasons that were vastly different from those of radical historians in Israel (Levy 1999). The question of comparability is thus a product of a variety of types of universalism.

The "universalization of evil," which is promoted by the mass media and appears within the context of new forms of remembrance specific to second modernity, has emerged in light of a variety of important political and historical phenomena. Within this context, the year 1989 is a watershed that marks the formation of new constellations of memory. This chapter examines the ways in which the iconographic power of the Holocaust has become a politically consequential force since the end of the Cold War. Paradoxically, it is precisely the Holocaust's limits of representation that have contributed to its decontextualization, enabling it to function as a model for "good and evil" or "guilt and innocence" in general. In this sense, the Holocaust provides a global point of reference for memory.

Within this context, the Americanization of the Holocaust plays a twofold role. On the one hand, the American media has turned the Holocaust into a product for consumption; on the other, it has transformed it into a universal imperative, making the issue of universal human rights politically relevant to all who share this new form of memory. We do not, however, want to fall back on the thoroughly instrumentalized idea that political interests and human-rights goals are fundamentally at odds with each other. Our aim is to determine how the Americanization of the Holocaust has played a role in making the remembrance of the event a globally relevant memory. The displacement of this historically specific event onto the future-oriented, global scene of politics, which provides a basis for universal human-rights agendas—thereby preventing another Holocaust—involves the deterritorialization of political sovereignty. The way in which a nation treats its citizens is now under the purview of a broader human-rights agenda. Contemporary politics is marked by a tension between international law, which guarantees the sovereignty of each state, and human rights, which limits that sovereignty. The question of who "owns" the Holocaust has become a key issue in this conflict.

This struggle is not played out solely on an international level, but often occurs within a specific national framework. Boundaries are no longer drawn strictly along national lines and do not necessarily follow the old divisions between left and right. They become blurred by generational differences and by the disappearance of the traditional division between private and public memory. In light of these developments, it is possible to speak of a *new culture of remembrance*. The increasingly vital role played by the Holocaust in German, American, and Israeli public remembrance is not the only factor here. Private forms of remembrance have also changed substantially. More and more, autobiographies, memoirs, films, oral testimony, video projects, and other media forms are becoming part of the public domain. The fact that memory is increasingly individualized and at the same time made public is a further sign of the diminished power of the state in determining how the Holocaust is remembered. This process of individualization not only indicates the fragmentation of memory cultures; it also signals the denationalizing of collective memory. On the one hand, memory becomes more concrete, with new biographies and individual faces of victims seeing the light of day. On the other hand, the humanizing of the victim allows for abstract identification. The universal and the particular do not simply form a new dichotomy; instead, the universal grows out of the particular. Thus, identification with individual experience has been a defining force in the de-territorialization of Holocaust memories.

There are many reasons for this. Often, the biological time frame is identified as a determining force in the revival of personal memories. The generation that lived through the Holocaust is in the process of dying out. The flood of memories in the past few years constitutes one final attempt to preserve as much as possible from this generation's storehouse of memories. As Nora points out, the role of historicizing and "archivizing" increases in importance as the memory *milieu* shrinks (Nora 1998: 5 ff.). Since the broadcast of the *Holocaust* series, television, movies, literature, and newspapers have replaced historical experts as a source of information about the Holocaust.

The Americanization of the Holocaust as Moral Imperative

When it comes to the "Americanization of the Holocaust," misunderstandings abound. Critics use such terms as "banalization," "trivialization," "Disney-fication," and even "McDonaldization" of the Holocaust (Cole 1999; Flanzbaum 1999; Junker 2000; Novick 1999; Rosenfeld 1997; Shandler 1999). This critique resonates with Frankfurt School criticism of America and what it perceives as mass culture. The new buzzword in Holocaust discourse is "instrumentalization," a reference to an ethically shady phenomenon ostensibly driven by economic or symbolic group interests (Finkelstein 2000). This flawed line of reasoning leads to a number of further assumptions. The critics who support it believe that a pure, complete, and immutable memory of the Holocaust exists that cannot be represented by the media. Consequently, products of the American mass market, such as the *Holocaust* series and *Schindler's List*, are relegated to a narrow group politics or dismissed as a product of the profit-driven culture industry. This assessment is enough to put many cultural critics off. The Frankfurt School's critique of the masses, especially the fascist masses, as the primary force behind the Nazi's' rise to power has been applied to the age of middle-class liberalism. As the argument goes, it is rational modernity that is instrumentalizing culture and turning it into a parasite. The traditional foundations of society, such as solidarity and community, have been shaken to their core. Furthermore, mass culture is a source of anxiety, because the questionable tastes of the uneducated have infiltrated every nook and cranny of modern life. Mass culture is vilified as a destructive force against reason, as a totalitarian project aimed at destroying autonomous, non-instrumentalized thought. The most common charge among critics is that the Americanizing of the Holocaust is making it into something vulgar. American market liberalism is pilloried in the name of European Republicanism. Thus, for many, anti-globalism is nothing but a form of old, aristocratic anti-Americanism in disguise, one that has been espoused by the right and left for a very long time (Diner 1993). Disdain for America was already common in the nineteenth century, particularly among the European cultural elite who had been stripped of their power. For them, Americanization was synonymous with the vulgarization of life.

According to this point of view, the marketing of the Holocaust is nothing but an American-dominated trivialization of the event. This critique is based on the biblical ban on images ("You shall not make for yourself a graven image": Exodus 20: 4–6). In the context of the Holocaust, this ban is often identified with critical theory's view that the event cannot be represented. Non-representability means sacredness, as in the sacredness of God. Therefore, representation of the unrepresentable cannot and should not be allowed (Hansen 1996). This view is shared by, among others, Claude Lanzmann. In his documentary film *Shoah*, Lanzmann seeks to discuss and reflect on the Holocaust without representing it.[1] The suggestion is that truth cannot be represented, especially by mass culture; it remains the property of experts such as Lanzmann or professional historians. This dichotomy between truth and the public sphere is not tenable, however. Further, rational discourse alone is not sufficient to present the public version of truth. Images and the emotional reactions they evoke are equally valid in the public arena.

It is precisely these mass products that can stir up emotion and that can make the general public sympathize with the suffering of others. Modernist critics are suspicious of such emotions; at the same time, however, they find fault with conventional memorials because they do not elicit precisely these emotional reactions. What form of remembrance, then, would be *absolutely* appropriate? Would it be, for instance, the German cult of atonement of the past few decades? Most likely not. Germany's state-sponsored Holocaust memorialization has been revealed lately as an exculpatory exercise that has more to do with Germany's culture of remembrance than with the actual event.

---

1. Lanzmann reiterated his position in March 2001 when he criticized a Paris photography exhibit on the concentration and death camps. As Lanzmann observed, "What is the role of photography? What can it engender? It is not about documentation, but about truth" (Riding 2001).

Popular culture, in all its hedonism, should not simply be dismissed as an instrument of social control and manipulation, for it can also function as an agent in the emancipation of cultural remembrance. Most people reflect on the Holocaust through those mediated mass images. At the same time, purists cringe at the thought of contaminating the memory of the Holocaust through the culture industry. In constantly insisting on the taboo against representation, however, they tend to avoid dealing with the content or the effect of popular films. An unbridgeable gulf opens up between the essence of the event and any adequate representation of it. What is more, the passive image of the consumer of mass culture is misleading. Contemporary viewers act as the interpreters of media messages. They imbue products of the American culture industry with meanings based on individual contexts (Katz and Liebes 1990). Viewers are able to maintain a critical distance from films and television, allowing them to look beyond the intentions of the directors who made them.

Steven Spielberg's 1993 film *Schindler's List* was used as the poster child for a critique of the "Holocaust industry" (Hansen 1996). This reception of the film is revealing in highlighting what is wrong with the approach, for the critics focused mainly on the film's sentimentalism and kitschiness. It was precisely these elements, however, that made the Holocaust accessible to a broad public. As we have noted, new models of identification emerged as interest grew in the Holocaust. In the case of *Schindler's List*, the film combines concrete historical material with a universal ethics. This "typically American" element is made possible through a vehicle for identification that is not so common: the *spectator*. Future-oriented American culture dislodges memory in a process of de-territorialization that enables Americans, Germans, and Israelis to be transformed from witnesses, perpetrators, and victims into spectators. The (third) role of the spectator overshadows that of the victim, which recedes into the background as an oppressed, tortured mass. The moral struggle revolves around the relationship to the victims: good versus evil, the spectator who intervenes against the wicked, horrifying evildoer. This passion play, which was staged so concretely in the case of Bosnia, found its fictional counterpart in *Schindler's List*. Like the oppressed and faceless masses in Bosnia, the Jews in Spielberg's films play a subordinate role and are reduced to objects. The real struggle is between Schindler and Goeth, the commandant of the Plaszow concentration camp. The true heroes of the film are the liberators and the survivors.

In contrast to those who abhor the universalizing and commercializing of the Holocaust, we view this process as a vital contribution to the development of a cosmopolitan memory. Can the Holocaust be consumed like any other product? Does it become neutralized, degraded, even forgotten in the process? If one clings to a traditional idea of politics that many social scientists still uphold, then the assumption is that consumerism is a depoliticizing force. This conception of politics is situated within the limiting framework of the nation-state. In second modernity, however, politics encompasses spheres other than the national—spheres that emerge from private and cultural realms (Beck 1993). Thus, we are ultimately confronted with a new approach to what politics is. This involves a reevaluation of the relationship between politics and mass culture. The latter cannot simply be written off because of a deep-seated anti-Americanism.

Young American visitors to Krakow and Auschwitz provide a case in point. In the past few years, Jewish cultural festivals have been held there, precisely in the area of the city called Kazimierz, which had a large Jewish population and later became famous through *Schindler's List*. The area is now a site for documentary films, performances of Klezmer music, tours, and talks; it has become a memorial site for Spielberg and for the Holocaust. One tour offers the opportunity to "retrace the trail of Steven Spielberg's *Schindler's List*," and for those who are not satisfied with the weepy sentimentalism of Kazimierz and want to see the "real sites," another tour advertises "daily tours to Auschwitz," with half-price tickets for students. Where 60,000 Jews once lived, only 150 inhabitants remain today. Tourism at Auschwitz is an important source of income for Krakow, as is the kitschy representation of the Jewish culture that was wiped out by the Nazis. The visitors are primarily young Americans and Israelis searching for traces of their heritage. Like so many Americans, they are historically unencumbered and are able to pass over the gravesites in Poland without much thought. Loud and disrespectful, which is common among people who do not feel the weight of history, the young Jewish Americans are the only lively element there. The sole functioning synagogue in the city is being transformed from a memorial site to a youth hangout. In Krakow, one can sense immediately that these young people come from a country where Jews live and where there is a living Jewish culture. They hedonistically snap up the half-price Auschwitz offers with a nonchalance that Europeans could only dream of. In Kazimierz, they are more interested in sites where *Schindler's List* was filmed ("And here's where Spielberg filmed the famous pogrom scene!") than in the real ghetto—testimony to the fact that the Holocaust has become, for them, a "commodity" and a part of their own history without being oppressive. Moral objectors will point to instrumentalization and commercialization, noting that the experience is not an authentic one. As Claude Lanzmann puts it, a "ring of fire" should surround the Holocaust (Lanzmann 1994); it should not be turned into a commodity, and it certainly should not be consumed lightly.

But why shouldn't it be, actually? Is pious respect more life affirming, and hence more "appropriate"? The defenders of morality would argue that commercialization taints our spirit and manipulates Holocaust remembrance. Mass culture, however, is a life-affirming pagan ritual. The frivolous economy, which is not even daunted by the Holocaust, uproots and de-territorializes traditional standards. It generalizes curiosity and democratizes taste and pleasure. These mechanisms are at play even when it comes to the representation and remembrance of the Holocaust—as well they should be if they are not to become the exclusive right of an elite few who think they have a monopoly on the proper forms of meaning, representation, and memory. The aristocratic rejection of so-called "mass culture" prevents one from encountering representational forms that fall outside the high culture–mass culture dichotomy. Public remembrance, it should be remembered, is not possible without technical reproducibility and mass consumerism. Admittedly, it is Spielberg who determines the view of the Holocaust that the young visitors walk away with. But it is precisely this alleged superficiality that enables these people to create a living, vibrant culture. What we are ultimately left with is not an eschatology of the Holocaust but, rather, vibrantly real human actions and emotions. The Americanization of the Holocaust, which dislodges the memory from a particular space or time, must not and should not be something "venerable."

So while many critics dismiss *Schindler's List*, the broader public considers it an authentic representation of the Holocaust. It was filmed on location in black and white, suggesting both authenticity and a connection to European cinema. In the movie, reality intermingles with fiction. The talk-show host Oprah Winfrey, whose programs usually highlight individual problems in everyday life, recommended the film, informing her viewers that it would turn them into "better people." The connection between Oprah and the Holocaust is not insignificant. Her show deals with alcoholism, child abuse, and other forms of victimhood; it celebrates and presents the victims as morally better people, placing the "survivors" on a moral pedestal. The term "survivor," which in Jewish thought is so closely tied to the Holocaust, is now frequently invoked to refer to victims of sexual abuse, recovering alcoholics, and other groups that have liberated themselves from traumatic victim roles. If one takes as a given that the meaning of the Holocaust is fundamentally collective and political, then this kind of reading is trivial and superficial. But this is not the only way to look at it. The other way—modern, Protestant, individualized (Americanized) way to look at it—is one-to-one in relation to the question: "What does the Holocaust do to me"? The story is supposed to appeal to the reader or viewer in such a way that she or he thinks, "What does it make me think? How does it make me feel? How can I possibly comprehend the enormity that seems beyond words?" To make an analogy to the church, this represents a desire for a one-to-one relationship to the Holocaust that is unmediated by priests. In other words, it is possible to relate to the Holocaust individually and psychologically rather than collectively and politically (if one understands the "political" as collective undertakings). If one believes that depoliticization is in essence wrong, then of course one must think that this is wrong, as well. This partly explains the anger that the Holocaust Museum or Spielberg often provoke. The depoliticization of the Holocaust is simply a reflection of the depoliticization of American culture—or, looked at from the other angle, of the individualization and decollectivization of its culture. The Holocaust is primarily an identity issue in America because everything is primarily an identity issue once individuality replaces collectivity as the ultimate reality of reference. What troubles so many intellectuals when they relate to the vocabulary of victimization—to those who "survive" alcoholism, child abuse, being orphaned, or living in poor neighborhoods, for example, typical topics of Oprah Winfrey's talk show—is the democratization of psychology. It is a psychology that anyone can apply and one that is best applied by (support) groups of normal people. In other words, it is a psychology that does not need therapists—like a religion that does not need priests. So when critics decry the victimology of the Holocaust, they are decrying people who treat historical events as personal rather than collective experiences, which is simply an everyday choice in a decollectivized society. They are decrying the way people describe their personal experiences in "uneducated" clichés. They call it "trivial," or "Americanized."

In this fashion, "survival" becomes a primary theme of Spielberg's Holocaust. The historical reality of the genocide only serves as a backdrop in the film, as an unspoken and assumed fact known by some, but certainly not all, viewers. Thus, viewers are made to believe that they are watching a historical film while they are really watching an American morality play for which the Holocaust provides the historical setting. At the same time, the universalized dramatic content of the film works to loosen the historical ties and points to the future rather than the past. Schindler is everyone who wants to save and liberate; Goeth is everyone who wants to kill; and the Jews stand for victims everywhere. Mass culture becomes a vehicle for memory, a public space accessible to all viewers, and a source for discussing ethical questions. Forming a nearly unanimously unified front as global defenders of high culture, critics declared the film trivial, oversimplified, too American, too positive—in a word, bad.[2] Daniel Goldhagen's *Hitler's Willing Executioners* elicited a similar critical reaction: The experts rejected it, while the public received it enthusiastically. This has nothing to do with disrespect for the victims. It does, however, help turn the Holocaust into a moral touchstone. One example of this transformation is the opinion expressed by President Bill Clinton, who recommended the film as a moral lesson.

2. For a review of various critical reactions to the film, see the articles in Loshitzky 1997.

For this reason, non-Jews can watch Schindler on the screen and cry; Germans can identify with the "good" German and escape the role of oppressor to take on that of observer or even liberator. The public sphere becomes the private, and vice versa. Thus, individual sensibilities are projected onto a public space and, from there, back to the individual. The result is not atomization but, rather, an individual formed by social forces. Instead of the old dichotomy between individual and society, we have the interpenetration of the two.[3] Thus, the decontextualization and individualizing of the Holocaust clearly has consequences in the public sphere. It does not take a huge leap to go from identifying with Schindler to taking the ensuing role of liberating Kosovo. Spielberg's film leaves behind the insecure territory of authentic memories for a space in which the viewers are engaged and can identify emotionally (Loshitzky 1997). In many respects, the global marketing of the film provides the framework in which the Holocaust as a historical event blends contemporary and future culture. This does not mean that the Holocaust disappears as a historical event. Rather, it is merged with the Spielberg production. People from different countries are then able to incorporate the event into their national discourses. It is no wonder that the film was a huge success outside the United States, with more than 25 million viewers in total. A few years after its theatrical release, *Schindler's List* once again hit the media, this time as a broadcast on American network television with no commercial interruptions, a rare practice reserved for special occasions.

In addition, the Holocaust Memorial Museum in Washington, D.C., opened the same year that *Schindler's List* was released. Like the film, the museum functioned as a universalizing mechanism. Just as the film takes a "positive" stance, with the unambiguous message that one can save others if one wants to, the museum tour ends with a strong message of liberation. Moral action is an individual matter of choice. This has nothing to do with "desk perpetrators" who were just following orders; it has to do with a conscious choice between good

---

3. One can trace this theoretical notion of the interpenetration of individual and society from Georg Simmel and Norbert Elias to Ulrich Beck and Elisabeth Beck-Gernsheim (2000).

and evil. In her assessment of Eichmann, Hannah Arendt observed that he "was not Iago and not Macbeth and nothing would have been further from his mind than to determine with Richard III to 'prove a villain'" (Arendt 1992 [1963]: 287). Arendt sought to depersonalize evil and situate it within the system of totalitarianism. She also believed that the question of evil was central to modernity. Spielberg, in turn, brought the issue back to the level of the individual. Goeth was Iago; he had decided to become evil. Spielberg repeatedly stated that the film was equally about Bosnians in Serbia and African Americans. When the film was shown in a primarily African American neighborhood in Oakland, for instance, a scandal erupted when some young black viewers laughed during the persecution scenes. This prompted Spielberg to go to Oakland and initiate a new course in the public schools there, "The Human Holocaust: The African American Experience." In this way, *Schindler's List* decontextualized Jewish memory by presenting the Holocaust as a backdrop for contemporary racism and intolerance.

Schindler's Homecoming

A few months after its American debut, *Schindler's List* was released in Germany, eliciting a similar set of reactions. Many critics rejected the "American trivializing of history," while the public identified with the movie, just as it would embrace Goldhagen's book two years later. Germans liked the movie for reasons similar to Americans': Perpetrators are transformed into spectators, and Schindler is a "good" German who saved Jews. Thus, spectators become saviors. The process of decontextualizing the Holocaust and making it into a universal story of suffering was very significant for Germany. The Holocaust, which originated in Germany and then returned after being reinterpreted by America, lost its seemingly unassailable national embeddedness. Of course, Germans interpreted the film quite differently from Israelis. In Germany, the role of the good German was most important, and it was precisely there that the decontextualized story, with its simplified view of good and evil, may have had its greatest effect. One can save others if one makes up one's mind to do so. Like their American counterparts, the German critics disapproved of the film's commercialization—which in Germany was mixed with anti-Americanism (Loshitzky 1997). German critics often quoted their American colleagues—above all, Jewish critics—to avoid charges of anti-Semitism. This tension between the critics and the public is noteworthy. It was apparent in almost every country in which the film was released and serves as further proof of the decline of a hierarchical culture of experts.

Spielberg in Israel

In Israel, as well, critics took issue with *Schindler's List* and tried to stave off the American vulgarization of the Holocaust (Bartov 2000; Breshet 1997). Despite this, or perhaps precisely because of it, the film enjoyed a certain amount of success among general audiences. Of greater significance for the present analysis, however, is the fact that the movie presented a narrative of Holocaust representation that was neither controlled nor instigated by the state. Spielberg was not the only one to break the state monopoly on Holocaust interpretation that had been so important for Israel. With the privatizing of Holocaust memories, a grassroots opposition to the monopoly had already begun to grow.

The reaction to *Schindler's List* in Israel is evidence that global and national factors can exist side by side. As competing stories emerge and private memories become part of public remembrance, the Israeli state's stronghold over the culture of remembrance is waning. Because a singular "public sphere" has given way to plural "public spheres" that do not necessarily conform to national boundaries, the state is forced to relinquish its role as the sole agent for transmitting memories. For Israel, the Americanization of the Holocaust points to a return (or a step forward) to long-denied diasporic existence. This path toward diaspora is not necessarily the same thing as the universalization of the Holocaust. In this case, what is strengthened is the specifically Jewish understanding of the Holocaust, which is not necessarily the same thing as the Israeli understanding. This discrepancy between Jewish (de-territorialized) and Israeli (territorialized) perceptions and memories becomes even more glaring in light of the Balkan crisis of the 1990s. That case is evidence of the fact that universalism and particularism are no longer mutually exclusive categories. Both exist simultaneously.

This tension is particularly evident in one of the most important Holocaust memorial rites—namely, the trips to Polish concentration camps for teenagers sponsored by the Israeli Education Ministry since 1988. Approximately 10,000 schoolchildren and young people participate in the so-called March of the Living, joining other, primarily Jewish, youths from all over the world to march from Auschwitz to Birkenau. For many young Israelis, this is an opportunity to wave the national flag and sing patriotic songs. The eight-day trip is carefully planned, and the participants are consciously kept away from other Polish regions.[4] They are on a "pilgrimage" in which their actual surroundings do not play a role. Treblinka, Auschwitz, Majdanek, and the Warsaw ghetto memorial are the main sites on this journey. As the Israeli Education Ministry states, these trips are about "emotional learning." One could also see them as an attempt to create a "tangible Holocaust." It is hard to ignore the irony of this situation: The goal of the journey is to strengthen the sense of territorial belonging among young Israelis, the so-called third generation; to cultivate their allegiance to Israel, they are taken from their homeland to the death camps. As one organizer puts it, "They leave as Israelis and return home as Jews." The tension between "there" and "here," between "homeland" and "exile," could not be more pronounced. The goal is to make young Israelis into better patriots and more self-aware Jews. During these trips, they are made to feel insecure and are told that only a strong state can ensure their safety. But as in the case of the Eichmann trial, the actual outcome is not what the state intended. Some of these young people do become more patriotic, and others probably return as universal humanists. The majority, however, most likely go "home" unchanged (Feldman 1995). Certainly, it is not in the state's power to control people's emotional reactions. By removing individuals from their familiar surroundings and letting them experience the Holocaust firsthand at the "original" sites, however, the state is inadvertently promoting the de-territorialization of the Holocaust. In the process, the young people begin to ponder what "Holocaust" means to them.

---

4. For an anthropological study of this event, see Feldman 1995; for critiques regarding the lack of a universal message in these trips, see Segev 1993.

This is confirmed in a 1999 study conducted in Israel, in which Jewish Israelis were asked about their personal "image of Germany" (Diner et al. 2000). The general findings indicate that most of the Israelis who participated in the study were neutral in their opinion of Germany. This is not to suggest that, fifty-five years after the Holocaust, Jewish Israelis have forgiven the Germans. Nevertheless, in an age of progressive globalization that has affected Israel, Germany no longer dominates collective memory. Relying on surveys to gain insight into collective processes of remembrance is problematic, of course. Many factors affect the answers, such as the general atmosphere of the day, moods that have little to do with the subject of discussion, and current events. Nevertheless, the survey allows us to reflect on possible cultural transformations and trends that may be at play among parts of the Jewish population in Israel. The gulf between the official culture of remembrance and the everyday experience of many people is widening. However, this does not suggest that official culture has become completely irrelevant.

When it comes to official recognition of the Holocaust, Germany has repeatedly come into the limelight because of reparations, the instating of diplomatic relations, the Eichmann trial, and the first Gulf War. As noted earlier, the images and emotions tied to Germany can surface at any moment in Israel. However, without a concrete occasion for stirring up the old images and complexes, a general sense of indifference is setting in. Most Israelis' knowledge of Germany is based on soccer, the German products that increasingly flood the Israeli market, and layovers in Germany while flying to ski resorts and other vacation spots in Italy. The Germany of Eichmann is slowly taking a back seat and being relegated to a space of myth. Each year, there are fewer and fewer survivors alive in Israel. Few take notice of elections for the chair of the Council of Jews in Germany, ongoing debates over Holocaust commemoration, or even revisionist attempts to put an end to Germany's official emphasis on commemorating the Holocaust as an integral part of its history. What, then, are the possible reasons for this shift in attitude?

In the past few years, the cultural landscape in Israel has been marked not so much by one homogenizing culture—one that, for instance, conjures images of Germany as evil to constitute itself internally—as by a series of sweeping internal struggles over cultural hegemony. Germany plays only a minor role in these struggles. For example, a total of 2 million people from the former Soviet Union with strong ties to their old homeland have now immigrated to Israel. Their image of Germany is most likely colored by old Soviet perspectives or is only very sketchy. In any case, this group of immigrants does not participate in historical remembrance to the extent that native Israelis do. In addition, Israeli intellectuals of African and Asian heritage are fighting for cultural recognition of their world and their histories and are not particularly focused on Germany. The self-identity of Arab citizens in Israel is not bound up with Germany in any significant way, either. Thus, memories connected to Germany must compete in an increasingly teeming marketplace of remembrance in Israel. This is happening as the cultural practices of many Israelis are coming into conflict with one another or are involved in a process of blending, exchange, or exclusion to claim legitimacy. Without relying too heavily on the metaphor of the "imagined" nation, one can maintain that the nation as a homogeneous cultural community does not exist. What does exist is the discrepancy between a coherent, unified culture that is desired and represented by a state-supported elite, on the one hand, and the plurality and variety of actual cultures and memories experienced by individuals, on the other. Every so-called national culture turns into a contest among ethnic, religious, and class-, generation- and gender-specific groups, all of whom are fighting for recognition. National culture is nothing but the product of this struggle. Israeli's image of Germany is, first and foremost, an Israeli issue, not a German one.

The results of the 1999 study point to a changed social reality involving the fragmentation of Israeli identity. Evening programming on Israeli television highlights this cultural fragmentation. There are programs and channels in Russian, Arabic, English, French, Turkish, Italian, and German (and even a few that are broadcast in Hebrew, the national language). But the demise of the old is also the harbinger of the new. Internal conflicts that place the images of external enemies in relative contexts do not herald the end of a "true" Israeli identity. Instead, they mark the beginning of a new one. Our thesis is that this new identity exists as part of a broader process of globalization.

That process involves the development of ethnic identities that do not conform to national boundaries and that in fact usurp the national from above and from below. To be an Israeli today, for instance, can mean that one reads Russian newspapers, watches Russian television, sees Russian theater, and listens to Russian rock music. At the same time, it means that one takes one's Oriental Jewish identity seriously and, in a paradoxical embrace of Western multiculturalism, that one rejects the West. Israeli identity includes non-Jewish Israelis, such as Palestinian citizens of Israel, who demand cultural autonomy. In the process, "Russians" become Israelis because they can continue to speak and read Russian. "Moroccans" become Israelis because they not only deeply despise the Russians but the entire establishment, which in their eyes is Western-oriented. Almost everyone is caught up in constantly reinventing the essence of his or her identity. The members of this post-national, global society are endlessly creating new categories and discarding old ones. The mix that results from this process should not be read as a sign of the failure of integration. Rather, it heralds the emergence of precisely the autonomy that is necessary for identity and integration to take hold in this new society. Hence, individuality in this globalizing and re-ethnicizing society is marked by overlapping interests as well as by conflicts. These identities, however, are not necessarily dependent on one homogeneous image of the enemy (e.g., Germany). The Israeli public sphere has become a space in which rifts can be overcome through conflict and in which certain forms of indifference and social distancing actually work in a positive way toward social integration. This means that old images of an enemy may slowly fade away but not that they must. As the study shows, people's attitudes toward Germany are marked by "indifference" even when compared with their attitude toward other countries. The conventional wisdom that a society is held together through a common conception of the Other is not necessarily true. Post-national societies hold together more effectively because they are split internally; this eases rather than intensifies tensions as conflict becomes the driving force behind integration. From the point of view of new Israelis, this means that they have more combinations at their disposal. They can experiment with numerous, overlapping identities and actually live them. As Israeli society opens itself up to forces that break down old national boundaries, it does not remain a closed space. The "enemy" was part of an old, nationally oriented collective consciousness. For many, however, "nation" is no longer synonymous with "society." Like many other groups, Russians cultivate their old heritage. The decisive factor is that the public sphere no longer has anything to do with "collective determination" in this sense. It is based not on solidarity or a sense of obligation but on conflictual coexistence.

Does Israel, then, represent the long-awaited end of history, the nation, and ethnicity? Hardly. But it is clear that the role of the state, which had been so central to Israeli identity for so long, is waning. The melting pot is slowly melting. One should not, however, confuse a pluralistic cultural system with a multicultural one. The Israeli state and the old elites, with their mono-cultural vision, are still powerful, even if they are facing a long and gradual decline. Thus, Israeli politics and society remain dependent on an old, traditional image of the enemy. That "enemy" is fate, predetermined and inexorable. Outsiders are either not mentioned or are ranked among the enemy; a shared history is to serve as the foundation for creating a shared set of values. Thus, cultural alternatives, and with them models of identity, arise that are played out beyond the borders of the national container. Inevitably, this has an effect on Holocaust remembrance. More and more changes are taking place as memories of the Holocaust are universalized, individualized, pluralized, and even ignored.[5]

Fragmented Memories

Pluralization goes hand in hand with making private memories public. This does not lead to the uncovering of new historical material in the sense of "objective" facts. Instead, the individual faces of a collective tragedy are brought to light. *Schindler's List* plays a pivotal

---

5. However, as events since the collapse of the peace process in 2000 and the increase in terror attacks on Israeli civilians have shown, Holocaust memory can come easily into play again when Jews in Israel feel threatened in their very existence. Terrorism mixed with an awareness of increased anti-Semitism in the world make it increasingly difficult for a beleaguered people to universalize, individualize, and pluralize the memories of the Holocaust. The opposite seems to be the case. The cosmopolitanization of memory is not fate, therefore, but dependent on political contingencies.

role in this context. His planned 2001 film about Anne Frank (which did not materialize), also sparked controversy. After the success of *Schindler's List*, Spielberg embarked on a video project, establishing the Survivors of the Shoah Visual History Foundation in 1994, involving the collection and recording of testimony. Over the past ten years, the Shoah Foundation has videotaped interviews with survivors and witnesses in fifty-six countries, and the archive has amassed nearly 52,000 testimonies in thirty-two languages. Michael Berenbaum, who headed the foundation until 1999 and served as director of the research institute at the U.S. Holocaust Memorial Museum, envisioned a global education program on the Internet. It was Spielberg's aim to exploit existing global communications technology to preserve the testimony in the most "de-territorialized" of places, virtual space.[6]

On the one hand, the project is about preserving memories of (and about) Holocaust survivors. As such, it is first and foremost a historically contextualized document. On the other hand, the project has taken on a much broader array of functions within the context of the politics of memory. The witnesses include not only Jews but also other victims as well as rescuers. One of the aims of the foundation is to cultivate tolerance, which is also a central objective of universalization. This corresponds to the mission of another well-known Holocaust institution, the Simon Wiesenthal Center in Los Angeles, and one of its most important offshoots, the Beit Hashoah Museum of Tolerance, which illuminates connections between the Holocaust and other instances of intolerance, such as acts of racism.

Spielberg was not the first to collect eyewitness accounts from Holocaust survivors. The earlier studies, however, were conducted at universities and research institutes and generally available to only a handful of experts.[7] Spielberg helped take the projects out of the university and make them available to the broader public. He has been criticized for this on a number of counts. Some accuse him of profiting from the Holocaust, the so-called commercialization argument, and

---

6. The website for the project is www.vhf.org.

7. An example is the "Fortunoff Video Archive," which was founded at Yale University in 1979, around the same time that the *Holocaust* miniseries was broadcast (Langer 1991).

of oversimplifying and trivializing the event. Others also pull out the "authenticity argument," claiming that the videotaped testimony has no historical value, since the survivors really cannot remember things accurately anymore. And, of course, there is the weightiest argument, the "Americanization argument," which dismisses the whole project because it comes from the United States. Among all of this criticism, however, there seems to be little recognition of the fact that a type of pact has been formed between popular culture and the survivors—a pact that excludes the so-called experts.

In the 1990s, Spielberg's popularization of a culture focused on victims and eyewitnesses spawned numerous documentary films about the memories of individuals and of particular groups. In addition to the fragmentation and privatization of memory, memory as such came under scrutiny. Historians are often critical of these projects, since what individuals remember often does not correspond to "what actually happened." An extreme example of this is the Wilkomirski case of 1995, involving the publication of a childhood memoir set in a concentration camp. The story, titled *Fragments*, was eventually discovered to be a fabrication.[8] Traumatic memories from early childhood cannot stand up to a factual—or even physical, in the sense of a connection to a particular place—account of reality. Historical remembrance escapes the event itself and thereby becomes accessible to a broader public, which in turn promotes universalization. The enthusiastic reception of Wilkomirski's book is proof that the Holocaust has become completely decontextualized and turned into a personal trauma with which anyone can identify. However, the fierce and angry reactions to the revelation that Wilkomirski invented his testimony demonstrate that a fine line still exists between fictionalized trauma and survivor memory.

Spielberg's video project helps to further blur the distinction between history and personal witnessing. The Holocaust is becoming a global code that no longer needs to be connected to history. The link between technology and memory, the blurring of authentic experience and its ideal representation, complete with international video distribution, take the Spielberg project to another level, which

---

8. For more details about this case, see Bartov 2000: 224–27 and Gourevitch 1999.

accelerates the growth of mass-culture-oriented memory. Through this process, alternative memories are awakened even for those who did not actually live through the event. The gulf between history and memory seems to widen.

These developments have numerous ramifications. In the past two decades, the memory boom has elicited a massive political (mostly nationalist) and academic reaction. The fragmentation of remembrance and publicizing of private memories creates a broad political sphere in which differing points of view on the past compete with one another. Thus, witness testimonies are at the same time historical sources and considered historically unreliable. (The Wilkomirski case is both the cause and the symptom of more widespread discontent.) The authenticity of these reports is often determined not so much by their accuracy as by their political context and the possibilities associated with it. Thus, in investigations of German compensation of Holocaust victims, eyewitness accounts by Jewish survivors from the first postwar decade were dismissed as unreliable (Stern 1992). At the time, it was said that these reports were too subjective to provide an accurate view of the past.[9] A similar attitude prevails when history and the law confront each other. Can justice, as well as the process of coming to terms with the past, be based on survivors' testimony? Can historians, whose narratives are often based largely on the memories of individuals or of groups formed of individuals, help ensure that justice is served (Frei et al. 2000)? It is no longer the Holocaust alone that stands before the court, but memory itself.

Another example, this one from Israel, illustrates how eyewitness accounts have been influenced by the popularization of the Holocaust and the extent to which their reception is based on a current political context. As mentioned, Holocaust remembrance in Israel has often become symbolically linked to the Israeli–Arab conflict. The victim role that has been readily embraced by Israelis has been used to justify political measures and has helped mobilize the Israeli population and influence world opinion. But even this is slowly beginning to

9. A project sponsored by the German government to research the persecution of *Volksdeutsche* (ethnic Germans) is based on an opposing view. In this case, eyewitness reports were considered essential in determining monetary compensation (Beer 1998).

change. The new historians have taken up the topic of the expulsion of Palestinians during the 1947–48 War of Independence and name it ethnic cleansing (Morris 1987). As we will analyze in more detail later, ever since the conflict in the Balkans, the term "ethnic cleansing" has increasingly become linked to the Holocaust. When this connection is made in Israel, it takes on a very special meaning. If one continues to insist that historians not simply rely on the archives of the oppressors but heed the voices of the victims, as well, then proximity to Holocaust discourse is not a mere accident. It becomes a political imperative.[10]

In the next section, we show how *Schindler's List* is just one example among many of the de-territorialization and individualization of memory. The development and reception of Holocaust remembrance is simultaneously embedded in a specific political context and functions as a general driving force for the de-territorialization of memory. The ongoing process of de-territorialization, which has accelerated at a rapid pace in the past two decades through the globalization of media images, is a central feature of self-reflexive collective memory in Second Modernity.

The United States and the Role of the Museum in Holocaust Remembrance

One must draw a distinction between an understanding of the Holocaust as the greatest crime against humanity, and thus as the greatest act of universal racism, and the Holocaust as the greatest act of anti-Semitism. The latter affects only Jews, whereas the former can affect anyone. The specifically American remembrance of the Holocaust emerged out of the tension between these two. The relationship between American Jews, who constitute 3 percent of the total

---

10. For an example of this, see Segev (2000), who describes a legal case in Israel that was ostensibly about a massacre committed by Israelis in 1948. To show solidarity with the historians who uncovered the massacre and were subsequently tried for slander, people held up posters that read, "Research, Educate, and Remember." For the controversy surrounding the role of the victim's perspective in history texts, see the correspondence between Martin Broszat and Saul Friedlander (1988), in which the German historian levels the charge that Jewish remembrance is mythic in nature.

population in the United States, and America as a state in which non-Jews form the vast majority plays a big role in this case. Survivors' memories have become a part of American memory, and the Holocaust has become a part of American history (Young 1997). Through its Americanization, the Holocaust is removed from its exclusively European point of reference and becomes de-territorialized.

The year 1993 was a decisive one in the de-territorialization process. After fifteen years in the works, the U.S. Holocaust Memorial Museum officially opened its doors in Washington, D.C.; one month later, *Schindler's List* opened in theaters across the country. From its inception, the museum highlighted the tensions between universalism and particularism (Linenthal 1995). Ultimately, both positions were adopted. Through his leadership role, Elie Wiesel, who insisted on the "singularity" of the Jewish catastrophe, tried to exclude other victim groups. The Armenians, for instance, wanted to be represented in the exhibit and were prevented from doing so by, among others, the Turkish government. Michael Berenbaum, the museum's former research director, stated that the goal of the museum was "to tell the story of the Holocaust in such a way that it would resonate not only with the survivor in New York and his children in San Francisco, but with a black leader from Atlanta, a Midwestern farmer, or a Northeastern industrialist" (Berenbaum 1990: 19).

The goal was clear: With regard to the past, the Holocaust should not be universalized or "humanized." The Germans were the criminals, and the Jews were the victims. But Berenbaum's project was also a clear expression of how American Jews wanted to transform the European-based Holocaust into part of mainstream American culture. A link was forged between the history of Jewish suffering and contemporary political and cultural institutions in America. This is underscored by the fact that the museum is situated on the Mall in Washington, alongside other national institutions. The Holocaust, which, apart from the liberation of concentration camps in western Germany, is only very indirectly related to the American past, has now become part of American history and tradition. Of course, this is also true in a negative sense: America stood for everything that negates the Holocaust. This is why the first thing that visitors to the museum see is a photograph of American soldiers liberating camp inmates. The nationalization and Americanization of the Holocaust contributed to its displacement from its historical and geographical framework. Jewish American ethnic politics, in turn, promoted its induction into an American national framework. Nationalization and Americanization are synonymous, in this case, with deterritorialization. Through its Americanization, Holocaust symbolism became linked to the dominant Christian culture in America (and the West), a situation that many Jews in America found problematic (Novick 1999: 11). The "Stations of Suffering" are reminiscent of the Via Dolorosa, and the cult of objects that prevails in the museum brings to mind the sacralization of suffering. It should be kept in mind, of course, that in the West Christianizing is synonymous with universalizing. This is particularly true in the United States: For the museum to be truly American, it must become "Christian" and hence, ultimately, universal.

This leads to the destabilizing of yet another dichotomy: that between Jewish particularism and Christian universalism, which is an essential component of Western modernity. Present-day cultures of remembrance are marked by the collapse of this dichotomy. Ethnic politics, particularly in the United States, has helped spur the universalizing of the particular. Dan Diner, whose argument rests on the old dichotomy, claims, "While the drive toward comparison, which also leads to the de-contextualized universalization of the crime, is in line with the Christian narrative, the insistence on singularity coincides with Jewish particularism" (Diner 1999: 249).

This analysis holds true for the so-called German–Jewish and the German–Israeli relationship. As we have shown, Jewish and German memories are dichotomous and cannot be bridged. The very meaning of being German means not to be Jewish. This is not the case in the United States, of course, where being Jewish and American can be inclusive. In the present day, this combination of a non-ethnic formal identity and the cultivation of ethnic memories (and lifestyles) has become more or less codified through a multicultural perspective. It is completely acceptable for Jews to be both Americans and Jews and for memories to be blended. What is more, since the dominant culture in America grew out of various forms of Protestantism that pluralized and individualized religion (Silver 1990), the Christianizing of the Holocaust in America is simultaneously a decollectivizing and therefore an individualizing event. This is apparent in Berenbaum's description, cited earlier, of his ideal Holocaust museum.

The Witnesses' Perspective

Holocaust remembrance, then, is situated between its meaning-producing function for a particularistic Jewish identity and its general role as a source of universalistic moral doctrine. It is precisely the particularization of the past and the universalizing of the future that enable these two positions to co-exist as mutually inclusive rather than exclusive conceptions. Neither the Yad Vashem Museum in Israel nor the official German memorial is based on the earlier "either-or" perspective. In the Israeli museum, "salvation" is provided by the Israeli state. In Germany, the victims are remembered, but the main focus is on the generations that came after the perpetrators. The Americanization of the Holocaust introduced a third role to that of victim and criminal—namely, the witness. In this privileged position, the witness or observer can choose either to identify with the victims or adopt the morally bankrupt role of the passive observer. This position of witnessing is a central feature of the politics of remembrance in Second Modernity, straddling the narratives of both oppressor and victim. Visitors to the museum in Washington begin with the liberation before turning to the Holocaust itself (Cole 1999: 152). They are thereby transformed from a collective of perpetrators into observers. This is perhaps also the reason behind the success of Daniel Goldhagen's book in Germany, which we will discuss in more detail later. In a brilliant move, Goldhagen relegated German collective guilt to the past, declaring contemporary Germans to be "innocent" observers since they had become Americanized. This third position of the witness is historically an American one, but it is possible for victims and oppressors to adopt it, as well. Goldhagen opened the door to this process in Germany, and a third generation, which is temporally as well as culturally removed from the Third Reich, is helping transform the country into "a collectivity of witnesses."

In Israel, the land of the victims, it is harder to set this process in motion. A small intellectual elite, which formed in reaction to Israel's state monopoly over the Holocaust, has tried to universalize the Holocaust for moral reasons. The third role of the observer has enabled this group to dislodge the Holocaust from the context of the nation-state and to humanize it. In some instances, Israeli occupiers were presented as the Nazis, and the Arabs were the Jews.[11] In the age of media-determined reality, the role of the observer and witness has become vital. Via the images broadcast into our living rooms every day, an increasingly large part of the "viewing audience" is being turned into witnesses.

Bosnia

In the last decade of the twentieth century, the reaction to the conflicts in the former Yugoslavia confirms that these fluid memories are not just superficial chatter. Through these conflicts, the memories have been given a framework. Discussions surrounding the role of the U.S. Holocaust Memorial Museum, as well as the fact that individual memory has become public, have also helped increase public awareness of the political role of memory. This became particularly clear one year before the opening of the museum, at the height of the Bosnian war. In his title for a series of *Newsday* articles, Roy Gutman referred to "Death Camps," bringing forward a central icon of the Holocaust by conjuring associations with the death camps of the Nazis.[12] The reports had a great impact: The international community was suddenly confronted with a new "Holocaust."

The trope that now equates Serbs with Nazis did not spring immediately from the facts. There was, unfortunately, nothing unusual about the scale of the atrocities in Bosnia. Worse things went on in many parts of the world during the same period. And the original understanding of the situation was not that one side was oppressing another, but that it sprung from the "irrational" and "ancient hatreds" that characterized the Balkans. The lesson of history at the beginning of the 1990s was that the problems were insoluble and intervention was doomed. What caught the public's attention was not so much

---

11. See, for instance, Sobol's stage drama *Arbeit macht Frei*, by the Akko-Theater Troupe; the film *Avanti Populo*; and a number of novels.

12. The articles appeared in book form under the title *Witness to Genocide* (Gutman 1993). For more on what motivated Gutman to write the articles, see Doubt 2000. In an interview at www.globetrotter.berkeley.edu/conversations/gutman, Gutman also explains that he did not see the camps himself, relying instead on eyewitnesses.

the war itself, or even the atrocities committed, but the fact that camps existed on European soil. It is the camps that make the Holocaust unique—not only for the survivors, but also as a metaphor for the Holocaust itself. Auschwitz is a symbol of a system of annihilation.[13]

Ironically, it was "pictures of Auschwitz" that provided proof that the world had stood by without intervening, even though these pictures were taken elsewhere. Most of the photographs and films of death camps were taken by the Allies after the liberation of Dachau, Buchenwald, and Bergen-Belsen. Perhaps the most penetrating images are those of British soldiers using bulldozers to pile bodies into mass graves at Bergen-Belsen (see Douglas 1995; Shandler 1999: chap. 1). These images have become a central symbol of indisputable moral facts. Connected to this symbolic context is the debate over whether the Allies should have bombed Auschwitz. In the U.S. Holocaust Memorial Museum, the decision not to bomb is clearly condemned.[14] For many, the failure to act became proof of the world's indifference to the fate of the Jews (Cole 1999: 150 ff.; Novick 1999: 54 ff.) When images of the camps in Bosnia were circulated, reference was made to this indifference, thereby strengthening the symbolic connection to Auschwitz, with the Serbs appearing as the Nazis in the eyes of the international community. It was not newspaper articles that secured this connection but a photograph, distributed by the British news service ITN, of an emaciated man looking at the camera from behind a fence. On 7 August 1992, the *Daily Mirror*, a popular British newspaper, ran the photograph on its front page under the headline "Belsen 92." The same image later appeared on the cover of *Time* magazine. A "frame" for memory had been found.

Using the photographic images of the Holocaust as a visual paradigm, Barbie Zelizer (1998) has examined why some images elicit particular reactions while others with similar themes leave viewers

---

13. For a variety of attempts by intellectuals to explain the Holocaust, see Traverso 1999.

14. The increasingly legalistic aspect of the reparations model is evident in a class-action suit against the U.S. government in which a group of survivors have asked for $40 billion in restitution because of the United States' failure to bomb Auschwitz. They allege that American passivity during World War II aided the murder of the European Jews (*New York Times*, 29 March 2001).

unmoved. Zelizer contrasts the international outcry against the conflict in Yugoslavia with the genocide in Rwanda, which received very little attention. Her explanation for this discrepancy rests on the fact that the Balkans are located in Europe and that the visual representation of concentration camps is linked to Holocaust iconography. Moral ideals are socially and culturally constructed, which, of course, makes them no less real or effective. The "image" of Auschwitz has a clear moral message: We recognize evil when we see it; if we do not put a stop to it, it is only because of our own moral failure. The images are proof of this fact.

Universal moral ideals are just as much a construction as are national moral ideals, and they are also just as real. For the Serbs to become Nazis, however, a further act of construction was necessary. Croatia and Albania were allies of Nazi Germany. Both were responsible for atrocities that gave even the Nazis pause, and the Croatians ran a concentration camp. The Serbs, however, were heroic opponents of the Nazis, refusing to give up even when the odds were against them. Many Serbs were slaughtered by the Nazi-allied Croats or died in the camps. Belgrade was bombed by the German Luftwaffe, and many Serbs had fought in the resistance and were murdered by the Nazis. In Jewish and Israeli memory, the Serbs were precisely the opposite of Nazis. With the rise of the Balkan conflict and the horrific fighting among various ethnic groups, however, a picture emerged that contradicted the moral assurance of "good" and "evil." This state of ambivalence and turmoil became heightened during the Kosovo conflict.

It was the images of the "concentration camps" that helped transform the Serbs into Nazis, although this alone did not spur anyone in the international community to intervene. No outside military intervention took place until 1999, during the Kosovo conflict. Nevertheless, the fact that the world had stood by during the fighting in Bosnia—yet another failure of not bombing Auschwitz—helped pave the way for the West to agree to intervene in Kosovo. At the time of the Bosnia conflict, the lessons of the Holocaust had led Germany to scale back its military, thus legitimating the decision not to get involved in the conflict. All this changed during Kosovo. Between 1992 and 1999, the former German collective of perpetrators was transformed into a collective of observers. "Never again Auschwitz" was now used as a call to bomb Belgrade. In this case, as well, the failure to intervene in Bosnia was key in spurring action.

In 1992, the assessment of the Serbs as Nazis was still being debated, and a number of Jewish groups took it upon themselves to sway public opinion. On 5 August 1992, precisely as images of the Serbian camps were distributed for the world to see, the three most prominent Jewish organizations—the American Jewish Committee, the American Jewish Congress, and the Anti-Defamation League—ran a full-page ad in the *New York Times* with the following message:

> Alongside the bloodstained names of Auschwitz, Treblinka, and other Nazi death camps, must now be added the names of Omarska and Brcko . . . Is it possible that, fifty years after the Holocaust, the nations of the world have decided to stand by passively and do nothing, claiming that they are helpless to do anything? . . . We hereby underline, that we are prepared to take all necessary steps, including the use of violence, to stop the madness and bloodshed.

Here, the Jewish organizations explicitly linked the Serbian and Nazi camps: The Serbs became the Nazis, and the Muslims were the Jews. Holocaust remembrance can be secured only by establishing clear ethical boundaries between victims and criminals, good and evil. As in the Holocaust, the victims must be completely "innocent." They were never political victims. The transference of the Holocaust onto Bosnia depoliticized the conflict. It is significant that it was the Jewish organizations that helped influence this process. The images could be universalized precisely because it was Jewish Americans who had successfully preserved and particularized the memories in the United States. On 22 December 1992, various Jewish organizations held a demonstration on the site of the Holocaust Memorial Museum, which was still under construction, to protest the atrocities being committed by the Serbs. At that time, however, the U.S. government, headed by President George H. W. Bush, as well as European governments, had no political interest in intervening in Bosnia.[15]

---

15. A vast amount has been written about the Balkan crisis and the violence it spurred. For a good overview, see the series of articles by Mark Danner in the *New*

During the dedication ceremony of the Holocaust Memorial Museum, Elie Wiesel directly addressed President Clinton to reiterate the connection between the Holocaust and Bosnia: "As a Jew, I am saying that we must do something to stop the bloodshed in that country! People fight each other and children die. Why? Something, anything must be done" (as cited in Linenthal 1995: 262).

As a Jewish survivor, Wiesel was putting his authority on the line by declaring solidarity with the Muslims in Bosnia. It should also be noted that the museum's planners had originally considered creating a "committee on conscience" as a watchdog to identify cases of genocide. The committee was to report directly to the president and Congress. On 26 April 1993, four days after the museum opened its doors, the American Jewish Congress ran another full-page ad in the *New York Times*, in which it directly entreated President Clinton to intervene in Bosnia. Among other things, the question was posed: "If the memories of Holocaust survivors do not move us to react to suffering and persecution in our time, what purpose does memory even have?" In addition to these entreaties, in March 1994 the museum organized an exhibition and lecture series titled, "Bosnia in the Light of the Holocaust." All of this still did not lead to action on the part of the United States and NATO, but the path had been laid for action in Kosovo.

Along the way, Srebrenica occurred, the largest massacre on European soil since World War II. Seven thousand Muslim men were brutally slaughtered by Serbian troops, right under the watch of a Dutch contingent of U.N. peacekeeping forces (see Doubt 2000; Honig and Both 1996). This incident tipped the scales. In the post–Cold War world, one takes claims of human-rights violations seriously. When people are murdered right in front of the cameras, the United States and NATO ultimately have no choice but to intervene—at least, when these massacres occur on European soil. If they do not, they face a rising credibility deficit. The consequences of the Holocaust, in the form of genocide and human-rights violations, have become too closely linked with the media-constructed, globalized

York Review of Books in 1997 and 1998, which were later published as a book (Danner 1999).

icons of *Schindler's List* and images of Bosnia. The U.S. Holocaust Memorial Museum participates in this type of construction, where non-intervention, as in Rwanda, highlights the negative side of contemporary human-rights politics.

In March 1994, ABC broadcast what was to become an influential documentary, *While America Watched: The Bosnian Tragedy*. The title itself is evocative of the Holocaust: the phrase "as America watched" had been used in reference to World War II. At that time, "watching" was considered something negative, which was confirmed by the "Bosnian tragedy" in the 1990s. In 1996, Reyak Hucanovicy's *The Tenth Circle of Hell: A Memoir of Life in the Death Camps of Bosnia*—an account that reads like a Holocaust memoir—was published. Not only did the phrase "death camps" appear in the title, but, more significant, the foreword was written by Elie Wiesel, who linked the two events.

It is correct to insist that the Holocaust is singular and that comparisons to other atrocities need to proceed from this premise. However, this is not the real issue. What is of greater significance in the present context is the way in which images of the Holocaust have become a symbol for an ethically driven politics in the global arena. At that particular historical junction, the images replaced the friend-or-foe iconography of the Cold War and of traditional nation-states, which recently have been resurrected. During the war in Bosnia, when military intervention was not yet an option, these new symbolic links and universally accepted values were still in the process of being defined. One should not look at the use of Holocaust representations during this conflict as merely an instrument of human-rights advocates who were willing to use any means possible to encourage military intervention. The old nation-based politics no longer pertains to these cases. What we are dealing with is an entirely new type of war (Kaldor 1999). In this new warfare, paramilitary units brutally attack the civilian population. As Mary Kaldor shows, these wars (of which the conflicts in the former Yugoslavia are a good example) are a result of a breakdown of states' legitimacy. According to Kaldor, legitimacy can be reinstated only through a cosmopolitan politics. Within this context, outside "intervention" begins to lose meaning as the borders between internal and external become blurred. After the demise of Cold War logic and the end of a concept of "war as revolution," the logic of war as genocide prevails (Shaw 1998).

The Holocaust is *the* genocide that led to the United Nations' convention against genocide in 1948. The Nazis waged war against the Jews; the Jews as such, not individual states, were the targeted enemies. The new wars might not be comparable to the horrors of Auschwitz. Nevertheless, they serve as an important model in a cosmopolitan society in which the media broadcast news of genocide into every living room. Dislodged from the context of the nation-state, memories of the Holocaust provided an answer to the global conflicts of Second Modernity during that particular period.

The Dispute over the Particular and Universal: The Goldhagen Debate

In the 1990s, Holocaust remembrance was marked by tensions be-tween the universal and the particular. Daniel J. Goldhagen's *Hitler's Willing Executioners*, which first appeared in the United States in 1996, is significant in this context. In what follows, we are not concerned with the specifics of public reactions to the book.[16] Instead, our fo-cus is on how the debates surrounding the book can be seen as part of a broader cultural transformation. The fact that this work, whose scholarly contribution was considered insignificant by many historians, had such an enormous impact makes it worthy of investi-gation. The success of the book also reveals the failure of historians to communicate the horrors of the Holocaust in a compelling way. In contrast to similar debates, the Goldhagen case is not based on an innovative model of interpretation, which in the past led to historio-graphical debates.

What was new about Goldhagen's contribution was not so much his thesis as the broader field surrounding its reception, which points to an increasingly self-reflexive discourse. From this perspective, the reactions to Goldhagen's book are a classic example of the culture of memory in Second Modernity. The book's content and its reception

---

16. The number of reviews written in English and German is too great for us to list here. Two broad overviews are Eley 2000 and Shandley 1998.

play a role in this context. Goldhagen's thesis cuts across the interpretive models that had been used until the book's publication. Goldhagen was less concerned with a structural, functional thesis of how the bureaucratic machine made it possible to carry out the Final Solution rationally and efficiently than with a type of "pre-scientific" question: Why were the Germans so evil? Goldhagen decontextualized this question. The issue of evil is central to his inquiry, as is the Germans' decision to become perpetrators. In his opinion, there had been no "thick description" of the Holocaust—the type of description that one finds, for instance, in autobiographies (Bartov 1997). The informed reader found Goldhagen's work reminiscent of Primo Levi, Jean Améry, Jorge Semprun, Elie Wiesel, Ka-Zetnik (who is mainly known in Israel), and many others who have produced this kind of "thick description." At first glance, Goldhagen's theoretical claims are a confusing jumble. On the one hand, he draws on a theory of voluntary action: Perpetrators act out of free will and choice. On the other hand, he essentializes this moral autonomy of the perpetrator as it is determined by ethnic German culture. Clearly, this thesis cannot be contained by scientific methodology, but it did correspond to the immediate experience of the victims of the Germans. The victims experienced the Germans not as abstract bureaucrats but as "willing executioners" who wanted to kill them because they were Jewish. One reason the book found huge success in the United States, where survivors have helped to shape the culture of remembrance, was the fact that, like Spielberg before him, Goldhagen echoed their experiences. His professional colleagues could not support his claims, because essentialism had been discredited among most historians. Goldhagen's essentialism, however, did not impede identification with the victims, and in Germany his work enjoyed a particularly enthusiastic reception. His thick description, dismissed by some critics as quasi-pornographic, enabled many readers to experience the Holocaust on an emotional level.

A line can be drawn from the *Holocaust* miniseries to *Schindler's List* to *Hitler's Willing Executioners* because of the feelings of empathy these three works arouse. Goldhagen's thesis also led to a revival of older theories of collective guilt, which Karl Jaspers had already discussed by 1945. As a product in the global market, Goldhagen was redefined on a local level. In America, the book helped Jewish Americans stem the tide of universalization (Rabinbach 1997); in Germany, it broke the historians' monopoly over Holocaust interpretation, thus helping to reach a broader audience, and it contributed to the globalizing of a sense of responsibility by encouraging identification with the victims. In Israel, in contrast, Goldhagen did not receive much public attention, because his thesis on German anti-Semitism was considered self-evident, and identification with the victims had become common since the Eichmann trial. In other words, his thesis did not resonate with the Israeli public because they saw it as redundant (Bartov 2000).

Thus, the significance of Goldhagen's book extends far beyond its immediate reception. At the time of its publication, it was still important to remark on the particularistic bent of the work. It stressed the singular nature of the Holocaust, identifying the perpetrators as "Germans," unlike Christopher Browning's (1992) stress on "Ordinary Men." Subsequently, the strict opposition between the particularistic and universalistic camps has become less relevant. In many respects, Goldhagen revived a position that had been prominent after the war but then became marginal. Historians of the structural-functionalist school largely neglected the role of anti-Semitism and focused on victims rather than perpetrators. In this sense, Goldhagen's book helped spark a renewed discussion about the Holocaust, both inside and outside academe. Goldhagen's personal shift in position is indicative of this more general transformation. Some of the reviews he wrote for the *New Republic* prior to publishing his own book provide insight into the process that led up to the particularist stance in *Hitler's Willing Executioners*. In his 1989 review of Arno Mayer's study of the Holocaust, Goldhagen claims that "[Nolte and Mayer] serve to dedemonize Nazism, to transform the Nazis into just another brutal regime: different in degree, but not in kind" (Goldhagen 1998: 44)

In Goldhagen's eyes, describing the Holocaust in such a way was unforgivable. A decade later, under the sway of the Kosovo crisis and as the Holocaust was becoming a catalyst for a renewed discussion about the scale and consequences of genocide, Goldhagen reversed his position. He did not go so far as to equate Milosevic with Hitler, but he did stress their similarities:

> Nevertheless, the Serbs have done as much as they could to remind the world of the Holocaust . . . And the horrific result is that, whether one calls it a genocide or not, all of the dead civilians are just as dead as the murdered Jews, Poles, Russians, and gays in Hitler's time. . . . The Serbian acts of terror only differ from those of the Nazis in terms of scale. (Goldhagen 1999: 17)

"Kosovocaust"

During the Kosovo crisis in 1998–99, the extent to which the Holocaust had become de-territorialized and an international political agenda prevailed became clear. This was the first time that the "lessons of the Holocaust," the protection of human rights, and the need to prevent genocide were invoked both at the highest political levels and as justification for military intervention. Seen in this light, Kosovo was a seminal moment in the process of universalizing the Holocaust. Conversely, this universalization was an important factor in the decision to use military force. This is not a tautology. It is a dialectical process in which temporally displaced, de-territorialized Holocaust memories become catalysts in shaping new political and cultural attitudes that no longer fit into the conventional rubric of the nation-state and particularistic–universalistic dichotomy.

In many respects, Kosovo was a global media event that, through implicit as well as explicit comparison to the Holocaust, took on the character of a moral struggle. On the one hand, military intervention was justified through the slogan "Never again Auschwitz," stressing the universalistic approach. On the other hand, references to the Holocaust, which had taken on a quasi-ritualistic dimension, sparked renewed debates about the viability of such comparisons. Public handling of the past itself became a topic of public discourse, which in turn bolstered the self-reflexive component of remembrance. At the same time, because of longstanding controversies based on individual national particularities, this universalization also led to the recontextualization of the Holocaust in relation to the internal realities of specific countries. It is on this level that global and local remembrances of the Holocaust meet.

Germany Liberates Auschwitz in Kosovo

The Kosovo crisis marked a transformation of Germany's official understanding of the Holocaust. For one thing, politicians started using Kosovo to make historical comparisons. The same critics who just a few years earlier had denounced such a move as an illegitimate instrumentalization of the Holocaust for political gain and as an attempt to re-nationalize German discourse now embraced it as an attempt to universalize memories of the Holocaust. During the first Gulf War, Helmut Kohl appealed to German history when he refused to send troops to the Middle East. Auschwitz was a symbol, among other things, for German militarism. In contrast, Chancellor Gerhard Schröder, Foreign Minister Joschka Fischer, and Defense Minister Klaus Scharping, all representatives of the German postwar generation, cited the lessons of the Holocaust to justify sending troops to Kosovo. What had happened between these two events? This transformation of memory was not so much the result of a new understanding of the Holocaust. There were other important factors, such as the often emotional debates about whether to deploy troops during the first Gulf War (as a member of NATO) and, above all, recalling the consequences of not taking action in Bosnia (and thus taking the illegitimate role of passive bystander). At the time of the Bosnian war, memories of World War II were still extremely vivid, but during Kosovo, images of a brutalizing Nazi Wehrmacht were decisively transformed into a humanitarian Bundeswehr, the military of the Federal Republic of Germany. This occurred precisely as the role of the Wehrmacht in the Holocaust was hotly debated, a debate sparked by a museum exhibit titled, "War of Annihilation: Crimes of the Wehrmacht, 1941–1944" (Bartov et al. 2002). From this perspective, intervention in Kosovo signaled not simply a departure from a longstanding pacifist tradition among a segment of the German left (above all the children of the '68 generation), a tradition that can be summarized by the slogan "Never again War." This slogan refers back to the Holocaust and to the militarism that many felt made that catastrophe possible in the first place. Hence, Germany's military action in Kosovo also marks a departure from the "criminal" Nazi Wehrmacht. These connections were reinforced in the debates surrounding Kosovo, when "Never again War" was replaced by "Never again Auschwitz." At the Green Party's convention on 13 May 1999, Joschka Fischer expressed this sentiment by declaring, "Auschwitz cannot be compared to anything else. Nevertheless, I support two fundamental principles: Never again war, never again Auschwitz; never again genocide, never again fascism. For me, the two are linked."[17]

In view of the unique meaning the Holocaust holds for Germans, one could at first glance interpret Fischer's words as a confirmation of the *Sonderweg* theory. In actuality, however, his statement signaled a de-contextualization and de-territorialization of Holocaust memories. The oft-mentioned "special responsibility" of Germany suddenly resonated with the Western, democratic global community. "Never again Auschwitz" no longer referred to the crimes committed by the Germans. Rather, it referred to the universal responsibility held by the entire collective of witnesses, understood in the way we described earlier. In this case, Auschwitz served as a metaphor for non-intervention, a memory that relied on Holocaust iconography but that also pointed to the failures of Bosnia. The Germans could be included within these fluid memories, as they had now posthumously joined the ranks of Auschwitz liberators.

Auschwitz had once been identified exclusively with Germans and Jews.[18] During Kosovo, the Holocaust was redefined for Germans (and by Germans) as a universal metaphor. Out of the guilt over past crimes grew a new sense of political and military responsibility for the future.

Ironically, it is the '68 generation of the "new left and the center-left," which became part of the ruling government at the end of the 1990s, that has worked toward realizing Kohl's goal of "normalization." This group articulates the needs of a generation for which the "national" past no longer elicits shame. It recognizes the growing need to construct a new image for Germany that does not hark back to the prehistory of the Federal Republic. The group's main goal

---

17. Excerpts from Fischer's speech are reprinted in *Süddeutsche Zeitung*, 14 May 1999.

18. Poles also made several attempts to appropriate the memory of Auschwitz. Most of these efforts resulted in public disputes. Various controversies arose about the construction of commercially based memorial sites and the Catholic church's attempt to "Christianize" the victims.

is to finish up with the National Socialist past, since that past is no longer considered the determining force in political deliberations. Now, the politics of remembrance is increasingly bound up with the history of the Federal Republic. The appropriate representation of the Holocaust, rather than the Holocaust per se, is at the center of debates.

This does no imply that the virtues of a collective memory that seeks to come to terms with the past have been forgotten. At this point, however, the Federal Republic has its own (pre)history—namely, the years before reunification. In the 1970s, appeals to continuity in history were rejected, because they were seen as perpetuating the German *Sonderweg*. Now, continuity refers to the preservation of the tradition that emerged during the Federal Republic. Holocaust remembrance has changed accordingly. In remembering the victims, Germany simultaneously commemorates the culture of remembrance of the past three decades. Consequently, the "proud" nation is no longer an ideological pipe dream of the right but an actual state-sanctioned political practice of the red–green coalition. Germany's postwar generation accepts its past—the decades-long insistence on "remembering as a form of liberation" seems to have worked—but it is no longer strongly hemmed in by these memories.

This shift in the object of remembrance becomes particularly apparent when one compares the public controversies that raged during the Kohl era to the muted reactions to Schröder's attempts at normalization. As an example, Schröder, a Social Democrat, was able to voice his summary opposition to the Wehrmacht exhibit. The exhibit challenged Adenauer's claim that there was a difference between the regular army and Hitler's special commando forces. In the tradition of Adenauer and Kohl, Schröder declared: "I have not seen [the exhibit], but I cannot accept the claim that a major part of an army could have committed such crimes" (Frankfurter Allgemeine Zeitung, 2 February 1999). We are not concerned so much with Schröder's political convictions as with the fact that his statement received little criticism. If Kohl had said the same thing a few years earlier, public protests and charges that he was trying to close the book on the past would have followed. More recently, this new air of openness has become evident in the revival of a statement that Kohl, the first chancellor born in the postwar era, did make about enjoying the "grace of late birth," which some interpreted as an attempt to avoid the issue of guilt. Within the same cohort and the same ruling coalition, we find the chancellor's qualified support of the "proud German" and the foreign minister's stress on Europeanization. In the meantime, Kohl has not received (or, at least, not yet) any credit for laying the groundwork for Schröder's normalization project. The same generation that criticized Kohl for supporting intervention in the Balkans—and particularly for drawing comparisons between what was happening there and Nazi crimes—later paved the way for a universalistic understanding of responsibility. Adopting a globalized approach to politics, this generation supported a similar type of intervention in Kosovo, with no apparent sense of contradiction. A "special sense of obligation" was invoked, referring not only to a specific national past, but also to the future. Germany's deployment of troops in Bosnia replaced the memories of crimes committed by the German military in the Balkans during the Nazi era. The process of universalizing the Holocaust is just as significant in this context: Kosovo was not merely the central focus within this new frame of reference; it was also a catalyst for the public consolidation of the Holocaust as a general point of reference for cosmopolitan memory.

Like Israel and the United States, Germany has experienced a pluralization of memories. In its case, as well, a process of individuation is apparent. If we look back to the postwar era of the 1950s and 1960s (see chapter 4), we notice that West Germany was inclined to individualize memories because of its tendency to remain silent about collective history. In the 1970s and 1980s, this process of de-nationalizing was spurred by the critiques of the new social movements and their search for new models of identity. In addition to these factors, which are connected to a generational shift, certain social transformations are helping to break the state's dominance over remembrance. As Germans start to realize that unemployment will play a key role in the new social reality, concerns about an unstable work environment are overshadowing a general interest in the "well-being of the nation."

In addition, shifting trends in immigration over the past four decades have contributed to the demise of the state monopoly over remembrance and to the pluralization of forms of remembering. Since the 1990s, the longstanding myth that Germany is "not a land of immigration" has been widely challenged. Of course, this does not mean that all Germans embrace "foreigners" (still the preferred term for referring to immigrants) with open arms. Nevertheless, there has been a transformation in the political arena and an end to a hegemonic society that, for two generations, has had ongoing contact with "foreign co-citizens." In schools and the workplace, and even through changes in culinary preferences, the presence of other ethnic groups can be seen everywhere. It is telling that since the 1990s, most opponents of dual citizenship—a hotly debated topic—have only seldom fallen back on the old ethno-cultural arguments. Instead, they have made individual appeals for integration and mobility (Levy 2001). This does not suggest that all Germans are open to the idea of a multicultural society or that these changes have automatically resulted in greater tolerance toward foreigners. However, multiculturalism is having an impact on the experiences and memories of a broad segment of the German population. This is very similar to the experience in Israel and the United States. In all three cases, particularized forms of memory have provided a foundation for later universal models of remembrance, which were perhaps unintended but nevertheless remain meaningful.

Kosovo and Israel

As noted, ethnic groups in Israel also function as communities of memory. Both Israelis and Palestinians considered Bosnia to be of direct strategic interest as well as significant to their politics of remembrance. Like Americans, Israelis tend to ignore things that do not affect them directly. There is little international news in Israel. In contrast to the United States, in Israel events in the Balkans went largely unnoticed in the early and mid-1990s. Too much was happening in the domestic arena—the Oslo Accords, the murder of Yitzhak Rabin, and the ensuing national elections—to follow the Bosnia conflict closely.

Despite this, various groups, with their specific memories and perceptions, were very quick to organize as things started to heat up in Kosovo. As noted, Jewish and Israeli memories are not necessarily identical in Israel. Israelis are often admonished not to universalize the Holocaust, and they have treated it as a traumatic event in Jewish history that cannot be used to draw universal lessons. Things became more complicated, however, when Kosovo entered the picture. During this conflict, the West had chosen to determine, through the use of force, who was good and who was evil, who was civilized and who was barbaric. As noted, many Jews considered the Serbs to be on the right side during the Holocaust, since they had saved Jews from the Croatians and Albanians. After all, had it not been Tito's partisans who had fought in the resistance against Hitler? Was it not true that Belgrade had been bombed by the Nazis? These memories of World War II shaped the image that many Israelis and Jews had of the Serbs. This image was shaken, however, by the first television broadcasts of the flood of refugees coming out of Kosovo. Israeli newscasters could not simply stand by and be trumped by CNN, the BBC, and SkyNews when these broadcasters echoed their governments in claiming that Kosovo was a second Holocaust. The resounding cry at the press conferences and on the news programs of the West was "Never Again."

In Israel, Holocaust survivors appeared on television to justify the claim that the Serbs, although they had saved Jews during World War II, were now Nazis, persecuting and murdering Jews (or Muslims). Many Israelis accepted this shift in perspective. Demonstrations were organized, and money was collected for the cause; a medical field unit was dispatched to Macedonia. Showing solidarity with the Kosovars enabled many Jews in Israel to merge their particularistic memories of the Holocaust with a universal, cosmopolitan humanism, without suffering the same kind of tensions that conflicts at home would cause. However, this seemingly ideal solution, in which the tension between the local and the global was resolved, did not take into account the issue of competing memories. The Palestinians watching the streams of refugees on television were not reminded of the Holocaust but of their own plight in 1948—their exile and their desire to return to a real or imagined homeland. This was something that left-leaning Israeli editorial writers tried to make clear to their readership.[19] For them, Kosovo was not about the Holocaust

---

19. Examples include Benveniste 1999 and Levi 1999.

but about the idea of "ethnic cleansing," which they wanted to apply to the 1948 Israeli War of Independence.[20] Many on the Israeli right, including members of the government, made a similar connection between Kosovo and 1948, albeit for different ends. They understood how precarious historical rights and claims of who owns holy sites can be and how deep-seated memories of historical injustices can remain among coexisting ethnic groups. The argument ran as follows: The Serbs made up only 10 percent of the population in Kosovo yet regarded Kosovo as the cradle of their ethnic and religious identity. Similarly, many right-wing Israelis were erecting settlements on the land of their forefathers in Hebron and East Jerusalem and thus considered the Serbs their spiritual brothers. If Kosovars could demand self-rule simply on the basis that they constituted the ethnic majority, then Palestinians could make the same demands. This would apply not only to the Occupied Territories—which many regard as sacred for Israel as Kosovo is for many Serbs. It would also pertain to parts of Israel proper, such as Galilee, where the majority of the population is Arab. According to the right-wing line of reasoning, if NATO bombed Serbia, it could bomb Israel on similar grounds.

In this case, Israeli memory prevails over Jewish memory. In postnational battles that were waged in the name of humanity itself, the distinction between friend and foe was expressed on a metaphoric level: good versus evil, light versus darkness, civilization versus barbarianism. For Israel, the road from Kosovo to Hebron reveals that memories cannot simply be instrumentalized, and that "collective" memory is neither homogeneous nor hegemonic. Above all, it reveals that the tension between local and global memory does—and, indeed, must—exist as a basic founding principle for Israel. By necessity, Jewish and Israeli memories compete with one another. This tension will help shape specific political, ethnic, and cultural conflicts in Israel in the years to come.

In contrast to other Western countries, in Israel religion and self-sacrifice are still social binding forces (Beck 1997). Here, First and

---

20. For a historical analysis of this war as "ethnic cleansing," see Morris 1987.

Second Modernity, exile and displacement, exist side by side in the same space, a phenomenon in which the memory of the Holocaust plays a role. The Holocaust happened "over there," whereas the "here" is what can prevent another such event from occurring. This means that tendencies toward individualization are by no means a foregone conclusion.

Since the end of the Cold War, Israel has not played the same strategic role for the United States. War is not something contained to specific geographic coordinates. It is ubiquitous, with new military coalitions constantly forming. Within the context of a global readiness to wage war, the memory of the Holocaust plays a vital role in the name of human rights and humanity. Through this cosmopolitanization process, Israel is losing its monopoly over the Holocaust. Media coverage, whether in the form of Spielberg's productions or of CNN's news coverage, has left its mark on the local culture of remembrance in Israel. Paradoxically, it was the Jewish organizations that once secured this monopoly in Israel. The Americanization of the Holocaust has not resulted in its becoming less Jewish, but it has certainly resulted in loosening its ties to Israel. Since 2000, with new conflicts erupting in the Occupied Territories, the deterritorialization of memory has led to accusations against Israel of human-rights violation. Under the watchful eye of the global media, this has resulted, as the Kosovo conflict did, in calls for outside military intervention.

Kosovo and the United States

The war in Kosovo played a decisive role in the United States and in the Americanization of the Holocaust. U.S. politicians—above all, President Clinton—explicitly referred to the Holocaust in arguing for military intervention in Kosovo. America's participation was justified primarily on moral grounds, spurred not just by ethnic cleansing but also by past failures to take action in protecting innocent civilians. The slogan "Never Again" referred both to the Holocaust and to America's slow reaction to the crisis in Bosnia. Kosovo provided an opportunity to turn "Never Again" into a guiding political principle on a global scale.

This is not to say, however, that the application of the Holocaust to Kosovo, as well as to other situations, did not meet with obstacles. Many people, including some survivors and those who insisted on the uniqueness of the Holocaust, continued to oppose universalization, fearing that it would lead to the trivialization of Nazi crimes. Others maintained that the very real dimensions of suffering experienced by the Kosovars and other victims could not be compared to the unfathomable scope of destruction wrought against the Jews. Such opposition was bolstered by various groups who cited various aspects of Holocaust memories: The Serbs repeatedly referred to their resistance to the Nazis and the Albanian collaborators; NATO air attacks were compared to Nazi attacks; Serbia's opponents compared ethnic cleansing in Kosovo with Nazi crimes and identified the Albanians as the new Jews.

Nevertheless, the prominent military and political role played by the United States, as well as America's stated moral mission, which grew out of its former passivity, tipped the scales in favor of military intervention. It was not the Holocaust as such but, rather, the mistakes of the past and the need to protect innocent civilians from genocide in the future that helped shape the argument. The particularistic commandment to remember the Holocaust was combined with the universal imperative actively to help groups in need.

The military conflicts of the 1990s illuminate the extent to which Western democracies have eschewed the old nation-state categories of earlier rhetoric. To be sure, "national interests" are still at stake, but they have been marked by a de-territorialized, cosmopolitan memory. In many respects, the 1991 Gulf War was still a classical war driven by national interests, since one state invaded another, thereby threatening the interests of other states. In another example, after the signing of the Dayton Peace Accords in 1995, which called for American troops to be stationed in Bosnia, President Clinton tried to win over American citizens by appealing to a sense of national duty and sacrifice:

> From our birth, America has always been more than just a place. America has embodied an idea that has become the ideal for billions of people throughout the world. Our founders said it best: America is about life, liberty and the pursuit of happiness.

In this century especially, America has done more than simply stand for these ideals. We have acted on them and sacrificed for them. Our people fought two world wars so that freedom could triumph over tyranny. After World War I, we pulled back from the world, leaving a vacuum that was filled by the forces of hatred. After World War II, we continued to lead the world. We made the commitments that kept the peace, that helped to spread democracy, that created unparalleled prosperity and that brought victory in the Cold War.

Today, because of our dedication, America's ideals—liberty, democracy, and peace—are more and more the aspirations of people everywhere in the world. It is the power of our ideas, even more than our size, our wealth and our military might, that makes America a uniquely trusted nation. (Clinton 1995)

Nine years later, George W. Bush would argue in the same manner, with one difference: His frame was not the Holocaust but international terrorism.

Clinton stressed the fact that, ultimately, the Holocaust was allowed to happen because America had decided to stay out of Europe's affairs. He also sought to describe America's new role in a global arena:

With the Cold War over, some people now question the need for our continued active leadership in the world. They believe that, much like after World War I, America can now step back from the responsibilities of leadership. They argue that to be secure, we need only to keep our own borders safe, and that the time has come now to leave to others the hard work of leadership beyond our borders. I strongly disagree. As the Cold War gives way to the global village, our leadership is needed more than ever because problems that start beyond our borders can quickly become problems within them. We're all vulnerable to the organized forces of intolerance and destruction, terrorism, ethnic, religious and regional rivalries, the spread of organized crime and weapons of mass destruction and drug trafficking. Just as surely as fascism and communism, these forces also threaten freedom and democracy, peace and prosperity. And they too demand American leadership.

But nowhere has the argument for our leadership been more clearly justified than in the struggle to stop or prevent war and civil violence. From Iraq to Haiti; from South Africa to Korea; from the Middle East to Northern Ireland, we have stood up for peace and freedom because it's in our interest to do so, and because it is the right thing to do. (Clinton 1995)

Subsequently, Clinton laid out the reasons for sending soldiers to Bosnia:

> Implementing the agreement in Bosnia can end the terrible suffering of the people, the warfare, the mass executions, the ethnic cleansing, the campaigns of rape and terror. Let us never forget a quarter of a million men, women and children have been shelled, shot and tortured to death. Two million people, half of the population, were forced from their homes and into a miserable life as refugees, and these faceless numbers have millions of real, personal tragedies, for each of the war's victims was a mother or daughter, father or son, a brother or sister. Now the war is over. American leadership created the chance to build a peace and stop the suffering. (Clinton 1995)

Clinton's appeal for national sacrifice did not resonate well with the American people. Everyone knew that military intervention should not result in American casualties, which directly influenced the decision not to send ground troops a few years later (Danner 1999).

With Kosovo, this new form of intervention—which the strategist Edward Luttwack (1996) calls "post-heroic warfare"—was taken to a higher level. Although human-rights violations were considered a legitimate basis for military intervention, they were not supposed to result in casualties for the intervening power. Free, liberal societies have the cultural means to recruit support for humanitarian interventions. But precisely because they are free and liberal societies, they want this intervention to be for free—that is, without victims on their own side. This has also determined military strategy. The new post-national and post-heroic wars are waged exclusively from the air (Ignatieff 2000), which has not turned out to be effective in preventing "ethnic cleansing." In Kosovo, such air campaigns kept the military from carrying out its mission of saving civilians.

It is very difficult to win wars against ethnic cleansing that are conducted in the name of moral universalism and motivated by the memory of the Holocaust. As subsequent developments have shown, they are more easily waged in the name of national security and preventing terrorism. Two concrete processes are at work here. Kosovo revealed how much warfare has changed in the past few decades, with civilians increasingly finding themselves at the epicenter of conflicts. While civilians constituted a minority among the victims of

World War II, about 80 percent of the victims in the new wars are civilians (Kaldor 1999; Shaw 1998).

With the end of the Cold War, the United States has remained a militarily oriented nation. The U.S. military budget is still higher than the budgets of all the NATO allies combined and significantly higher than those of its enemies (Becker 2000). After the Vietnam debacle and the end of the standoff between East and West, wars must and should be waged with as few casualties as possible to be considered legitimate. A major problem in Second Modernity remains—namely, how to be a liberator without having to pay the price. The wars that the United States has engaged in since the Cold War (the 1991 Gulf War, Bosnia, and Kosovo) did not result in any American fatalities. In 1993, the deaths of eighteen American soldiers in Somalia caused the United States immediately to pull its troops out of the country. The same factor that determined the cultural and political reasons for intervention (i.e., compassion for the innocent victims) also prevents the deaths of "one's own" soldiers.

Another characteristic of the new warfare in Second Modernity has to do with transnational legitimacy, which is secured by forming military coalitions (Ignatieff 2000). National contingents still exist within these troops, but the acting force is NATO. Such a constellation leaves little room for heroism based on national particularities.

In addition, tension exists between a military ideal of sacrifice and a hedonistic civil one. In Second Modernity, the West has continued to cultivate an idea of the nation, but it has had increasing difficulty in mobilizing the majority of the population militarily for this purpose. Benedict Anderson (1991) proposes conducting a "sociological test" to gauge the authenticity of a value system: In a globally oriented world, are people prepared to sacrifice themselves in the name of national ideals? We would add: Are people prepared to sacrifice themselves for ideals that extend beyond the individual nation? The question is not an easy one. Intervention in Kosovo—which occurred in the wake of inaction during the Bosnian massacre, which in turn can be symbolically linked to the Holocaust—is evidence of the fact that some people are willing to act even when the stakes do not concern their individual nation. They are not eager, however, to engage in ground combat, as they did in previous wars. As Anderson puts it, liberal principles do not entail the heroic ideals of death. He considers the willingness to sacrifice an inherent force of the "imagined community" of the nation. Many critics of global culture see this lack of emotional engagement as proof of its superficiality.

This unwillingness to sacrifice does not by any means suggest that global culture is without memory, as Anthony Smith (1990, 1995) maintains. Quite to the contrary: It is precisely the global memory of the great wars, and above all of the Holocaust, that moves many people to worry about their "own affairs" and not think so much about national themes anymore. Individuals whose principles extend far beyond their own nation rely on global memory. What frequently moves them to action is news about human rights abuses based on ethnic identity. Liberal, individual-oriented societies whose memory is based on the principle of "Never Again," however, take their time in discussing issues and are not readily willing to sacrifice their lives. This is something that every "ethnic cleanser" knows. Cosmopolitan memory of the Holocaust is oriented toward life and survival, not toward death. As Max Weber notes, political communities are defined by their willingness to engage in violence (Weber 1962; see also Beck 1997: 387 ff.). Memories of exactly this readiness for violence may lead to traumatic experiences that, in turn, reinforce the impulse to engage in violence. When these experiences are situated outside the perimeters of the nation, however, they can result in the opposite—namely, an unwillingness to engage in violence. This makes any intervention that is not connected to "national interests" all the more problematic. Paradoxically, the same mechanisms that lead to a willingness to intervene can also lead to unwillingness to do so. In the West, memories of the Holocaust have made many people into sympathetic, compassionate individuals. This fact does not, however, necessarily motivate them to condone the sacrificing of lives, as evidenced in Europe's popular and principled objections to war as such.

An increase in war and Holocaust memories, new forms of warfare, and de-territorialized concern for others are characteristic of Second Modernity. Comparisons with the Holocaust arose unintentionally; the charge of instrumentalization or imposition by outside forces is not valid here. World War II was as much a conflict among nations as it was a war against the Jews (Davidowicz 1975). Both struggles occurred simultaneously and were interconnected, but they remain discrete events. Although both were initially clumped together, in Second Modernity a division exists between war memories, on the one hand, and Holocaust memories, on the other. The Holocaust was not, however, a classic international conflict and it was not "ethnic cleansing." Ironically, from today's perspective, it was precisely the opposite. Jews were taken out of the Nazi-occupied territories and rounded up in various places to be murdered. Destruction, not persecution, was the goal.[21] The moment the Holocaust became universalized, it could no longer legitimately be distinguished from ethnic cleansing.

Second Modernity and "Distanced Sympathy"

We stress the change in the military's self-understanding to point to a new connection between nationalism and solidarity in Second Modernity. Nationalism is first and foremost an ethic of the heroic victim. In Second Modernity, people are no longer as willing to sacrifice their lives. At the same time, compassion toward those who suffer and are caused harm has grown in contemporary societies (Boltanski 1999). Further, the circle of those who are deemed worthy of such compassion is expanding (Sznaider 2001). These two attitudes are constantly at odds with each other: compassion and the unwillingness to become the heroic victim—or, in Weberian terms, the tension between the ethics of ultimate ends and the ethics of responsibility.

This has nothing to do with a neoliberal glorification of the market. Rather, it stems from an awareness that the market is not just a means for organizing economic relationships. It also leads to emotional and cognitive changes that redefine the ethical relationship between strangers. The market brings strangers together to form a dense web of social relationships; it transforms friends as well as enemies into strangers. This process of estrangement is accompanied by a rise in certain feelings, such as compassion, in bourgeois society (Sznaider 2001). Democracy and equality among individuals on an official level play an important role here by providing the necessary conditions

---

21. For the historical differences between the Holocaust and ethnic cleansing, see Diner 1999: 195–249.

for cultivating such feelings. Political freedom and equality are not anathema to the market; they are integral components of it. Like material goods, ideal goods and principles must be able to circulate freely via open avenues of communication. Only those individuals who have access to information can imagine the suffering of others and, consequently, might feel compassion toward them.

In First Modernity, compassion rarely extended beyond an individual's immediate social and cultural borders. Social boundaries determined moral boundaries. For capitalist democracies, however, suffering is no longer a hopeless situation. It is a tragedy that must be rectified (and often can be). Since "good" can no longer be defined in Second Modernity, what remains is to define the "bad" as evil. Suffering is bad; compassion toward others helps combat it. The sympathetic individual of Second Modernity does not lose himself in the process of sympathizing and does not want to sacrifice his own life. Compassion does not mean negation of the self. On the contrary, only those individuals who have a sense of "self" and thus of their own individual interests are able to generalize this sense and extend it to strangers. Individualism and altruism are not mutually exclusive. Together, they form the foundation for a bourgeois Second Modernity.

Thus, de-territorialization in global life does not mean the end of compassion. Global organizations and globally oriented people have become the purveyors of global compassion. Amnesty International has succeeded in making torture victims' cries heard wherever people are able and willing to listen. CNN and other media organizations bring us news about human suffering from the remotest regions of the world. The number of groups who demand our sympathy keeps growing and is no longer limited to our own immediate circle. On a cognitive level, the media is responsible for this phenomenon; on a normative level, a global human-rights discourse legitimates it. Transnational institutions have codified international human rights, providing a reference point for a diverse number of groups. The cosmopolitan memory of the Holocaust, which has grown out of the intermingling of local realities and global concerns, acts as the transnational symbol for human-rights abuse and the need to protect those rights. Debates over how one should "properly" remember the

Holocaust are a sign of increased compassion in global society. In America, the Holocaust has long been a universal experience that calls forth universal compassion, a sentiment that is increasingly being adopted elsewhere. The troops in Kosovo are part of a long-term trend when it comes to global compassion. Among other things, the generalized Holocaust perspective, "Never again Auschwitz," provided a justification for it.

We are, of course, aware that this can have an opposite effect and result in emotional distancing. Examples abound of how selective perceptions and, hence, memories can be—one need only think of Africa as the "forgotten continent," or of the millions of children who starve to death every year. Paradoxically, it is the global media that makes us aware of the "limits" of global compassion, as well. The circle of those in need of compassion is expanding, and people in need are forced to compete for the attention of the global audience. The viewers' attention span is short, while the lists of victims are extremely long. Thus, de-territorialized compassion is not evenly distributed (directly and equally) to all victims. It does, however, open up a global forum and under certain circumstances can make people aware of the suffering of others as well as of the world's failure to notice suffering in the past. The issue of human rights has become an integral part of national identity and a dominant *topos* for gaining legitimacy in the eyes of the international community. Consequently, paying lip service to solidarity has been replaced by a normative injunction that developed democracies would find hard to defy. Cosmopolitan memory, which is often the source of distanced compassion in the first place, is a byproduct of news about others' pain and suffering. Such news may seem cynical when it appears alongside mass marketing ads and entertainment programs, but to make an apathetic public compassionate, one must know how much suffering it is able and willing to confront.

"Ethnic Cleansing"

The Kosovo conflict—or, more precisely, its reception—marks a watershed in national remembrance. The political and cultural meaning of the national container is transformed by globalization. This results not in the disappearance of the nation but, rather, in the rise of the global as a context and means for national cultures to define themselves. In brief, the popularization of the term "ethnic cleansing," the controversies surrounding it, and the historical transformation of its meaning are evidence of this trend. What appears at first glance to be a neutral, clear description of despicable combat methods on closer inspection presents itself as a semantic minefield in which the basic elements of national sovereignty are questioned.

The term "ethnic cleansing" has been a rallying cry in international politics since the beginning of the 1990s. The conflicts in the former Yugoslavia have greatly contributed toward defining the specifics of the term—the violent persecution of a people, including murder, torture, and rape—within an international political and legal frame of reference. The fact is all too often overlooked that the forced migration of populations, grouped by race, ethnicity, religion, or other criteria, was formerly considered a legitimate practice in the formation of a nation-state (Preece 2000). In the first half of the twentieth century, such acts of "cleansing" were part of the effort (and the ideal) of drawing territorial borders in line with a homogeneous nation. In contrast to the Holocaust and other instances of mass murder, the main goal of ethnic cleansing is to preserve the identity of a territory or of a particular population. The removal of a minority group, whether it be for ethnic or religious reasons, is a means to an end (in contrast to genocide, in which the annihilation of the minority is an end unto itself). Ever since Woodrow Wilson introduced the idea of "national self-determination" in 1919, which linked the concept of the political community to the independent state, ethnic cleansing has played a central role in international peacekeeping. At that time, the transfer of populations was considered a legitimate method for creating homogeneity within the national territory. The dominant normative function of this perspective is still apparent in the theories of nationalism touted by both defenders and critics of modernization. According to this view, the homogenization of the nation and of territory is a defining characteristic of modern states (Gellner 1983). Such an understanding of politics, based as it is on the national container, has undergone a radical shift since the end of the Cold War. In the past ten years, the international outcry against ethnic cleansing is proof of a normative shift within the international community.

Before 1948, ethnic cleansing was still considered a legitimate way to create international stability; later, it was not (Preece 2000). This is evidence of how new attitudes toward the appropriateness of certain security measures affect the precarious relationship between national and international law.

Since 1948, there have been numerous attempts to combat state discrimination against minorities by implementing international law and imposing sanctions. With the expansion and institutionalization of international law in the past three decades, groundbreaking changes have taken place. Among them are the de-territorialization of sovereign jurisdiction and the concomitant transformation of national sovereignty through international law. The rise of international law is thus indicative of a change in national sovereignty. This notwithstanding, the state is still the central organ for putting political principles into practice, even if those principles often transcend the national container to privilege a cosmopolitan outlook.

With the increase in international forums, which are now endowed with legal and political authority, moral and legal rulings concerning the treatment of minorities have been de-territorialized. Human-rights watches, close observation of armed conflicts, and military intervention are all indicators of new conceptions of international legitimacy. These signal a new solidarity that reaches beyond national borders (Preece 2000). The conflicts in Yugoslavia in the 1990s are no longer compared to the Balkan conflicts during the two world wars. Instead, a symbolically powerful connection is drawn between genocide and the Holocaust. Who is still aware of the fact that the "Great War," World War I, determined the collective memories of nations, ultimately leading to a rise in national chauvinism that culminated in World War II? The memory of the Holocaust superimposes itself on these forms of remembering. International condemnation of ethnic cleansing and forced migration now occurs with the Holocaust as backdrop. The de-territorialization of Holocaust memories opens up to an abstract and hence universally accessible terrain on which cosmopolitan memories can form. This force has evolved, by and large, because of the Americanization of the Holocaust. In the process, a global norm has been established, with human-rights conventions as a guiding principle in international peace- and wartime politics.

The Holocaust Forum in Stockholm and its Consequences

The globalization of this norm and the cosmopolitanization of Holocaust memories are now key components of European politics. The Holocaust is free of any moral ambiguity, and its universal form, coming out of America, has helped Europeans redefine themselves. This was obvious during the 2000 Holocaust Conference in Stockholm, which brought together representatives from more than forty nations. High-ranking politicians from numerous European states participated in the conference to discuss how Europe could "imagine" itself as a community of values. The need to avoid another Holocaust provided a foundation for (official) European memory. Contemporary concerns, such as fighting neo-Nazism, also played a role in anchoring European memory to the Holocaust. The conference helped make this a legitimating model for future military as well as nonmilitary forms of intervention. Here, the formerly sacrosanct nation was made subordinate to the symbolic power of a victim-centered, cosmopolitan memory.

This process has forced Europe to face an entirely new situation. The Holocaust took place in Europe; at the present moment, it is taking a more prominent position than any other event connected to World War II. During the war, nations fought against one another, and Germany was defeated by the Allies. During the Holocaust, it was the ethno-nationalism of Germany and its allies that sought to destroy the "nationless" Jewish culture. After the war, most Europeans identified themselves, for opportunistic reasons, as resistance fighters against the Nazis (Judt 1993). The Nuremberg trials heightened postwar awareness of the need to ensure that National Socialism would never resurface in any form. But this cosmopolitan interpretation, which was imposed from above by the Allies, was interrupted by the Cold War. The Cold War in turn led to an East–West split that displaced the issue of the Holocaust and "re-nationalized" its memory. Nevertheless, the "Western" world was unified not simply through common interests but also through common values. The end of the Cold War fundamentally altered the parameters of the postwar period and made the creation of a de-territorialized, cosmopolitan value system possible.

The memory of the Holocaust is an essential aspect of this development. This is not just a memory that spawns foundational myths oriented toward the past; it is, more significantly, a future-oriented memory. Attempts at post-national solidarity usually arise in response to protests and media coverage of far-reaching environmental dangers. With the Balkan conflicts a new type of danger arose—namely, genocide, which forced Europe to revisit the Holocaust. Cosmopolitanism also creates a space for an ethical politics that can no longer be based purely on the national collective, making cosmopolitan memory possible. Since the Holocaust was itself an attack on cosmopolitanism, it is the event that best expresses the value of cosmopolitanism.

The declaration of the Stockholm International Forum on the Holocaust highlights this fact and institutionalizes the characteristics of a de-territorialized, cosmopolitan memory that we have been analyzing. The universalistic goals of the declaration are laid out in Article 1:

> The Holocaust (Shoah) fundamentally challenged the foundations of civilization. The unprecedented character of the Holocaust will always hold universal meaning. After half a century, it remains an event close enough in time that survivors can still bear witness to the horrors that engulfed the Jewish people. The terrible suffering of the many millions of other victims of the Nazis has left an indelible scar across Europe as well. [22]

Article 2 stresses the importance of the witnesses and of those who came to the victims' aid. It is an appeal to play an active role in determining the fate of innocent victims. True compassion knows no bounds and is never passive:

> The magnitude of the Holocaust, planned and carried out by the Nazis, must be forever seared in our collective memory. The selfless sacrifices of those who defied the Nazis, and sometimes gave their own lives to protect or rescue the Holocaust's victims, must also be inscribed in our hearts. The depths of that horror, and the heights of their heroism, can be touchstones in our understanding of the human capacity for evil and for good.

---

22. For the entire text, see www.holocaustforum.gov.se.

It is obvious that the reference here is not only to World War II. By situating the earlier deeds within a moral context of good and evil, the statement is also aimed at contemporary Europeans, appealing to them to perform similarly selfless acts if necessary.

Explicit reference to this future-oriented memory is made in Article 3:

> With humanity still scarred by genocide, ethnic cleansing, racism, anti-Semitism and xenophobia, the international community shares a solemn responsibility to fight those evils. Together we must uphold the terrible truth of the Holocaust against those who deny it. We must strengthen the moral commitment of our peoples, and the political commitment of our governments, to ensure that future generations can understand the causes of the Holocaust and reflect on its consequences.

Here, the connection between the Holocaust and ethnic cleansing in Yugoslavia provides a springboard for a future-oriented memory.

In the final article of the declaration, the de-territorialized moral lesson that can and must be drawn from the Holocaust is described:

> It is appropriate that this, the first major international conference of the new millennium, declares its commitment to plant the seeds of a better future amidst the soil of a bitter past. We empathize with the victims suffering and draw inspiration from their struggle. Our commitment must be to remember the victims who perished, respect the survivors still with us, and reaffirm humanity's common aspiration for mutual understanding and justice.

The other articles of the declaration are educational and commemorative in nature. The immediate goal is to ensure that the Holocaust becomes an integral part of the European school curriculum. In addition, the project contributes to the creation of a European memory culture, which is urgently needed, given the present controversies about establishing a common culture. Once again, the Holocaust works to de-territorialize memory because it conforms so unequivocally to categories of good and evil. In this way, nationally based memories are transformed through commemoration based on universal principles. It is noteworthy that agreement can be reached about this process precisely when individual countries are no longer grappling with their own actions during the war.

With this declaration, the Holocaust became officially anchored in European memory. Since the end of the Cold War, the Holocaust has become the new founding moment for Europe. It is, of course, no coincidence that this moment followed in the wake of the Americanization process. An annual day of remembrance (27 January, commemorating the liberation of Auschwitz) is now observed in many countries throughout Europe. Significantly, the commemoration of Auschwitz was the first new memorial day to be established in the new millennium. Its importance is underscored by the debate that erupted in Great Britain when Holocaust Memorial Day was first celebrated in 2001.[23] Many people criticized the Memorial Day as too narrowly focused on German crimes while ignoring "other" acts of genocide, such as the mass murder of Armenians at the hands of the Turks, and as playing down the history of British anti-Semitism.[24]

The effects of these developments extend beyond Europe and the United States to include places that had no direct geographical or historical connection to the Holocaust. Japan serves as a good example. The war crimes and massacres perpetrated by the Japanese during World War II cost millions of lives in China, Korea, Indonesia, the Philippines, and Singapore. As is often the case with such historical topics, a good deal of controversy has centered on determining the exact number of dead. Some estimate the death toll to be as high as 50 million (Kristof 1998). Until recently, Japan refused to apologize, seeing itself instead as the victim of American nuclear aggression. This is slowly starting to change, however. A number of publications mark this shift in attitude, including Iris Chang's *The Rape of*

---

23. For a representative piece, see Hutton 2000. For the British government's official representation, see www.holocaustmemorialday.gov.uk.

24. That was in 2000. Four years later, the same conference pushed its drive towards universalization even further. The name of the 2004 conference was "Preventing Genocide: Threats and Responsibilities." The Holocaust was pushed completely into the background. The theme now was to prevent injustice in the future. (For a short statement of the conference agenda, see www.preventinggenocide.com/files/declaration.pdf.) Even more, Israel was depicted as one of the major culprits in conducting genocide. The Israeli government decided to lower the rank of its participating delegation, and many delegates directed their criticism against the Bush administration. With the divisions among European and American/Israeli perceptions, we can see how cosmopolitanized memory is realigned along new fault lines.

Nanking: The Forgotten Holocaust of World War II (1997).[25] In addition, an international organization has been formed, the Global Alliance for Preserving the History of World War II in Asia (AOHWA), whose website documents Japan's crimes. Japan's neighbors have not forgotten, of course, and refuse to accept Japan's portrayal of itself as an innocent victim of nuclear war. China and Korea have museums that document Japanese crimes and still consider Hiroshima appropriate punishment for Japan's acts of aggression.

In contrast to the slaughter of the Jews, the massacres committed by Japan were part of the war. Despite historiographical attempts to include the Holocaust as part of the war experiences, it is clearly a separate event. The Holocaust remains the exception—an exception that has become the norm in Second Modernity for victims of all types of aggression. Hiroshima has always been officially justified by the United States as a necessary evil to bring the war to a speedier conclusion. (Similarly, the Allies justified their air raids on Hamburg and Dresden as a mixture of military tactics and revenge for Germany's aggression.) These cases are also being absorbed into the master narrative of the Holocaust. According to this narrative, there are no "guilty" victims in Second Modernity, only innocent ones. This perspective is part of the greater cosmopolitanizing mechanism of Second Modernity. All victims have become Jews. This explains why Japan has shown some readiness to apologize for its crimes and offer restitution (Barkan 2000). Like Germany, it can join the ranks of victims only if it officially declares itself a perpetrator.

Reflexive Memory: Reflections on the Controversy over the "Real" Anne Frank

Let us return briefly to the question of Anne Frank, the girl who became a Holocaust icon. Could Anne Frank perhaps be the personal Holocaust symbol of Second Modernity? Why and how has she become the personification of the Holocaust? More than half a million people visit the Anne Frank house in Amsterdam each year, and numerous traveling exhibits all over the world relate her story. From

---

25. The subtitle of the book explicitly connects Japanese and German atrocities.

the first publication of the book to the stage and film productions in the late 1950s, the diary has been available in a great variety of forms. Since the 1980s in particular, American interest in Anne Frank's story has been rekindled. In 1985, a musical based on her story titled *Yours, Anne* was staged. With the passing of time, Anne Frank's status as the most important symbol of the Holocaust has only grown. For a long time now, Anne Frank has signified not only the Holocaust as a historical event or her own personal memories. Instead, contemporary debates tend to focus on her representative role. From the very beginning, controversy has surrounded the proper presentation of her diary. This was especially true in the case of the stage adaptation, which prompted Meyer Levin to criticize Goodrich and Hackett's version for obscuring the story's Jewish element. [26]

Authenticity does not stem the tide of interpretation or of political and cultural transformations, however. Renewed debates in the past decade reveal how much memories have changed. It is not questions about authenticity that are at the center of these debates but, rather, question about the accuracy of memories—more specifically, the memory of memories. To put it another way, the debate is no longer about the Holocaust but about its representation and its political and cultural consequences. Jon Blair's 1995 film *Anne Frank Remembered* highlights this reflexivity. In the film, as well as in Wendy Kesselman's 1997 adaptation of Goodrich and Hackett's *The Diary of Anne Frank* for Broadway, the debates from the 1950s are presented as part of a revisionist interpretation. The diary is re-contextualized, and the "non-Jewish" version is corrected.

All of this sparked a debate among some American intellectuals as to whether the Holocaust should be presented as a specifically Jewish experience or accepted as a didactic tool for communicating

---

26. A further point of debate concerned passages deleted by Otto Frank, which included sexually explicit descriptions and had to do with Anne Frank's troubled relationship with her mother. With the publication of the critical edition in 1986, the problem seemed to be solved. It was later revealed, however, that Otto Frank had deleted an additional five pages of the original manuscript shortly before his death in 1980. Nevertheless, the critical edition put out by the Netherlands Institute for War Documentation provides authentic insight into the diary as written by Anne Frank.

universal values.[27] What is often overlooked in these debates is the fact that these two positions are no longer mutually exclusive. As we have seen, with the rise of cosmopolitanism in Second Modernity, the dichotomy between particular and universal memory has disappeared. In light of this, the revisionist position that reintroduces the Jewish component is no longer necessarily a particularistic one. In today's context, particularistic claims frequently take on universal significance. This brings us back to our thesis—namely, that as representative of the foreign, the Jewish experience provides a paradigm for shaping new ethical models in Second Modernity. At the same time, the diary retains its metaphorical power and has been consciously applied to other situations. In the 1990s, a number of diaries inspired by Anne Frank contributed to the storehouse of moral and ethical pronouncements—for example, Zlata Filipovic's *Zlata's Diary: A Child in Sarajevo* (1995), which was written during the war in Bosnia. The universality of Anne Frank's book lies precisely not in its historical specificity and corresponding memories of the past. It is coming to represent much less a past characterized by evil than a message for the future that transcends the past. This bears the mark of memory in Second Modernity—namely, that it consciously takes up the past to form new memories for the future.

---

27. See, for instance, the debate among Cynthia Ozick, Ralph Melnick, and Ian Buruma in *New York Review of Books* in 1998 and 1999.

7

The Consequences of
Cosmopolitan Memory

WHAT HAPPENS WHEN historical time is no longer in sync with national time? When memory is no longer determined by a closed collective and becomes fragmented, multifarious, and as unreliable as individual memory? Memories are no longer coherently tied to place and time. They are losing their solidity and are becoming liquid.[1] This does not mean that they will disappear completely, or that cosmopolitan societies are devoid of memory or even arbitrary. As we have shown, they emerge from national memories, refer back to them, transform those old memories, fall back on them, and so on, but they never disappear completely. From this perspective, new limits are placed on the "imagining" of memories. At the same time, these imagined memories have very real consequences, which provide new forms of security. Like the original sin inherited by Christians, Europeans, and, above all, Germans, the memory of the Holocaust supplies, in its hybrid incarnations, a new form of security by providing a gauge for personal suffering.

Second Modernity and globalization are also associated with Jews, which is perhaps one reason that opposition to it is often vocal and emotionally laden, at times bordering on xenophobia. In First Modernity, Jews were accused of being rootless cosmopolitans and thus not patriotic, which is exactly the situation that the State of Israel rectified. This very rootlessness, however, has become precisely the desired alternative for people who no longer can or want to situate themselves

---

1. For "liquidity" as a metaphor of today's modernity, see Bauman 2000.

within the particular spatial and temporal coordinates of a nation. We are not referring here to the "citizens of the world" as conceived by Kant and other Enlightenment thinkers. Nor are we proposing globalization as the brainchild of peripatetic social scientists who either embrace Enlightenment thought as a liberating utopia or denounce it as a nightmarish loss of community. Instead, what we have is a concrete realization of cosmopolitanism formed from historical experience, political contingencies, and cultural developments. This type of cosmopolitanism constitutes the horizon of values and experience for a growing number of individuals.

The changing relationship between national and cosmopolitan memory is shaped by two decisive historical developments: 1) from the memory of World War II, which in the past ten years has focused less on the war itself than on the Holocaust as the "emblem of the 20th Century" (Diner 1999); and 2) from social memory of the fall of the Iron Curtain, which signaled the end of the of the postwar period. Both factors accelerate the process in which memory becomes cosmopolitan in that they put in question the "imagined community of the nation." Today, the focus is not only on a "friend-versus-foe" dichotomy. It is on victims—victims without heroes. Without heroes, cracks appear in the national container. The nation is narrated and conceived not in a heroic account but, rather, through skeptical memories that abjure the earlier whitewashing of the past.

In the nineteenth century, the "invention of the nation" was based on conceptions of heroism and founding myths that were conveyed through "traditional" and "exemplary" forms of narratives (Rüsen 1982). In contrast, World War II, the Holocaust, and, later, a self-critical historical narrative were all deeply etched in the European consciousness in the second half of the twentieth century. While traditional and exemplary narratives borrow from history to promote foundational myths, the critical narrative relies on history to question national tradition.

It is also necessary, however, to look at non-European narratives, because Europe and the United States are no longer alone determining historical narratives. Charles Maier (2000) has argued that, in non-Western countries in the second half of the twentieth century,

European imperialism and colonialism played a greater rol͜ cal narrative than the Holocaust. Hannah Arendt (1958) attemp͵ identify a common context for these disparate historical phenomen͏ Drawing the connection between colonialism and the Holocaust, as well as subsequent reparations, demands a cosmopolitan approach. Within a global context, what are the links between colonialism and the Holocaust? For one thing, they are linked by a mutual concept of "human rights." When the United Nations passed the Universal Declaration of Human Rights in 1948 as a globally binding standard, the memory of the Holocaust was still very immediate.[2] It is hardly conceivable that the declaration would have been proclaimed without the Holocaust, even though the Holocaust at the time was regarded as one among many events connected to the war. The memory of the Holocaust problematizes the conception of a "universality" of human rights, however. Protection of human rights entails a limiting of individual states' sovereignty (as the bombing of the Federal Republic of Yugoslavia proved in 1999), and new institutions have been created that would be unthinkable without human-rights conventions (the International Criminal Court, to name a recent and prominent example). Human-rights directives are meant to protect those people who are persecuted by the state in which they live, precisely the form of protection that was denied to Jews in World War II. Human rights and their violation create a moral space in which there is no longer any uncertainty. The oppressed must be "innocent" and the oppressors "evil," a global religion in which Jews and Nazis serve as the basic prototypes. Consequently, those who claim that their rights have been violated create a connection between their suffering and that of the Jews, and their oppressors become likened to Nazis. This connection was successfully made in the case of Kosovo. "Never again Srebrenica" was not enough; the slogan heard around the world was "Never again Auschwitz," which presented itself as a historical paradigm for instances where citizens were stripped of their rights and murdered by their "own" state. The Holocaust is an example of how "civil rights," as envisioned by Thomas Hobbes, one

---

2. For a summary of the debates about the passage of the Universal Declaration of Human Rights, see Ignatieff 1999.

...s of First Modernity, are no longer adequate in ... for individuals. Consequently, after the Holo-
...guidelines were implemented to protect citizens
...s.

..., that the concept of human rights that is growing
...lightenment (which is why the Holocaust stands
... f the Enlightenment) harks back to a "European"
experience. The limiting of state sovereignty, however, is not a purely European and American phenomenon. After the war, the same Western nations that signed the declaration were held accountable for human-rights violations in their colonies. The socialist states that signed were also confronted with accusations of human-rights infringements. During the Cold War, it was not possible to implement global human-rights policies. Subsequently, however, transnational organizations such as Amnesty International and Doctors without Borders have served as human-rights watchdogs in the most distant regions of the world. Even opponents of the declaration are required to abide by it and devise their own, often contrary, sets of rules. Specific moral viewpoints are then incorporated into the globalized system of reference. Those who can present themselves as "innocent victims" are deemed in the "right." Thus, it is becoming increasingly difficult to ignore these international agreements, even if some view them as part of the Western system of domination. The mass media see to it that news about infractions is communicated in "deterritorialized" fashion around the world.

Besides de-territorialization, another feature of cosmopolitan memory is reflexivity. Reflexivity is evident in the reversed relationship between history and memory. Memories have a strong emotional component, whereas history is supposed to be limited to an analytical understanding of the past (Nora 1996). Today, the majority of Europeans rely on memory when it comes to thinking about the nation and its heroic victims. Historically based memories of the nation exist, but they are no longer driven exclusively by emotional content. Instead, what is often debated in determining a national self-image is the way in which those memories are articulated in public discourse. Seen in this light, national identity is no longer a dominant (or dominating) collective ideology based on a mythological past. Instead, it presents itself as a conscious choice that speaks to individual preferences for certain memories. These choices are not arbitrary, however. Our thesis is that they are increasingly driven by the way in which the Holocaust is remembered. Historic remembrance of the Holocaust (and its future-oriented inclusion of genocide and ethnic cleansing) has become a symbol for a critical national stance toward the past. As such, it has repressed the mythological memory of the heroic nation. The new types of mythological memories are oriented toward victims rather than perpetrators or heroes. The Holocaust thus now serves as a universal "container" for memories of myriad victims. This has also resulted in the "universalizing of evil."

We are not claiming, of course, that Second Modernity progresses in a continuous, linear fashion to replace the nation. Rather, we approach this as a dialectic process between the global and the local. Specifically, this is a process that is often fraught with conflict and that emerges from the opposition between globalization and the nation-oriented model of First Modernity. Despite—or, maybe, precisely because of—the resistance of the nation, concrete transnational trends are appearing that reflect a cosmopolitan orientation.

Memories Oriented toward the Past and the Future

De-territorialization and the accompanying cosmopolitan memory appear in different forms based on different temporal models. We distinguish here between memories that refer back to the past and ones that point to the future. In First Modernity, reference to the past bolstered the myth of national continuity. In Second Modernity, collective memories often follow a self-reflexive model that demythologizes first religion and then the nation while at the same time it is cognizant of discontinuities. Cosmopolitan memory also means that the future is no longer mechanistically driven by the past. Like the present, it is unpredictable (Beck and Bonss 2001). Collective memory in Second Modernity is freed from naturalized categories (e.g., the nation) and turns toward symbols (e.g., the Holocaust) to try to come to terms with an uncertain future rather than to celebrate a certain past. This becomes programmatic for a world full of insecurities:

> All concepts can be shaped according to one's perspective, whether it be from the point of view of the past, present, or future. The presence

of the past is different from that of the future ... the notion of one "present society" is wrong, since the present becomes in principle ambiguous. It is split between the present-past and the present-future. (Beck and Bonss 2001: 12)

The future is also no longer what it used to be—namely, a linear process propelled by the concept of progress. In terms of theories of memory, the legacy of the Holocaust is an important marker in the transition from First to Second Modernity. This is not a smooth transformation; it is riddled with conflicts and uncertainties connected to the dwindling power of the nation as a producer of meaning. Thus, it is no accident that, since the 1990s, the concept of collective memory has also changed. In many respects, interest has shifted to the collective memories of national, regional, and local entities from the earlier dominant *topos* of nationalism.

In Germany, the theme of the nation has had negative connotations since 1949 because of the history of National Socialism. Until reunification, attempts to reverse this trend were thwarted.[3] It is thus questionable whether one could even come up with a unified culture (*Leitkultur*) in Germany that is positive and would not simply serve to exclude the Other. This kind of self-criticism, which before the Cold War could be dismissed as unique to the German case, has now become the norm throughout Europe. Critically revisiting the past has crept in even in countries where the concept of the national was considered something positive (e.g., France). The homogeneity of national time is disrupted by the present time of the "Other." Thanks to immigration, demographic shifts, and the demands of multicultural societies with a post- and trans-nationalist bent, alterity now plays a vital role. Of course, this does not signal the complete demise of the nation, just as religion did not disappear completely with the transition to First Modernity. Since the uncertainties and insecurities associated with the shift from First to Second Modernity persist, the nation and other imagined communities must share the same space. This does not mean, however, that they share the same time. We must tread cautiously at this point, however, for neither modernity

---

3. See the Historians' Dispute and the vehement criticism of Kohl's treatment of history in Maier 1988.

nor any subsequent era marks an absolute end to religions and to cultural identities. Nevertheless, these identities undergo a type of transformation that allows them to blend with other religions and identities. The walls of dogmatism are crumbling. This is the opportunity that cosmopolitanism has opened up for many people. In this way, the virtual Holocaust has had unexpected consequences.

Given these developments, the nation as a homogeneous entity can no longer be easily mobilized. Cosmopolitan memory exists as one among many forms of memory. The future-oriented function of memory that we have described is by no means the only aspect of contemporary memory, but it represents a temporary reorientation. Examples of memories still oriented toward the past include the preoccupation with legacies and traditions; interest in genealogy; nostalgia; and, as mentioned, the obsession with collective memory.

The year 1989 symbolizes not only the end of the postwar era; it also determines the memory of the prewar years. The end of the postwar era has now also become part of history and, as such, plays a role in identity formation. What we have here is a shift in which the nation no longer plays a vital role in terms of autobiographical memory. After 1989, the nation was either discredited or replaced with a transnational orientation. Which past are we commemorating? The foundational myth of the postwar era, now fueled by a consumer-oriented ideology and practice and, since the 1990s, by the revived legacy of the Holocaust, is working to unravel the nationalist myths of the prewar era. Memories of the Holocaust vacillate between the deeds (or misdeeds) of specific nations during the war and countries' subsequent failure to come to terms with their past actions in a critical fashion.

Thus, future-oriented cosmopolitan memory can become part of the foundation for an emerging global civic society. In contrast to the cosmopolitans of the eighteenth century, this is not simply about the experiences of and exchanges between intellectuals. It is about values transmitted through the mass media, nation-states, and supranational institutions. These norms, which are now globally "available," are reaching an increasingly large audience and are thereby becoming more democratic. Globalization promotes these developments, and conversely, the acceptance of such norms is a necessary prerequisite for participating in globalization. States that seek to withdraw from this process suddenly find themselves under "global" pressure. To this day, for instance, Turkey has refused officially to recognize the genocide of the Armenians in 1915 and to apologize for the killings. Its refusal to offer reparations is more striking when the Armenian genocide is classified within the categories of the Holocaust—and when it is even regarded as a precursor to the slaughter of the Jews (Mazower 1998). For Turkey to acknowledge this would mean having to concede that even Turkey's heroic past is built on a "legacy of sin."[4] This would also push World War I as a "European catastrophe" back into the limelight. In this way, the Holocaust becomes a European, not just a German, problem. A new European awareness of its past as a "dark continent" is emerging.[5] One consequence of this development is that it allows Germany to be "normal" again. The things that conservative historians, in their debates about the "past that won't go away," tried but failed to accomplish are now anchored at an institutional level. This was brought into sharp relief when German fighter jets flew over Kosovo.

The Stockholm conference underscored the connection between the specifically Jewish experience of the Holocaust and the new mission that Europe has set for itself. In his closing speech, German's cultural affairs minister, Michael Naumann, stressed this connection:

> In the Holocaust, the dehumanization of politics under totalitarian terror became horrifically evident. Historical reflection cannot master the past—the past is over. Rather, the legacy of this genocide demands from the present an answer to the central question: What constitutes the dignity of humanity if not that of life? How can it be protected from future genocidal attempts? In the remembrance of the Holocaust we must find the right answer for politics and society of future history. (Naumann 2000)

Holocaust remembrance is marked by various taboos in different countries. Nevertheless, it is no coincidence that the memory of the Holocaust is playing an increasingly central role in a transnational, global arena. As we have noted, Jews, or more specifically, their

4. For a comparison of the Holocaust and the Armenian genocide, see Melson 1992. For an account of current political conflicts of interest, see Mazower 2001.

5. See Mazower 1998. For an analysis connecting World War I to the Holocaust, see Bartov 2000.

media representations, are the most important carriers—indeed, the very personification—of cosmopolitan memories. As the ultimate attempt to eradicate cosmopolitanism, the Holocaust is *the* defining tragedy for Jews (and precisely not for political victims). That is the social foundation for the historical "uniqueness" of the Holocaust, which was often translated and reinterpreted in moral terms. This is why no other catastrophe could play the same role in the memory of Second Modernity. A moral significance is attached to the Holocaust that is separate from its historical and territorial origins.

As an emblem of remembrance for the twentieth century, the Holocaust is shaping forms of remembrance for the future. Our perspective on the century that recently came to a close becomes clearer if one keeps in mind Maier's distinction between moral and structural narratives:

> The growing emphasis on metaphoric truths guarantees that the 20th century will remain a vital historical point of reference. My position is not that the historical period will not be considered important, but rather that its significance will lie in meaning-producing, moral narratives, not in structural or analytical ones.... Century markers often provide the chronological boundary for what we recognize as moral narratives.... The 20th century is not, first and foremost, a chronological unity; it is a moral epoch. (Maier 2000: 811–12)

This distinction explains why the "lessons" of the Holocaust stem not from an actual historical awareness—which historians like to claim as their own—but from the possibility of spreading, via the media, a moral narrative.

Maier distinguishes between two moral narratives. One of them comes out of the West and is determined by the Holocaust and by Stalinism; the other comes from the "rest of the world," a reference to non-Western civilizations. In the global age, these different narratives blend together. This becomes obvious if one looks at the case of Israel. The Jewish Holocaust was always considered a problematic event in the eyes of Arab intellectuals, since many considered it a means for Israel to legitimate its oppression of the Palestinians. Since Israel often compared the Arabs to Nazis (see chapter 5), the Holocaust often met with denial from Arabs. During the 1990s and in the aftermath of the Oslo Accords, this equation began to change. The first step was the recognition of the Holocaust as a problem of European modernity, for which the Palestinians in the Middle East had to pay the price.[6] The Europeanization of the Holocaust—which was, of course, influenced by the theories of the Frankfurt School and by Zygmunt Baumann's analysis—enables Arabs not only to recognize the Holocaust but also to take a position similar to that of the "new historians." This marks the culmination of a universalizing process that, with its emphasis on expulsion, ironically is also a Europeanization. It was bolstered by the willingness of Israeli critics to put the 1947–48 flight (the so-called Nakbah) and expulsion of Arabs from Palestine on par with the Holocaust.[7] Mutual recognition of suffering universalizes the Holocaust in a way that enables the Palestinians to present themselves as victims, as well. This becomes even more apparent on a symbolical level when Palestinians adopt the same rituals used in the Israeli Holocaust Remembrance Day to commemorate the Nakbah—namely, observing two minutes of silence throughout the Occupied Territories.

The cosmopolitan understanding of the Holocaust is transposed onto other conflicts, as well—above all, in addressing the Holocaust against the "Other" (regardless of the fact that the West continues to focus on the Jewish victims). Stalinism, Nazism's main European competitor, is often referred to as the "Red Holocaust" (Courtois et al. 1999; Rothenhäusler and Sonderegger 2000). We should mention at this point that the Holocaust is not being used here on a purely metaphorical level, as a way to refer to all catastrophes. As we have shown in this chapter, memories of the Holocaust have now become associated with very concrete political and legal procedures. As Maier notes, the Holocaust narrative has retained its force "less because of the existence of contemporary horror scenarios than because it is associated with due legal process, reparations, and debates about the appropriate form of historical remembrance" (Maier 2000: 827).

---

6. For a change in attitude about the Holocaust among Arab intellectuals, see Bashara 1995; Saghiyeh and Bashir 2000; Said 1999.

7. For examples of Israeli proponents of this position, see Gur-Zeev 1999; Kimmerling 1998.

According to Maier, this means that the Western narrative about the Holocaust has finally come to a close.

We, however, have reached the opposite conclusion. It is precisely the foreseeable end to autobiographical remembrance of the Holocaust—which has come into the limelight once more with the most recent legal battles and reparation payments—and the global transformation of these memories that has made the Holocaust, as a mode of remembering, cosmopolitan. The Holocaust sets the parameters for de-territorialized memoryscapes in Second Modernity, provides a model for national self-critique, serves to promote human rights as a legitimating principle in the global community, and plainly offers a negative example of dealing with alterity.

Conclusion

Given all this, how can we now conceive of the future? The security of a future that grows out of a homogeneous past no longer exists; the future can no longer be thought of using the old model of the past. Through their "imagined" security, national and ethnic memories sparked resistance and thus led to new insecurities. The cultural foundations of Second Modernity are built on the institutions of First Modernity. Cosmopolitan memory, which is establishing itself in Europe as the new "European remembrance," grows out of a plurality of national and ethnic memories. In the immediate aftermath of World War II, the war and its atrocities were downplayed in the public culture of remembrance. Modernization meant, among other things, conceiving of a new future, and the view was forward-looking. We have shown how these processes have played out under different circumstances, albeit with some similarities, in German, American, and Israeli society. In all three cases, what resulted was a silence surrounding the Holocaust. The Cold War split the political world into opposing camps and led to coalition-building among countries. The Holocaust then became embedded in the national politics of those individual states. Cultural processes, however, often are not reliable partners in politics, and ethnic-group politics, coupled with popular culture, is a powerful enough force to introduce an alternative remembrance of the Holocaust. After the fall of the Berlin Wall and the search for cultural reorientation, images of the Holocaust were taken out of their original historical context to serve as a symbol of "evil" per se. They became mutable and liquid as a way to quell the fears that pervaded the new epoch. The transition from First to Second Modernity is thus accompanied by a new cultural understanding of the Holocaust—an understanding that assigns to it a new value as a cultural fundament. In becoming increasingly cosmopolitan, the world needs a cosmopolitan type of memory, which the Holocaust can provide.

New European remembrance of the event, which the United States and Israel have also had a hand in shaping, breaks down the boundaries between "inner" and "outer." As is the case with national borders, the borders of memory are constantly being redrawn. Just as "ethnicities" are constituting themselves independently of the nation-state, collective memory is forming in new places. One of these places is the "dark continent" of Europe. The past is wiped out because countries can no longer simply declare themselves neutral or claim that they were enemies of Nazism; now, everyone is guilty. Sweden's and Switzerland's history of neutrality has come under scrutiny. An effort has been under way for some time now to look more closely at the resistance movement in France; Eastern Europe has also jumped on the bandwagon.[8] Now, Europe is considered the aggressor, with the European Jews as the victims. The old formula in which Germany was the "guilty" party implied that the rest of Europe was "innocent." Now everyone is guilty. Because they defy the old national boundaries, memories of the Holocaust are situated at the junction of First and Second Modernity. These memories must be approached in a new way. The unrepresentability of the Holocaust, the monstrous atrocity, the helplessness of the victims, the indifference, and also, quite frequently, the collaboration of the "bystanders" have all helped imbue the event with an iconic significance as a benchmark for moral judgment. The dichotomy of helpless victims and gruesome criminals offers a sense of moral assurance and security—perhaps the only remaining security in the new, uncertain world of Second Modernity.

---

8. For an overview of this trend, see the analyses of individual countries in Deak et al. 2000.

Thus, the Holocaust has become the bitterest reminder of the consequences of national self-certainty in First Modernity. The heroic (national) narrative can no longer claim a monopoly and is now complemented by a skeptical (self-reflexive) cosmopolitan orientation. Auschwitz, as modernity's breakdown in civilization and as the frontier between civilization and barbarism, corresponds to the civilizational break, the uncertainty about one's own world, and, above all, about the discontinuities that characterize Second Modernity.

Nevertheless, the question arises as to whether this cultural openness and its structures of consciousness can actually be institutionalized or whether cosmopolitanism will have to make due without any concrete cosmopolitan institutions. In addition to debates, museums, and memorials, the increase in restitution claims by the most diverse groups of victims against past and present perpetrators is an important institutional feature of a cosmopolitan set-up. Amends can and should be made in the face of wrongdoing.

Reparations, Forgiveness, and Guilt as Pillars of Reflexive Modernization

Memories of the Holocaust are both a catalyst and a model for an increasingly prevalent global politics that is focused on "guilt" and "forgiveness." While the Holocaust is a key component, this does not suggest that its memory should be understood as a timeless totality. Over the course of time, various fragments of the event are highlighted as cosmopolitan, and the memories proper are loosened from their origins to become independent. As mentioned, 1989 was a watershed in the formation of memory cultures. This temporal icon represents a break in so-called postwar history. It seems that the political changes and the fall of dictatorships in that year spawned new forms of guilt and atonement. Reparations, appearing in a universalized form that is no longer connected to the original process of negotiations between Israel and Germany in the 1950s, are now vital components of Second Modernity. Growing de-nationalization and de-territorialization of models of collective identity lead to the creation of moral interdependence, which, in turn, is based on cosmopolitan memories. With this, spaces for constituting new "communities of fate" open up and take root outside the boundaries of the nation-state. This growing politics of reparations can serve as a normative alternative to more traditional forms of solidarity and belonging. Elazar Barkan (2000) has termed this the "new guilt of nations." Barkan delineates a new international ethics that is characterized not just by seeking to bring others to justice but, above all, by countries' willingness to admit to their own guilt—a second Enlightenment, so to speak. In the present context, it will certainly come as no surprise that it is Germany, with its willingness to provide reparations, that provides the model for this process. Germany not only made reparations to the "winners" of the war, but also—and this is what is radically new about these reparations—to the "losers," the victims.[9] This opened the door for the claims of other victim's groups, from the aboriginal peoples of Australia to the Japanese interned by Americans during World War II to the victims of Japanese aggression. The list continues to grow.

The national catastrophe of the Holocaust was removed from its historical context and reformulated in a global context. Today, when an admission of guilt is accompanied by material repayment, it is the Holocaust and its reparations—the Jewish and German memories—that have provided this global phenomenon with an institutional framework. According to John Torpey (2001), the Holocaust and its globalization have set the standard for such demands. Despite the long prehistory of reparations for war crimes, the general trend toward offering compensation to groups because of past injustices is above all a result of reactions to the Holocaust.

A politics of "forgiveness," which Arendt upheld as a political principle at the end of the 1950s as a way to render politics more pragmatic, is now emerging into the limelight. Nothing is permanent; every decision can be reversed. In this way, politics becomes an act of beginning—that is, religious creation translated into politics. (Arendt 1958). Although Christian in its origins, forgiveness has abandoned its Christian container. When a Japanese minister apologizes to Koreans

---

9. It thus comes as no surprise that an anti-Semitic rhetoric has sought to delegitimize the reparations payments and the demands for restitution as so-called war profiteering. The groups who level such charges overlook the radical shift that enabled such reparations to be made in the first place.

or Chinese, he adopts a "Christian" language, although the cultures in question are not part of the biblical or the European tradition. It is difficult in such cases to escape this ethic.

Despite the European origins of forgiveness and the dominance of the West, it would be false to see this as a new form of "moral imperialism." The discourse of making amends is based not on an absolute, universalist ethics but, rather, on cultural negotiations with the Other. This cultural dialogue entails a rethinking of the ruling dichotomy between globalism and localism in First Modernity, as well as that of universalism and particularism. The trend toward reparations is being fueled not only by a generalized legal concept, but also by the smallest common denominator that takes into account local particularities. This often entails an ad hoc conception of justice that, in embracing the global culture of human rights, determines various negotiations between local demands and universal expectations.

All this does not mean that we live in a world free of "interests." Rather, it is a world in which the line between ideals and material interests is blurred. Our global world is, of course, also a capitalist one. Moral cosmopolitanism is closely linked to market cosmopolitanism. When one talks about reparations, one is talking about money. Linking the Holocaust to money has always been considered problematic.[10] In some world views, money and commerce are seen as the right hand of the devil. Nevertheless, there continue to be cases today in which non-Jewish groups are trying to gain compensation for former injustices with money. One principle of global ethics has been made concrete through the universalization of the Holocaust: Victims can expect reparations from the guilty party.

Money does not right past wrongs, of course, for we still live under the sway of a pre-bourgeois idea that honor and dignity have no price. Ironically, this is one of the oldest anti-Semitic arguments. According to this logic, Jews never had any honor and dignity, for they were always after money. Nevertheless, in the 1950s many Jews in Israel and elsewhere refused "blood money" because they adhered to these ideas of honor. If money does not buy honor and dignity, then what

---

10. See Finkelstein 2000 for a bitter leftist critique of the commercialization of the Holocaust.

can be done? In the pre-bourgeois world, one restored one's honor by seeking revenge against one's enemy or his people, but this is not an option today. Money is the means for promising amelioration, even if it does not buy forgiveness. At the very least, in a bourgeois society based on equality, financial compensation forces former enemies to negotiate a contract, thereby altering the course of their relationship. Thus, one should not look for contradictions where none exist. In the twenty-first century, "paid pardons" are part of Second Modernity.

We would like to point here to a unique feature of German monetary reparations. During the negotiations between Konrad Adenauer and David Ben-Gurion, the relationship between the two nations they represented was at stake. The individuality of the victims was relevant to the extent that it was possible to group them according to national identity. (That is also a reason that the Sinti and Roma were skipped over when it came to financial compensation.) In this sense, Israel was recognized at least symbolically as representing all Jews, and the Federal Republic of Germany was the mouthpiece of the German nation, despite—or, perhaps, precisely because of—the division of Germany. In the Eichmann trial, the defendant stood accused in the name of the Jewish people. In contrast to this state-propelled process, today's politics of reparations is not exclusively national; it is often initiated by private parties. To an even greater extent, legal cases involve the misdeeds of states rather than individuals. The plaintiffs are often heterogeneous groups that organize through class-action suits against states, businesses, and institutions. While the indictments are frequently aimed at specific nations, the plaintiffs are often from more than one country.

The proliferation and privatization of reparations politics points to an attenuation of the national frame of reference. Material compensation is surely not the only area in which national law is being supplanted by international human-rights guidelines. For example, in discussing immigration and citizenship issues, Yasemin Soysal talks about the separation of civil rights and territorial membership (Soysal 1994). As Soysal notes, the extension of social and civil rights to noncitizens grows out of global norms that are based on ideas of the "individual person," not their nationality. This explanation is in line with the promulgating and institutionalizing of human rights through various nongovernmental organizations. The consolidating of the European Union and other transnational organizations also works to promote international forums of justice. This not only provides an institutional foundation for taking legal action. It also provides a global human-rights discourse through which states can legitimate themselves. What we have, then, is a de-territorialized model of legitimation that is not hemmed in by national boundaries. What is at stake is not only bringing the past into the present, but also the projection of a common form of remembrance for the future. That projection is sustained by a cosmopolitan orientation that grows out of recognition of the particular and the institutionalization of the universal.

We will end on a cautionary note. Cosmopolitan memory also produces old–new enemies. The battle is not only over the past, but also over the future. But which future is meant? Opponents of cosmopolitanism seek to usher in a renaissance of counter-modernity. Tradition is on the rise again. Xenophobia and the essentializing of one's own identity are being pedaled alongside the repertoire of memories. What role does the Holocaust play in all this? In Israel, it is used to uphold the friend–foe dichotomy; in Germany, it is used to maintain an opposition between a "good" and "bad" *Sonderweg*. It can even lead to an outright denial of the Holocaust. In the United States, counter-modernity serves to hone an image of America as liberator, thus promoting the violent unleashing of "God's Country" as savior nation throughout the world.

Nevertheless, one must ask: Is the twenty-first century realizing the promises set forth by the Enlightenment thinkers of the eighteenth century? Can the ideals of the intellectual elites be rendered democratic? Can precisely the "catastrophic" twentieth century (or the century of catastrophes) serve as a mnemonic foundation to achieve these goals? Can a perspective be formed that pits the universal cosmopolitan state of mind against the particular attributes of the nation? Whatever one's opinion of globalization, it cannot be denied that the victims of particularism are benefiting from a new openness in the world and a form of justice that often represents their only hope (and protection) against the forces of national exclusionism. Who says that globalization is perfect, anyway?

Bibliography

Adenauer, Konrad. 1949. *Verhandlungen des Deutschen Bundestages. Stenographische Berichte*, 1949/5/27, 30.

Adorno, Theodor W. 1959. "Was bedeutet: Aufarbeitung der Vergangenheit." Pp. 10–28 in Theodor W. Adorno, *Erziehung zur Mündigkeit*. Frankfurt: Suhrkamp.

———. 1989. *Studien zum autoritären Charakter*. Frankfurt: Suhrkamp.

Adorno, Theodor W., and Max Horkheimer. 1999 (1944). *Dialectic of Enlightenment*. New York: Continuum.

Adorno, Theodor, W., Else Frenkel-Brunswik, and Daniel J. Levinson. 1950. *The Authoritarian Personality*. New York: Harper.

Albrow, Martin. 1996. *The Global Age*. Stanford, Calif.: Stanford University Press.

Alexander, Jeffrey. 2002. "On the Social Construction of Moral Universals: The Holocaust from War Crime to Trauma Drama." *European Journal of Social Theory 5*, no. 1: 5–85.

Andersen, Arne. 1997. *Der Traum vom Guten Leben: Alltags- und Konsumgeschichte vom Wirtschaftswunder bis Heute*. Frankfurt: Campus.

Anderson, Benedict. 1991. *Imagined Communities: Reflections on the Origin and Spread of Nationalism*. London: Verso.

Arendt, Hannah. 1950. "Social Science Techniques and the Study of Concentration Camps." *Jewish Social Studies 12*: 49–64.

———. 1958 (1951). *The Origins of Totalitarianism*. London: Allen and Unwin.

———. 1992 (1963). *Eichmann in Jerusalem*. New York: Penguin Books.

Assmann, Aleida. 1999. *Erinnerungsräume: Formen und Wandlungen des kulturellen Gedächtnisses*. Munich: C. H. Beck.

Assmann, Jan. 1991. "Die Katastrophe des Vergessen. Das Deuteronomium als Paradigma kultureller Mnemotechnik." Pp. 337–55 in *Mnemosyne. Formen und Funktionen der kulturellen Erinnerung*, ed. Aleida Assmann and Dietrich Harth. Frankfurt: Fischer.

Baer, Ulrich, ed. 2000. *Niemand zeugt für den Zeugen: Erinnerungskultur nach der Shoah*. Frankfurt: Suhrkamp.

Barber, Benjamin R. 1995. *Jihad versus McWorld*. New York: Random House.

Barkan, Elazar. 2000. *The Guilt of Nations: Restitution and Negotiating Historical Injustices*. New York: W. W. Norton.

Bartov, Omer. 1996. *Murder in Our Midst: The Holocaust, Industrial Killing, and Representation*. New York: Oxford University Press.

———. 1997. "Kitsch and Sadism in Ka-Tzetnik's Other Planet: Israeli Youth Imagine the Holocaust." *Jewish Social Studies* 3, no. 2: 42–75.

———. 1998. "Defining Enemies, Making Victims: Germans, Jews, and the Holocaust." *American Historical Review* 103, no. 3: 771–816.

———. 2000. "Reception and Perception: Goldhagen's Holocaust and the World." Pp. 33–87 in *The "Goldhagen Effect": History, Memory, Nazism-Past*, ed. Geoffrey Ely. Ann Arbor: University of Michigan Press.

Bartov, Omer, Atina Grossman, and Mary Nolan. 2002. *Crimes of War: Guilt and Denial in the Twentieth Century*. New York: New Press.

Bashara, Azmi. 1995. "The Arabs and the Holocaust." *Zemanim* 53: 54–71 (in Hebrew).

Bauman, Zygmunt. 1989. *Holocaust and Modernity*. Cambridge: Polity Press,
———. 2000. *Liquid Modernity*. London: Polity Press.

Beck, Ulrich. 1992. *Risk Society: Towards a New Modernity*, trans. Mark Ritter. London: Sage Publications.

———. 1993. *Die Erfindung des Politischen*. Frankfurt: Suhrkamp.

———. 1997. *The Reinvention of Politics: Rethinking Modernity in the Global Social Order*, trans. Mark Ritter. Cambridge: Polity Press.

———. 2000. "The Cosmopolitan Perspective: The Sociology of the Second Age of Modernity." *British Journal of Sociology* 51, no. 1: 79–105.

———. 2002. "The Cosmopolitan Society and its Enemies." *Theory, Culture and Society* 19, nos. 1–2: 17–44.

———. 2004. *Der Kosmopolitische Blick oder Krieg ist Frieden*. Frankfurt: Suhrkamp.

Beck, Ulrich, ed. 1998. *Perspektiven der Weltgesellschaft*. Frankfurt: Suhrkamp.

Beck, Ulrich, and Wolfgang Bonss, eds. 2001. *Die Modernisierung der Moderne*. Frankfurt: Suhrkamp.

Beck, Ulrich, and Johannes Willms. 2004. *Conversations with Ulrich Beck*, trans. Michael Pollak. Cambridge: Polity Press.

Beck, Ulrich, Anthony Giddens, and Scott Lash. 1994. *Reflexive Modernization: Politics, Tradition and Aesthetics in the Modern Social Order*. Stanford, Calif.: Stanford University Press.

Becker, Elizabeth. 2000. "Chief Themes of Military Budget: Modernizing and Troop Welfare." *New York Times*, 8 February.

Beck-Gernsheim, Elisabeth. 2000. *Juden, Deutsche und andere Erinnerungslandschaften*. Frankfurt: Suhrkamp.

Beer, Mathias. 1998. "Im Spannungsfeld von Politik und Zeitgeschichte. Das Großforschungsprojekt 'Dokumentation der Vertreibung der Deutschen aus Ost-Mitteleuropa.'" *Vierteljahreshefte für Zeitgeschichte* 3: 345–91.

Benjamin, Walter. 1969. *Illuminations.* New York: Schocken.

Benveniste, Meron. 1999. "Seeking Tragedy." *Haaretz*, 16 April.

Berenbaum, Michael. 1990. *After Tragedy and Triumph: Essays in Modern Jewish Thought and the American Experience.* Cambridge: Cambridge University Press.

Berg, Nicolas. 2003. *Der Holocaust und die Westdeutschen Historiker. Erforschung und Erinnerung.* Göttingen: Wallstein Verlag.

Berger, Stefan. 1997. *The Search for Normality: National Identity and Historical Consciousness in Germany since 1800.* Providence, R.I.: Berghahn Books.

Bernstein, Michael Andre. 1994. "The Schindler's List Effect." *American Scholar* 63, no. 3: 429–32.

Bodemann, Michal Y. 1996. *Gedächtnistheater. Die jüdische Gemeinschaft und ihre deutsche Erfindung.* Hamburg: Rotbuch Verlag.

———. 2000. "Vom Vorspiel auf dem Theater zum ökumenischen Gottesdienst." *Frankfurter Allgemeine Zeitung*, 24 August.

Boltanski, Luc. 1999. *Distant Suffering.* Cambridge: Cambridge University Press.

Bosworth, R. J. B. 1993. *Explaining Auschwitz and Hiroshima: History Writing and the Second World War, 1945–1990.* New York: Routledge.

Boyarin, Daniel, and Jonathan Boyarin. 1993. "Diaspora: Generation and the Ground of Jewish Identity." *Critical Inquiry* 19: 693–726.

Brandt, Willy. 1970. *Verhandlungen des Deutschen Bundestages. Stenographische Berichte*, 1970/6/51, 2566.

Breshet, Haim. 1997. "The Great Taboo Broken: Reflections on the Israeli Reception of Schindler's List." Pp. 193–212 in *Spielberg's Holocaust: Critical Perspectives on Schindler's List*, ed. Yosefa Loshitzky. Bloomington: Indiana University Press.

Broszat, Martin, and Saul Friedlander. 1988. "Briefwechsel." *Vierteljahreschrift für Zeitgeschichte* 36: 339–72.

Browning, Christopher. 1992. *Ordinary Men: Reserve Police Battalion 101 and the Final Solution in Poland.* New York: HarperCollins.

Buruma, Ian. 1994. *Wages of Guilt: Memories of War in Germany and Japan.* New York: Farrar, Straus & Giroux.

———. 1999. "The Joys and Perils of Victimhood." *New York Review of Books*, 8 April.

Calhoun, Craig, Paul Price, and Ashley Timmer, eds. 2002. *Understanding September 11.* New York: New Press.

Carter, Erica. 1997. *How German Is She? Postwar German Reconstruction and the Consuming Woman.* Ann Arbor: University of Michigan Press.

Castells, Manuel. 1996. *The Rise of Network Society.* Oxford: Blackwell.

Chang, Iris. 1997. *The Rape of Nanking: The Forgotten Holocaust of World War II*. New York: Basic Books.

Cheah, Peng, and Bruce Robbins, eds. 1998. *Cosmopolitics: Thinking and Feeling beyond the Nation*. Minneapolis: University of Minnesota Press.

Clifford, James. 1994. "Diasporas." *Cultural Anthropology* 9, no. 3: 302–38

Clinton, William J. 1995. "Why We're Sending Troops to Bosnia," televised speech, 27 November, available at www.dtic.mil/bosnia/army/pres_bos .html and www.cnn.com/us/9511/bosnia_speech/speech.html.

Cohen, Robin. 1997. *Global Diasporas: An Introduction*. London: UCL Press.

Cole, Tim. 1999. *Images of the Holocaust: The Myth of the "Shoah Business."* London: Duckworth.

Courtois, Stephane, Nicolas Werth, and Jean-Louis Panne. 1999. *The Black Book of Communism: Crimes, Terror, Repression*, ed. Mark Kramer, trans. Jonathon Murphy. Cambridge, Mass.: Harvard University Press.

Dabag, Mihran, und Kristin Platt, eds. 1995. *Generation und Gedächtnis. Erinnerungen und kollektive Identitäten*. Opladen: Leske and Budrich.

Danner, Mark. 1999. *The Saddest Story: America, the Alliance and the Catastrophe in the Balkans*. New York: Pantheon.

Davidowicz, Lucy. 1975. *The War against the Jews*. New York: Seth Press.

Dayan, Daniel, and Eliahu Katz. 1992. *Media Events: The Live Broadcasting of History*. Cambridge, Mass.: Harvard University Press.

Deak, Istvan, Jan Gross, and Tony Judt, eds. 2000. *The Politics of Retribution in Europe: World War II and Its Aftermath*. Princeton, N.J.: Princeton University Press.

Deutsch, Karl W. 1966. *Nationalism and Social Communication*. New York: MIT Press.

Diner, Dan. 1993. *Verkehrte Welten. Antiamerikanismus in Deutschland*. Frankfurt: Eichborn Verlag.

———. 1995. "Cumulative Contingency: Historicizing Legitimacy in Israeli Discourse." *History and Memory* 7: 147–67.

———. 1996. *America in the Eyes of the Germans: An Essay on Anti-Americanism*. Princeton, N.J.: Markus Weiner.

———. 1997. "On Guilt-Discourse and Other Narratives: Epistempological Observations Regarding the Holocaust." *History and Memory* 9: 301–20.

———. 1999. *Das Jahrhundert verstehen: Eine universalhistorische Bedeutung*. Munich: Luchterhand.

———. 2000. *Beyond the Conceivable: Studies on Germany, Nazism, and the Holocaust*. Berkeley: University of California Press.

Diner, Dan, Natan Sznaider, and Mina Tzemah. 2000. *Israelis und Deutsche: Die Ambivalenz der Normalität*. Tel Aviv: Friedrich-Ebert-Stiftung.

Don-Yehiya, Eliezer. 1993. "Memory and Political Culture: Israel's Society and the Holocaust." *Studies in Contemporary Jewry* 9: 139–62.

Doubt, Keith. 2000. *Recovering Justice: Sociology after Bosnia and Kosovo.* Boulder, Colo.: Rowman and Littlefield.

Douglas, Lawrence. 1995. "Film as Witness: Screening Nazi Concentration Camps before the Nuremberg Tribunal." *Yale Law Journal* 105: 449–81.

Dubiel, Helmut. 1999. *Niemand ist frei von der Geschichte: Die nationalsozialistische Herrschaft in den Debatten des Deutschen Bundestages.* Munich: Hanser.

Eley, Geoff, ed. 2000. *The Goldhagen Effect: History, Memory, Nazism—Facing the German Past.* Ann Arbor: University of Michigan Press.

Elias, Norbert. 1996 (1989). *The Germans,* trans. Eric Dunning and Stephen Mennell. New York: Columbia University Press.

Fargo, Uri. 1989. "Hazehut ha-yehudit shel noar yisraeli, 1965–1985 (The Jewish identity of Israeli youth)." *Yahadut Zemaneinu* (Contemporary Judaism) 5: 259–85.

Faulenbach, Bernd. 1993. "Problems des Umgangs mit der Vergangenheit im vereinten Deutschland: Zur Gegenwartsbedeutung der jüngsten Geschichte." Pp. 175–91 in *Deutschland, eine Nation—doppelte Geschichte: Materialien zum deutschen Selbstverständnis,* ed. Werner Weidenfeld. Cologne: Verlag Wissenschaft und Politik.

Featherstone, Mike. 1995. *Undoing Culture: Globalization, Postmodernism and Identity.* London: Sage.

Feldman, Jackie. 1995. "Über den Gräbern mit gehisster Fahne Israels— Die Struktur und Bedeutung israelischer Jugendreisen nach dem Polen der Schoah." In *Dass Auschwitz nicht noch einmal sei. Zur Erziehung nach Auschwitz,* ed. Helmut Schreier and Matthias Heyl. Hamburg: Krämer.

———. 2002. "Marking the Boundaries of the Enclave: Defining the Israeli Collective through the Poland 'Experience.'" *Israel Studies* 7, no. 2: 84–114.

Filipovic, Zlata, and Christina Pribichevich-Zoric. 1995. *Zlata's Diary: A Child's Life in Sarajevo.* New York: Penguin Books.

Finkelkraut, Alain. 1997 (1984). *The Wisdom of Love.* Lincoln: University of Nebraska Press.

Finkelstein, Norman. 2000. *The Holocaust Industry.* New York: Verso.

Fischer, Fritz. 1967. *Germany's Aims in the First World War.* London: Chatto and Windus.

Flanzbaum, Hilene. 1999. "The Americanization of the Holocaust." *Journal of Genocide Research* 1, no. 1: 91–104.

Frei, Norbert. 1997. *Vergangenheitspolitik: Die Anfänge der Bundesrepublik und die NS-Vergangenheit.* Munich: Beck.

———. 2002. *Adenauer's Germany and the Nazi Past: The Politics of Amnesty and Integration.* New York: Columbia Press.

Frei, Norbert, Dirk van Laak, and Michael Stolleis, eds. 2000. *Geschichte vor Gericht: Historiker, Richter und die Suche nach Gerechtigkeit.* Munich: Beck.

Friedlander, Saul, and Adam Seligman. 1994. "The Israeli Memory of the Shoah: On Symbols, Rituals, and Ideological Polarization." Pp. 356–71 in *NowHere: Space, Time and Modernity*, ed. Roger Friedland and Deirde Boden. Berkeley: University of California Press.

Friedman, Jonathan. 1990. "Being in the World: Globalization and Localization." *Theory, Culture and Society* 7: 311–28.

Friedrich, Jörg. 2002 *Der Brand: Deutschland im Bombenkrieg 1940–1945*. Munich: Propyläen.

Gebhardt, Winfried, ed. 2000. *Events: Soziologie des Außergewöhnlichen*. Opladen: Leske and Budrich.

Gellner, Ernest. 1983. *Nations and Nationalism: New Perspectives on the Past*. Ithaca, N.Y.: Cornell University Press.

Giddens, Anthony. 1990. *The Consequences of Modernity*. Cambridge: Polity Press.

Gilroy, Paul. 1993. *The Black Atlantic: Modernity and Double Consciousness*. Cambridge, Mass: Harvard University Press.

———. 2000. *Between Camps: Nations, Cultures and the Allures of Race*. London: Penguin Books.

Goldhagen, Daniel Jonah. 1996. *Hitler's Willing Executioners: Ordinary Germans and the Holocaust*. New York: Alfred A. Knopf.

———. 1998. "Why Did the Heavens Not Darken?" *New Republic*, 17 April, 39–44.

———. 1999. "Eine 'deutsche Lösung' für den Balkan." *Süddeutsche Zeitung*, 30 April, 17.

Gorni, Yosef. 1998. *Between Auschwitz and Jerusalem*. Tel Aviv: Am Oved (in Hebrew).

Gourevitch, Philip. 1993. "Behold Now Behemoth—The Holocaust Memorial Museum: One More American Theme Park." *Harper's Magazine*, vol. 287, no. 1718, 55–57.

———. 1999. "The Memory Thief." *New Yorker*, June 14, 48–68.

Gur-Zeev, Ilan. 1999. "Palestinians and the Memory of the Holocaust and the Nacba." Pp. 99–123 in *Philosophy, Politics and Education in Israel* (in Hebrew). Haifa: Haifa University Press.

Gutman, Roy. 1993. *Witness to Genocide*. New York: Macmillan.

Habermas, Jürgen. 2001. *The Postnational Constellation: Political Essays*. Cambridge: Polity Press.

Hacohen, Malachi Haim. 1999. "Dilemmas of Cosmopolitanism: Karl Popper, Jewish Identity and Central European Culture." *Journal of Modern History* 71: 105–49.

Halbwachs, Maurice. 1980. *The Collective Memory*. New York: Harper and Row.

Hannerz, Ulf. 1995. "Cosmopolitans and Locals in World Culture." Pp. 237–52 in *Global Modernities*, ed. Mike Featherstone, Scott Lash, and Robert Robertson. London: Sage.

Hansen, Miriam Bratu. 1996. "Schindler's List Is Not Shoah: The Second Commandment, Popular Modernism, and Public Memory." *Critical Inquiry* 22: 292–312.

Heineman, Elizabeth. 1996. "The Hour of the Woman: Memories of Germany's 'Crisis Years' and West German National Identity."*American Historical Review* 101: 354–95.

Herbert, Ulrich. 2000. *National Socialist Extermination Policies: Contemporary German Persepectives and Controversies*. New York: Berghahn Books.

Herf, Jeffrey. 1997. *Divided Memory: The Nazi Past in the Two Germanies*. Cambridge, Mass.: Harvard University Press.

Hertzberg, Arthur. 1998. *Jews: The Essence and Character of a People*. San Francisco: Harper.

Herzl, Theodor. 1989 (1896). *The Jewish State*, trans. Sylvie D'Avigdor. New York: Dover.

Hobsbawm, Eric. 1996. *The Age of Extremes: A History of the World, 1919–1991*. New York: Vintage Books.

Hobsbawm, Eric, and Terence Ranger. 1983. *The Invention of Tradition*. Cambridge: Cambridge University Press.

Hollinger, David. 2001. "Not Universalists, Not Pluralists: The New Cosmopolitans Find Their Own Way." *Constellations* 8, no. 2: 236–48.

Honig, Jan Willem, and Norbert Both. 1996. *Srebrenica: Record of a War Crime*. London: Penguin.

Hucanovicy, Reyak. 1996. *The Tenth Circle of Hell: A Memoir of Life in the Death Camps of Bosnia*. New York: Basic Books.

Huntington, Samuel. 1996. *The Clash of Civilizations and the Remaking of the World Order*. New York: Simon and Schuster.

Hutton, Patrick. 1993. *History as an Art of Memory*. London: University Press of New England.

Hutton, Will. 2000. "We Have Blood on Our Hands." *The Observer* (London), 21 January.

Huyssen, Andreas. 1980. "The Politics of Identification." *New German Critique* 19: 117–36.

———. 1995. *Twilight Memories: Marking Time in a Culture of Amnesia*. New York: Routledge.

———. 2000. "Present Pasts: Media, Politics, Amnesia." *Public Culture* 12, no. 1: 21–38.

Iggers, Georg. 1997. *Historiography in the Twentieth Century: From Scientific Objectivity to the Postmodern Challenge*. Hanover, N.H.: Wesleyan University Press.

Ignatieff, Michael. 1999. "Human Rights: The Midlife Crisis." *New York Review of Books*, 20 May, 58–62.

———. 2000. *Virtual War: Kosovo and Beyond*. London: Chatto and Windus.

———. 2001. "The Danger of a World without Enemies: Lemkin's Word." *New Republic*, 26 February.

Jarausch, Konrad, and Hannes Siegrist. 1997. *Amerikanisierung und Sowjetisierung in Deutschland 1945–1970*. Frankfurt: Campus.

Jaspers, Karl. 1961 (1946). *The Question of German Guilt*, trans. E. B. Ashton. New York: Capricorn Books.

Judt, Tony. 2000. "The Past Is Another Country: Myth and Memory in Postwar Europe." Pp. 293–323 in *The Politics of Retribution in Europe*, ed. Istvan Deak, Jan Gross, and Tony Judt. Princeton: Princeton University Press.

Junker, Detlev. 2000. "Die Amerikanisierung des Holocaust." *Frankfurter Allgemeine Zeitung*, 9 September.

Kagan, Robert. 2004. "A Tougher War for the U.S. Is One of Legitimacy." *New York Times*, 24 January.

Kaldor, Mary. 1999. *New and Old Wars: Organized Violence in a Global Era*. London: Polity.

Katz, Elihu, and Tamer Liebes. 1990. *The Export of Meaning: Cross-Cultural Readings of Dallas*. New York: Oxford University Press.

Katz, Steven. 1993. *The Holocaust and Comparative History*. New York: Leo Baeck Institute.

Kettenacker, Lothar, ed. 2003. *Ein Volk von Opfern? Die neue Debatte um den Bombenkrieg 1940–45*. Berlin: Rowohlt Berlin.

Kimmerling, Baruch. 1998. "The Nakhba." *Theory and Criticism* 12–13: 33–36 (in Hebrew).

Köhler, Lotte, and Hans Saner, eds. 1985. *Hannah Arendt–Karl Jaspers Briefwechsel 1926–1969*. Munich: Piper.

Kristof, Nicholas. 1998. "The Problem of Memory: The Danger of Living History." *Foreign Affairs*, vol. 77, no. 6, 37–49.

Kushner, Tony. 1997. "'I Want to Go on Living after My Death': The Memory of Anne Frank." Pp. 3–25 in *War and Memory in the Twentieth Century*, ed. Martin Evans and Ken Lunn. New York: Berg.

Lagrou, Pieter. 1997. "Victims of Genocide and National Memory: Belgium, France and the Netherlands, 1945–1965." *Past and Present* 154: 107–41.

Landsberg, Alison. 1997. "America, the Holocaust, and the Mass Culture of Memory: Toward a Radical Politics of Empathy." *New German Critique* 71: 63–87.

Langer, Lawrence. 1991. *Holocaust Testimonies: The Ruins of Memory*. New Haven, Conn.: Yale University Press.

Lanzmann, Claude. 1994. "Why Spielberg Has Distorted the Truth." *Le Monde*, reprinted in *Guardian Weekly*, 3 April, 14.

Lash, Scott, and John Urry. 1994. *The Economies of Signs and Spaces*. London: Sage.

Lemkin, Raphael. 1944. *Axis Rule in Occupied Europe: Laws of Occupation, Analysis of Government, Proposals for Redress*. Washington, D.C.: Carnegie Endowment for International Peace.

———. 1946. "Genocide." *American Scholar* 15 (March): 227.

Levi, Gideon. 1999. "Kosovo: It Is Here." *Haaretz*, 4 April.

Levinas, Emmanuel. 1990. *Difficult Freedom: Essays on Judaism.* London: Athlone Press.

Levinson, Hannah. 1981. "The Television Series 'Holocaust' in Israel." *Journal of Political Education* 4, no. 2: 151–66.

Levy, Bernard-Henri. 1999. "Ein paar Versuche, in Deutschland spazierenzugehen." *Frankfurter Allgemeine Zeitung*, 17 February, 50.

Levy, Daniel. 1999. "The Future of the Past: Historiographical Disputes and Competing Memories in Germany and Israel." *History and Theory* 38: 51–66.

———. 2001. "The Politicization of Ethnic German Immigrants: The Transformation of State Priorities." Pp. 289–304 in *Ethnic Migration in 20th Century Europe: Germany, Israel and Russia in Comparative Perspective*, ed. Rainer Münz und Rainer Ohliger. London: Frank Cass, 2003.

Levy, Daniel, and Natan Sznaider. 2004. "The Institutionalization of Cosmopolitan Morality: The Holocaust and Human Rights." *Journal of Human Rights* 3, no. 2: 143–57.

Liebman, Charles, and Eliezer Don-Yehiya. 1983. *Civil Religion in Israel: Traditional Judaism and Political Culture in the Jewish State.* Berkeley: University of California Press.

Linenthal, Edward. 1995. *Preserving Memory: The Struggle to Create America's Holocaust Museum.* New York: Penguin.

Loshitzky, Yosefa. 1997. *Spielberg's Holocaust: Critical Perspectives on Schindler's List.* Bloomington: Indiana University Press.

Lübbe, Hermann. 1983. "Der Nationalsozialismus im deutschen Nachkriegsbewusstsein." *Historische Zeitschrift* 236: 579–99.

Lüdtke, Alf, et al., eds. 1996. *Amerikanisierung: Traum und Alptraum im Deutschland des 20. Jahrhunderts.* Stuttgart: Steiner.

Luttwack, Edward. 1996. "Post-Heroic Military Policy." *Foreign Affairs*, vol. 75, no. 4, July–August, 33–44.

Maier, Charles. 1988. *The Unmasterable Past: History, Holocaust, and German National Identity.* Cambridge, Mass.: Harvard University Press.

———. 2000. "Consigning the Twentieth Century to History: Alternative Narratives for the Modern Era." *American Historical Review* 105, no. 3: 807–31.

Marrus, Michael. 1998. "The Holocaust at Nuremberg." *Yad Vashem Studies* 26: 5–41.

Mason, Tim. 1979. *Intention and Explanation in Nazism, Fascism and the Working Class.* Cambridge: Cambridge University Press.

Mazower, Mark. 1998. *Dark Continent: Europe's Twentieth Century.* New York: Alfred A. Knopf.

———. 2001. "The G-Word." *London Review of Books*, vol. 23, no. 3, 7.

Meinecke, Friedrich. 1963 (1946). *The German Catastrophe: Reflections and Recollections*, trans. S. B. Fay. Boston: Beacon Press.

Melson, Robert. 1992. *Revolution and Genocide: On the Origins of the Armenian Genocide and the Holocaust*. Chicago: University of Chicago Press.

Meyer, John, et al. 1997. "World Society and the Nation-State." *American Journal of Sociology* 103: 144–81.

Miles, William. 2001. "Report on an International Symposium: Third World Views of the Holocaust." *Journal of Genocide Research* 3, no. 3: 511–13.

Milgram, Stanley. 1973. *Obedience to Authority*. New York: Harper and Row.

Mitscherlich, Alexander and Margarete. 1975 (1967). *The Inability to Mourn: Principles of Collective Behavior*, trans. Beverly R. Placzek. New York: Grove Press.

Moeller, Robert G. 1996. "War Stories: The Search for a Usable Past in the Federal Republic of Germany." *American Historical Review* 101: 1008–48.

Mommsen, Hans. 1983. "Die Realisierung des Utopischen: Die Endlösung der Judenfrage im Dritten Reich." *Geschichte und Gesellschaft* 9: 381–420.

Morris, Benny. 1987. *The Birth of the Palestinian Refugee Problem: 1947–1949*. Cambridge: Cambridge University Press.

Moses, Dirk A. 2003. "Revisionism and Denial." Pp. 337–70 in *Whitewash: On Keith Windschuttle's Fabrication of Aboriginal History*, ed. R. Manne. Melbourne: Black.

Mosse, George L. 1990. *Fallen Soldiers: Reshaping the Memory of the World Wars*. New York: Oxford University Press.

Müller-Schneider, Thomas. 1994. *Schichten und Erlebnismilieus. Der Wandel der Milieustruktur in der Bundesrepublik Deutschland*. Wiesbaden: Deutscher Universitätsverlag.

Naumann, Michael. 2000. "Closing Speech." Delivered at the Stockholm International Forum on the Holocaust, Stockholm, 26–28 January, available at: www.holocaustforum.gov.se / conference / official_documents / speeches / naumann_eng.htm.

Nederveen Pieterse, Jan. 2003. *Globalization and Culture: Global Mélange*. Lanham, Md.: Rowman and Littlefield.

Noelle, Elisabeth, and Erich Peter Neumann, eds. 1956. *Jahrbuch der öffentlichen Meinung 1947–1955*, vol. 1. Allensbach: Verlag für Demoskopie.

Noelle-Neumann, Elisabeth, ed. 1984. *Allensbacher Jahrbuch der Demoskopie 1984–1992*. Munich: Saur.

Noelle-Neumann, Elisabeth, and Peter Neumann, eds. 1981. *The Germans: Public Opinion Polls, 1967–1980*. Westport, Conn.: Greenwood Press.

Nolte, Ernst. 1966. *Three Faces of Fascism: Action Française, Italian Fascism, National Socialism*. New York: Henry Holt.

Nora, Pierre. 1989. "Between Memory and History: Les Lieux de Memoire." *Representations* 26: 1–21.

————. 1996. *Realms of Memory, Volume 1: Conflicts and Divisions.* New York: Columbia University Press.

————. 1998. *Zwischen Geschichte und Erinnerung.* Frankfurt: Fischer.

Nordau, Max. 1909. *Zionistische Schriften,* ed. Zionistisches Aktionskomitee. Cologne: Jüdischer Verlag.

Novick, Peter. 1999. *The Holocaust in American Life.* New York: Houghton Mifflin.

Ofer, Dalia. 1996. "Linguistic Conceptualization of the Holocaust in Palestine and Israel, 1942–53." *Journal of Contemporary History* 31, no. 3: 567–95.

Olick, Jeffrey K. 1993. "The Sins of the Fathers: The Third Reich and West German Legitimation, 1949–1989." PhD. diss., Yale University, New Haven, Conn.

Olick, Jeffrey K., and Daniel Levy. 1997. "Collective Memory and Cultural Constraint: Holocaust Myth and Rationality in German Politics." *American Sociological Review* 62: 921–36.

Olick, Jeffrey K., and Joyce Robbins. 1998. "Social Memory Studies: From 'Collective Memory' to the Historical Sociology of Mnemonic Practices." *Annual Review of Sociology* 5, no. 24: 105–40.

Ong, Walter J. 1995. *Orality and Literacy: The Technologizing of the Word.* New York: Routledge.

Ozick, Cynthia. 1997. "Who Owns Anne Frank?" *New Yorker,* vol. 73, 6 October, 76–87.

Pappe, Ilan. 1994. *The Making of the Arab–Israeli Conflict: 1947–51.* London: Tauris.

Peled, Yoav, und Gershon Shafir. 1996. "The Roots of Peacemaking: The Dynamics of Citizenship in Israel, 1948–1993." *International Journal of Middle East Studies* 28: 391–413.

Popper, Karl R. 1996 (1945). *The Open Society and Its Enemies.* London: Routledge.

Preece, Jennifer Jackson. 1998. "Ethnic Cleansing as an Instrument of Nation-State Creation: Changing State Practices and Evolving Norms." *Human Rights Quarterly* 20: 817–42.

Rabinbach, Anson. 1997. "From Expulsion to Erosion: Holocaust Memorialization in America since Bitburg." *History and Memory* 9, no. 1–2: 226–55.

Ravitzky, Aviezer. 1996. *Messianism, Zionism, and Jewish Radicalism.* Chicago: University of Chicago Press.

Raz-Krakotzkin, Ammon. 1993. "Exile within Sovereignty: Toward a Critique of the 'Negation of Exile' in Israeli Culture." *Theory and Criticism* 4: 23–55 (in Hebrew).

Reichel, Peter. 1995. *Politik mit der Erinnerung: Gedächtnisorte im Streit um die nationalsozialistische Vergangenheit.* Munich: Hanser.

————. 2001. *Vergangenheitsbewältigung in Deutschland. Die Auseinandersetzung mit der NS-Diktatur von 1945 bis heute.* Munich: Beck.

Riding, Alan. 2001. "Memoir of the Camp: Images of the Unspeakable Horror Stir Voices of Debate." *New York Times*, 14 March.

Ritzer, George. 1993. *The McDonaldization of Society: An Investigation into the Changing Character of Modern Life*. Newbury Park, Calif.: Pine Forge Press.

Robertson, Roland. 1992. *Globalization: Social Theory and Global Culture*. London: Sage.

———. 1995. "Glocalization: Time-Space and Homogeneity-Heterogeneity." Pp. 25–44 in *Global Modernities*, ed. Mike Featherstone, Scott Lash, and Roland Robertson. London: Sage.

Rosenfeld, Alvin H. 1991. "Popularization and Memory: The Case of Anne Frank." Pp. 243–78 in *Lessons and Legacies. The Meaning of the Holocaust in a Changing World*, ed. Peter Hayes. Evanston, Ill.: Northwestern University Press.

———. 1997. "The Americanization of the Holocaust." Pp. 119–50 in Alvin H. Rosenfeld, *Thinking about the Holocaust: After Half a Century*. Bloomington: Indiana University Press.

Rothenhäusler, Paul, and Hans-Ueli Sonderegger. 2000. *Erinnerung an den Roten Holocaust*. Roth: Werner.

Rousso, Henry. 1991. *The Vichy Syndrome: History and Memory in France since 1944*. Cambridge, Mass.: Harvard University Press.

Rüsen, Jörn. 1982. "Die vier Typen historischen Erzählens." Pp. 514–606 in *Formen der Geschichtsschreibung*, ed. Reinhardt Koselleck and Jörn Rüsen. Munich: Fink.

Sa'adah, Anne. 1998. *Germany's Second Chance: Trust, Justice, and Democratization*. Cambridge, Mass.: Harvard University Press.

Saghiyeh, Hazem, and Saleh Bashir. 2000. "Universalizing the Holocaust." *Haaretz*, 21 February (in English).

Said, Edward. 1999. "Bases for Co-Existence." Available at: www.one-state .org/articles/1997/said.htm (last viewed 14 June 2005).

Sassen, Saskia. 2001. *The Global City: New York, London, Tokyo*. Princeton, N.J.: Princeton University Press.

Scarry, Elaine. 1985. *The Body in Pain: The Making and Unmaking of the World*. New York: Oxford University Press.

Schlant, Ernestine. 1999. *The Language of Silence: West German Literature and the Holocaust*. New York: Routledge.

Schulze, Hagen, and Etienne François. 2000. *Deutsche Erinnerungsorte*. Munich: Beck.

Schuman, Howard, and Jaqueline Scott. 1989. "Generations and Collective Memory." *American Sociological Review* 54: 359–81.

Schwartz, Barry. 2000. *Abraham Lincoln and the Forge of National Memory*. Chicago: University of Chicago Press.

Segev, Tom. 1993. *The Seventh Million: The Israelis and the Holocaust*. New York: Hill and Wang.

———. 2000. "The Teddy Katz Trial." *Haaretz*, 2 December (in English).

Shafir, Gershon. 1989. *Land, Labor and the Origins of the Israeli–Palestinian Conflict, 1882–1914.* Cambridge: Cambridge University Press.

Shandler, Jeffrey. 1999. *While America Watches: Televising the Holocaust.* New York: Oxford University Press.

Shandley, Robert, ed. 1998. *Unwilling Germans: The Goldhagen Debate.* Minneapolis: University of Minnesota Press.

Shapira, Anita. 1998. "The Holocaust: Private Memories, Public Memory." *Journal of Jewish Studies* 4, no. 2: 40–58.

Shaw, Martin. 1997. "Globalization and Post-Military Democracy." Pp. 26–48 in *The Transformation of Democracy*, ed. Anthony McGrew. Cambridge: Polity Press.

Silberstein, Laurence. 1999. *The Postzionism Debates: Knowledge and Power in Israeli Culture.* New York: Routledge.

Silver, Allan. 1990. "The Curious Importance of Small Groups in American Sociology." Pp. 61–72 in *Sociology in America*, ed. Herbert Gans. Newbury Park, Calif.: Sage.

Simmel, Georg. 1978 (1900). *The Philosophy of Money*, trans. Tom Bottomore and David Frisby. London: Routledge and Kegan Paul.

———. 1999 (1908). *Soziologie: Untersuchungen über die Formen der Vergesellschaftung.* Frankfurt: Suhrkamp.

Smith, Anthony. 1990. "Towards a Global Culture?" *Theory, Culture and Society* 7: 171–91.

———. 1995. *Nations and Nationalism in a Global Era.* Cambridge, Mass.: Blackwell.

Sombart, Werner. 1911. *Die Juden und das Wirtschaftsleben.* Munich: Duncker.

Soyinka, Wole. 2000. *The Burden of Memory, the Muse of Forgiveness.* New York: Oxford University Press.

Soysal, Yasemin N. 1994. *Limits of Citizenship: Migrants and Postnational Membership in Europe.* Chicago: University of Chicago Press.

Stern, Frank. 1992. *The Whitewashing of the Yellow Badge: Anti-Semitism and Philosemitism in Postwar Germany*, trans. William Templer. Oxford: Pergamon Press.

Stürmer, Michael. 1986. "Geschichte im geschichtslosem Land." *Frankfurter Allgemeine Zeitung*, 25 April.

Sznaider, Natan. 1998a. "Vom Wehrbürger zum Einkaufsbürger. Konsum und Nationalismus in Israel." *Soziale Welt* 49: 43–56.

———. 1998b. "Are Israeli Young People Apolitical? The Latent Politics of the 1990s." Pp. 7–19 in *Israeli Youth's Attitudes toward Personal, Social and National Issues.* Tel Aviv: Israeli Institute for Economic and Social Research.

———. 2001. *The Compassionate Temperament: Care and Cruelty in Modern Society.* Boulder, Colo.: Rowman and Littlefield.

Tester, Keith. 1999. "The Moral Consequentiality of Television." *European Journal of Social Theory* 2, no. 4: 469–83.

Thompson, John. 1995. *The Media and Modernity: A Social Theory of the Media.* Cambridge: Polity Press.

Tomlinson, John. 1999. *Globalization and Culture.* Chicago: University of Chicago Press.

Torpey, John. 2001. "'Making Whole What Has Been Smashed': Reflections on Reparations." *Journal of Modern History* 73, no. 2: 333–61.

Traverso, Enzo. 1999. *Understanding the Nazi Genocide: Marxism after Auschwitz,* trans. Peter Drucker. London: Pluto Press.

United Nations. 1948. "Convention on the Prevention and Punishment of Genocide," available at: www.hrweb.org/legal/genocide.html.

Walker, R. B. J. 1990. "Sovereignty, Identity, Community: Reflections on the Horizons of Contemporary Political Practice." Pp. 159–218 in *Contending Sovereignties: Redefining Political Community,* ed. R. B. J. Walker and S. H. Mendlovitz. Boulder, Colo.: Lynne Rienner Publishers.

Weber, Max. 1962. *Basic Concepts in Sociology,* trans. H. P. Secher. New York: Greenwood Press.

Weitz, Yechiam. 2000. "Ben-Gurions Weg zum 'Anderen Deutschland' 1952–1963." *Vierteljahresheft für Zeitgeschichte* 48: 255–79.

Wildt, Michael. 1996. *Vom kleinen Wohlstand. Eine Konsumgeschichte der Fünfziger Jahre.* Fischer: Frankfurt.

Winter, Jay. 1995. *Sites of Memory, Sites of Mourning: The Great War in European Cultural History.* Cambridge: Cambridge University Press.

Wuthnow, Robert. 1987. *Meaning and Moral Order: Explorations in Cultural Analysis.* Berkeley: University of California Press.

Yablonka, Hanna. 1999. *Survivors of the Holocaust: Israel after the War.* New York: New York University Press.

Yerushalmi, Y. H. 1983. *Zakhor: Jewish History and Jewish Memory.* Seattle: University of Washington Press.

Young, James. 1993. *The Texture of Memory: Holocaust Memorials and Meaning.* New Haven, Conn.: Yale University Press.

Zelizer, Barbie. 1998. *Remembering to Forget: Holocaust Memory through the Camera's Eye.* Chicago: University of Chicago Press.

Zertal, Idith. 1998. *From Catastrophe to Power: Holocaust Survivors in Israel.* Berkeley: University of California Press.

Zerubavel, Yael. 1995. *Recovered Roots: Collective Memory and the Making of Israeli National Tradition.* Chicago: University of Chicago Press.

Zimmermann, Moshe. 1994. "Israels Umgang mit dem Holocaust." Pp. 387–406 in *Der Umgang mit dem Holocaust,* ed. Rolf Steininger. Vienna: Böhlau.

Zuckermann, Moshe. 1998. *Zweierlei Holocaust: Der Holocaust in den politischen Kulturen Israels und Deutschlands.* Göttingen: Wallstein.

Index

Adenauer, Konrad, 74, 75, 77, 81, 103, 168, 206

Adorno, Theodor, 42–43, 93n.11

African Americans: national identity and, 24; relationship with Jewish populations, 113, 114–15

air campaigns: Hamburg and Dresden, 188; Hiroshima, 39, 188; in Kosovo, 176

Alexander, Jeffrey, 5

"alienation," of Marx, 41

American Jewish Committee, 159

American Jewish Congress, 159, 160

American Jews: Cold War and, 115–16; relationship with African Americans, 113, 114–15; victimhood claims of, 114–15

Americanization of the Holocaust, 9, 12–13, 82, 109–11, 153–54; Anne Frank and, 60–63; cosmopolitan memory and, 183; criticisms of, 134; *Holocaust* TV miniseries and, 116–17; Jewish versus Israeli perceptions of, 143; Kosovo conflict and, 173; mass images and, 135–37; misunderstanding of, 134–35; Spielberg's video project and, 150; universalization of evil and, 132–33. See also *Holocaust* (TV miniseries); *Schindler's List* (movie); universalization

Améry, Jean, 163

Amnesty International, 180, 194

Anderson, Benedict: on authenticity of value system, 177–78; "horizontal community" and, 37; on imagined communities, 32–33

Anne Frank Remembered (movie), 189

"anomie," of Durkheim, 41

Anti-Defamation League, 159

antifascism, 83; in Germany, 111

anti-Semitism: criticism of Israel viewed as, 108; in European consciousness, 114; racism versus, 114; reparations and, 204n.9, 205–6

antiterrorist measures, civil rights and, 19

anti-totalitarianism, 81

Arab–Israeli conflict. *See* Israeli–Arab conflict

Arabs: compared with Nazis, 199–200; expulsions of (1947–48), 152, 200, 200n.7; on Holocaust, 200, 200n.6; in Israel, 146. *See also* Palestinians

Arafat, Yasir, 108

Arendt, Hannah: assessment of Eichmann, 142; on "banality of evil," 43, 43n.1, 111, 112; on colonialism, 193; on Eichmann trial, 110; on Enlightenment and National Socialism, 110–11; on human condition, 44; on Israel as sovereign nation, 106; on Nazi crimes, 68; political and social theory of, 42; social-science study techniques of, 110

Argentina, 5

Armenian genocide, 153, 198, 198n.4

Asia: emigrants from, 146; preserving war memories in, 188

assassinations, in 1960s, 113

assimilation, 16

Assmann, Aleida, 34

Assmann, Jan, 33

atomic bomb, 39–40, 93, 188

atonement, German cult of, 135